Studies in European Literature

BEING

THE TAYLORIAN LECTURES

SECOND SERIES

1920–1930

DELIVERED BY

EDMUND GOSSE · F. Y. ECCLES · H. THOMAS
EDMUND G. GARDNER · J. G. ROBERTSON
ÉMILE LEGOUIS · JOHN BAILEY
H. A. L. FISHER · ABRAHAM FLEXNER
OLIVER ELTON · P. E. MATHESON

Essay Index Reprint Series

BOOKS FOR LIBRARIES PRESS
FREEPORT, NEW YORK

First Published 1930
Reprinted 1969

STANDARD BOOK NUMBER:
8369-1232-2

LIBRARY OF CONGRESS CATALOG CARD NUMBER:
76-90673

PRINTED IN THE UNITED STATES OF AMERICA

CONTENTS

THE University of Oxford, by decree of Convocation of 28 June 1917, accepted offers of £400 five per cent. War Stock from Professor Sir Charles Firth and £100 of the same Stock from the late Professor Joseph Wright, and directed that the said Stock should be applied to the formation of a permanent Fund to be called the Taylorian Special Lectures Fund, the income of which should be used by the Curators of the Taylor Institution in providing Special Lectures on subjects connected with Modern European Literature.

The practice of the Curators has been to appoint one Lecturer annually. Provision was made for publication, and the present volume contains all the lectures delivered on the foundation since 1920.

The Curators hope that the publication of these lectures will contribute to the study of foreign letters beyond as well as in the University, and they wish to express their gratitude to the distinguished scholars who, by accepting the post of Lecturer, have enabled them to carry out the intentions of the founders.

The Taylorian Lecture

1920

MALHERBE

and the

Classical Reaction

in the

Seventeenth Century

By

EDMUND GOSSE, C.B.

MALHERBE AND THE
CLASSICAL REACTION

In contemplating the chart of literary history we are confronted by phenomena which more or less closely resemble those marked on the geographical map. The surface is not uniform, but diversified by ups and downs of the feature that we call taste or fashion. A special interest attaches to what may be described as the watersheds of literature, the periods which display these changes of direction in thought and language. I propose to bring before you briefly some characteristics of one of the most saliently marked of all these points of alteration, that which led irresistibly and imminently to the classical school, as it is called, in France, and from France ultimately to the whole of Europe. Before doing so, I must draw your attention to the fact that while most of us are led to give special heed to movements which tend, like the Romantic renaissance of poetry in England two centuries later, to the emancipation and even the revolution of literature, that of which I am about to speak was deliberately introduced in the interests of law and order, and was in all its features conservative, and, if you choose to call it so, retrogressive. It did not aim at enlarging the field of expression, but at enclosing it within rules, excluding from it eccentricities and licentious freaks, and rendering it subservient to a rigorous discipline. In this University, where the practice of poetry is now conducted with so much ardour and with such audacity of experiment, you may or may not, as you please, see any parallel between the condition of France in 1595 and our own condition to-day. My purpose is, with your leave, to describe the former without criticizing the latter.

The sixteenth century had been a period of great activity in the literature of France, where the interaction of two vast forces, the Renaissance and the Reformation, had introduced wholly new forms of expression into the language. Prose had started from its mediaeval condition into full modernity in Calvin, and then in Montaigne. In poetry, with which we are concerned to-day, there had existed since 1550 the brilliant and feverish army of versifiers who accompanied Ronsard, 'the Prince of Poets', and claimed with him to have created out of the rude elements of the Middle Ages a literary art which linked modern France directly with ancient Greece. While England was still languishing under the early Tudors, and Italy had grown weary of her burst of chivalrous epic, France gave the world the spectacle of a society palpitating with literary ambition. Ronsard's magnificent audacity had conquered for poetry, an art which had hitherto enjoyed little honour in France, the foremost position in the world of mental activity. Verse, which had been treated as a butterfly skipping from flower to flower, was now celebrated by the Pléiade as a temple, as a sunrise, as the apotheosis of the intellect. Immensely flattered by being suddenly lifted to the status of a priesthood, all the budding versifiers of France, who a generation earlier would have withered into insignificance, expanded into affluent and profuse blossom. By the year 1560 it was 'roses, roses all the way', but the misfortune was that the flowers were foreign, had been transplanted from Greece and Rome and Italy, and were not really native to the soil of France.

During the next generation, under conditions with which we have no time to occupy us to-day, there was a steady, indeed an almost precipitous decline in the quality of French verse. If we turn to our own literature of half a century later, we see a parallel decline in the drama down from Shakespeare to Shirley and the later disciples of Ben Jonson. We all know how disconcerting it is to pass from the sheer beauty of the great Elizabethans to the broken verse and the mixture of flatness and violence of the lesser poets of the Commonwealth. But in France the decadence had been still more striking, because of the extremely high line adopted by Ronsard and Du Bellay in their prose manifestos. The doctrine of the Pléiade had been as rigorous and lofty as a creed in literature could well be, and it rose to an altogether higher plane than was dreamed of by the English critics half a century later. No dignity, no assurance of high and pure poetic resolution could surpass the apparent aim of the manifestoes of 1549. Frenchmen, it seemed, had nothing to do but follow these exalted precepts and to produce the most wonderful poetry which the world had seen since the days of Pindar and Sappho. We cannot to-day enter into the question why these high hopes were almost immediately shattered, except so far as to suggest that excellent principles are sometimes insufficient to produce satisfactory practice. We have to look abruptly this afternoon into the conditions of French poetry in the last years of the sixteenth century, and to realize that those conditions had brought French literature to a point where reform was useless and revolution was inevitable.

There was no slackening—and I ask your particular attention to this fact—there was no slackening in the popularity of the poetic art.   There existed, in 1595, as great a crowd of versifiers as had been called forth fifty years earlier by the splendour of the Pléiade.   A feature of poetic history which is worthy of our notice is that an extreme abundance of poetical composition is by no means necessarily connected with the wholesomeness and vigour of the art at that moment.   There was a crowd of poets in France during the reign of Henri IV, but they were distinguished more by their exuberance and their eccentricity than by their genius.   I shall, in a few moments, endeavour to give you an idea of their character.   In the meantime, let us be content to remark that the exquisite ideals of the Pléiade had degenerated into extravagant conventionality, into which an attempt was made to infuse life by a spasmodic display of verbal fireworks.   The charm of sobriety, of simplicity, was wholly disregarded, and the importance of logic and discipline in literature ignored and outraged.   The earlier theory, a very dangerous one, had been that poetry was the language of gods rather than of men, that it was *grandiloquentia*, an oracular inspiration.   Being above mankind in its origin, it was not for mortal men to question its authority.   It possessed a celestial freedom, it was emancipated from all rules save what it laid down for itself.   Let us see what was the effect of this arrogance.

The scope of imaginative literature as practised by the Pléiade had been curiously narrow, so much so that it is difficult to distinguish the work of different hands except by the dexterity of the technique.   The odes and pastorals of the lesser masters are just like those of Ronsard, except that Ronsard is very much more skilful.

But by the close of the century there was a wide divergence between the various poets in their themes and their points of view. Two of them greatly excelled their contemporaries in eminence and popularity, and these two were as unlike each other in substance as it was easy for them to be. The elder of these two was Salluste du Bartas, a writer whose quartos are now allowed to gather dust on the shelves, and who, when he died in 1590, was, with the exception of Tasso, the most eminent European writer of verse. His influence on English poetry in the next generation was immense. Translations of his works by Joshua Sylvester and others had begun to appear before his death, and were extremely popular. Du Bartas possessed qualities of intellect and art which are by no means to be despised, but his taste was execrable. He wished to create a national religious poetry on a large scale, and he has been called the 'Milton manqué de la France'. Du Bartas is all relinquished to evangelical and moral exhortation, and his immense *Les Semaines*, besides being one of the longest, is the most unblushingly didactic encyclopaedia of verse that was ever put forth as a poem. He had a very heavy hand, and he sowed with the whole sack. Our own Bishop Joseph Hall of Norwich, who called him ' some French angel, girt with bays ', described Du Bartas as—

> The glorious Sallust, moral, true, divine,
> Who, all inspirèd with a holy rage,
> Makes Heaven his subject, and the earth his stage.

In his own time his myriad admirers preferred him above ' golden Homer and great Maro '. His earnestness and his cleverness—among other things he was the first man after the Renaissance to see that the obsession of the heathen gods was ridiculous in a Christian

literature—his abundance and his vehemence, made Du
Bartas a very formidable figure in the path of any
possible reform.

As an instance of the violence of fancy and gaudy
extravagance of language which had become prevalent
with the decline of the Pléiade, I will now present to
you what I select as a favourable, not a ridiculous,
example of the art of Du Bartas. He wishes to paraphrase the simple statement in Genesis that, on the
fourth day, God set the stars in the firmament of heaven
to give light upon the earth. This is how he does it:

> Even as a peacock, prickt with love's desire,
> To woo his mistress, strutting stately by her,
> Spreads round the rich pride of his pompous vail,
> His azure wings and starry-golden tail,
> With rattling pinions wheeling still about,
> The more to set his beauteous beauty out,—
> The Firmament, as feeling like above,
> Displays his pomp, pranceth about his love,
> Spreads his blue curtain, mixt with golden marks,
> Set with gilt spangles, sown with glistening sparks,
> Sprinkled with eyes, speckled with tapers bright,
> Powdered with stars streaming with glorious light,
> To inflame the Earth the more, with lover's grace
> To take the sweet fruit of his kind embrace.

Our first impression of such a passage as this is one of
admiration of its colour and of its ingenuity. It is more
than rich, it is sumptuous; the picture of the wheeling
peacock is original and brilliantly observed. But there
commendation must cease. What could be meaner or
less appropriate than to compare the revolution of the
starry firmament as it proceeded from its Creator's
hands with the strut of a conceited bird in a poultry-
yard? The works of Du Bartas are stuffed full with
these strained and fantastic similes, his surface sparkles
with the glitter of tinsel and pinchbeck. At every turn

something majestic reminds him of an embroidery, of a false jewel, of something picturesque and mean. The planets, in their unison, are like the nails in a cart-wheel; when darkness comes on, heaven is playing at blind man's buff; the retreat of the armies of the King of Assyria reminds the poet of a gamekeeper drawing his ferret. He desires the snow to fall that it may ' perriwig with wool the bald-pate woods '. All is extravagant and false, all is offensive to the modesty of nature.

Du Bartas is stationed at the left wing of the army of poets. The right is held by Philippe Desportes, whose name has recently been made familiar to us by Sir Sidney Lee's investigations into the extraordinary way in which his works were pillaged in his lifetime by our Elizabethan sonneteers. Even Shakespeare seems to have read, and possibly imitated, Desportes's *Amours de Diane*. The producer in vast quantities of a kind of work which is exactly in the fashion of the moment is sure of a wide popular welcome, and the cleverness of Desportes was to see that after the death of Ronsard French taste went back on the severity of Du Bellay's classicism, and returned to the daintiness and artificial symmetry of the Petrarchists. It has been said that to the Italians of the sixteenth century Petrarch had become what Homer was to the Greeks and Virgil to the Latins. He was the unquestioned leader, the unchallenged exemplar. This infatuation, which spread through Europe, is of importance to us in our inquiry to-day, for Petrarch was really the worm, the crested and luminous worm, at the root of sixteenth-century poetry. It was extremely easy to imitate the amorous conceits of the Italian imitators of Petrarch, and of these imitators in France by far the most abundant, skilful, and unwearying was Philippe Desportes, to whom Petrarch's ingenious elocution appeared, as it appeared to all the critics of Europe, ' pure beauty itself '.   By the close of the century it was no longer the greater Italians, such as Francesco Molza, who represented at its height the victorious heresy of Petrarchism, it was a Frenchman, of whom our own great lyrist, Lodge, in his *Margarite of America* in 1596, wrote ' few men are able to second the sweet conceits of Philippe Desportes, whose poetical writings are ordinarily in everybody's hand '.   Desportes exercised over the whole of Europe an authority which surpassed that of Tennyson over the British Empire at the height of his reputation.

Here, then, was another and still more formidable lion couched at the gate of poetry to resist all possible reform.   The career of Desportes had been one of unbroken prosperity.   He had become, without an effort, the wealthiest and the most influential person of letters of his time.   His courtly elegance had enabled him to be all things to all men, and although a priest of unblemished character, he had attended one Valois king after another without betraying his inward feelings by a single moral grimace.   He had found no difficulty in celebrating the virtues of Henri III, and the anecdote about him that is best known is that he had been re-warded with an abbey for the homage of a single sonnet. He had exaggerated all the tricks of his predecessors with a certain sweetness and brilliance of his own, which had fascinated the polite world.   The best that can be said of Desportes is that he was an artificer of excellent skill, who manufactured metrical jewellery by rearranging certain commonplaces, such as that teeth are pearls, that lips are roses, that cheeks are lilies, that hair is a golden network.   But I will give you his own statement of his aim, not attempting to paraphrase his remarkable language. Desportes gives the following account of his ambition :

> I desire to build a temple to my chaste goddess. My eye shall be the lamp, and the immortal flame which ceaselessly consumes me shall serve as candle. My body shall be the altar, and my sighs the vows, and I will intone the service in thousands and thousands of verses.

What a ridiculous confusion of imagery! Here we have a man whose body is an altar, and whose eye—one of whose eyes—is a lamp, and whose passion is the candle in that lamp, and whose mouth and throat are detached from his body, and are preforming miracles in the vicinity. This is to take Desportes at his worst, and it is only fair to admit that the reader who winnows the vast floor of his work will find some grains of pure gold left. But the mass of these sonnets and odes and madrigals is extraordinarily insipid and cold, the similes are forced and grotesque, and everywhere pedantry takes the place of passion. When there is beauty it is artificial and affected, it is an Alexandrine beauty, it is the colour of the dying dolphin.

Such was the poetry which occupied the taste of France at the close of the sixteenth century, and whether its form was brief and amorous, as in the sonnets of Desportes, or long-winded and hortatory, as in the sacred epics of Du Bartas, it was uniformly exaggerated, lifeless, and incorrect. In all its expressions it was characterized by an abuse of language, and indeed, in the hands of the poets of the late Valois kings, the French tongue was hurrying down to ruin. One curious vice consisted in the fabrication of new phrases and freshly coined composite words. Of these latter, some one has counted no fewer than 300 in the writings

of Du Bartas alone, and Professor Paul Morillot has
observed that the licence which the poets of that age
indulged in has been the cause of subsequent poverty
in that direction, French having received and rejected
such a glut of new and useless words as to have lost all
appetite for additions of vocabulary.   Another vice of
the period was the ceaseless cultivation, in season and
out of season, of a sort of antithetical wit.   The sincerity
of nature was offended at every turn by the monstrous
cleverness of the writer, who evidently was thinking far
more about himself than about his subject.   Here is an
example :

Weep on, mine eyes, weep much, ye have seen much,
And now in water let your penance be,
Since 'twas in fire that you committed sin,

and so on, with wearisome iteration of the hyperbole.
We were to suffer from the same disease fifty years
later, when a great English poet, capable of far nobler
things, was to call the eyes of St. Mary Magdalene

Two walking baths, two weeping motions,
Portable and compendious oceans.

An excellent grammarian, M. Ferdinand Brunot, has
remarked that at the end of the sixteenth century
a lawless individualism—and in this term he sums up
all the component parts of literature, style, grammar,
treatment, and tone—had set in ; that everybody had
become a law to himself ; and that the French language
was suffering from the incessant disturbance caused by
'the fantastic individuality of writers' both in prose and
verse.

This chaotic state of things, which threatened French
literature with anarchy and French logic with bankruptcy,
was brought to a stand-still and successfully confronted

by the energy and determination of a single person. I recollect no other instance in the history of literature in which one individual has contrived to stem the whole flood of national taste. Of course, an instinct of French lucidity and reasonableness must have been ready to respond to the doctrine of the new critic, yet it is none the less certain that through the early years of the struggle there remains no evidence of his having been supported by any associate opinion. I dare say you recollect a famous Japanese print which represents a young lady standing on the edge of a cliff, and gazing calmly out to sea while she restrains the action of a great plunging horse by simply holding one of her feet down upon the reins. In the same way the run-away Pegasus of France was held, and was reduced to discipline, by the almost unparalleled resolution of a solitary man. This was François Malherbe, whose name, but perhaps very little else, will be familiar to you. I hope to show you that this poet, by the clearness of his vision and his rough independence, brought about a revolution in literature which was unparalleled. He cut a clear stroke, as with a hatchet, between the sixteenth century and all that came after it down to the romantic revival at the beginning of the nineteenth century, and he did this by sheer force of character. Malherbe was not a great poet, but he was a great man, and he is worthy of our close consideration.

François Malherbe was a Norman; there is a hint of the family having come from Suffolk, in which case the name may have been Mallerby, but we need not dwell on that. His parents were Calvinists, and he was born at Caen in 1555. This was, you observe, between the births of Spenser and Shakespeare; and Rabelais was just dead. Cervantes was eight years old, Lope de Vega

was to be born seven years later. We ought to notice
these dates : they give us a sense of what was preparing
in Europe, and what was passing away ; a great period
of transition was about to expand. Until he was thirty
years of age Malherbe appears to have taken no
interest whatever in poetry ; he was a soldier, a military
secretary, a man of business. Then he went to live in
Provence, where he read the Italian verse fashionable
in his day, and began to imitate it. The kindest and
most enthusiastic of his later disciples told Tallemant that
Malherbe's early poems were ' pitiful '. We can judge
for ourselves, since at the age of thirty-two he published
a paraphrase, or rather a series of selections from
Tansillo's *Lagrime di San Pietro*. The bad poets of
the age were lachrymose to the last degree. Nothing
but the honour of addressing you to-day would have
induced me to read these ' Tears of St. Peter '. I have
done so, and have even amused myself by paraphrasing
some of them, but these I will not inflict upon you. It
is sufficient to assure you that up to the age of forty the
verses of Malherbe were not merely, as Racan put it,
pitiful, but marred by all the ridiculous faults of the age.
After all, I must give you a single example. This is
translated literally from ' The Tears of St. Peter ' :

Aurora, in one hand, forth from her portals led,
Holds out a vase of flowers, all languishing and dead ;
And with the other hand empties a jar of tears ;
While through a shadowy veil, woven of mist, and
    storm,
That hides her golden hair, she shows in mortal form
All that a soul can feel of cruel pains and fears.

At what moment Malherbe observed that this was
a detestable way of writing, and conceived the project
of a great reversal of opinion, we do not know. His

early life, and just that part of it on which we should like light to be thrown, remains impenetrably obscure. But we do know that when he arrived in Paris he had formulated his doctrine and laid out his plan of campaign. At Aix-en-Provence he had been admitted to the meetings of a literary society, the chief ornament of which was the celebrated orator and moralist Du Vair, who ought perhaps to be considered as in some directions the master of Malherbe. The ideas of Du Vair have been traced in some of Malherbe's verses, and the poet afterwards said, in his dictatorial way, 'There is no better writer in our language than M. Du Vair.' It was probably the dignity of the orator's attitude and the severity of his taste in rhetoric which encouraged the poet to adopt a similar lucidity and strenuousness in verse. The two men, who were almost exactly of the same age, may perhaps be most safely looked upon as parallel reformers, the one of French verse, the other of French prose.

Few things would be more interesting to us, in our present mood, than to know how Malherbe, arriving in Paris at the mature age of fifty, set about his revolution. He found the polite world tired of frigid conceits and extravagant sentimentality, above all tired of the licence of the poets and the tricks which they were taking with the French language. There was undoubtedly a longing for order and regularity, such as invariably follows a period of revolutionary lawlessness, but no one was giving this sentiment a voice. What was wanted after such a glut of ornament and exuberance was an arbiter and tyrant of taste who should bring poetry rigidly into line with decency, plainness, and common sense, qualities which had long been thought unnecessary to, and even ridiculously incompatible with, literature of a high order.

All this we may divine, but what is very difficult to understand is the mode in which Malherbe became the recognized tyrant of taste. It was not by the production, and still less by the publication, of quantities of verse composed in accordance with his own new doctrine. Malherbe had hesitated long in the retirement of the country, waiting to be summoned to Court. Somehow, although he had published no book and can scarcely have been known to more than a handful of persons, he had a few powerful friends, and among them, strange to say, three poets whose work was characteristic of everything which it was to be Malherbe's mission to destroy. These were the Cardinal Du Perron, Bertaut, and Vauquelin de la Fresnaye. They formed the van of the poetical army of the moment, and it is a very curious thing that these three remarkable writers, each of whom remained faithful to the tradition of Ronsard, should have welcomed with open arms the rebel who was to cover Ronsard with ridicule. With a divine simplicity, they opened the wicket and let the wolf in among the sheep. They urged the King to invite Malherbe to Court, and, when His Majesty delayed, Malherbe very characteristically did not wait for a summons. He came to Paris of his own accord in 1605, was presented to Henri IV, and composed in September of that year the long ode called a ' Prayer for the King on his going to Limoges'. This is the first expression of classical verse in the French language.

In those days the intelligent favour of the King did more for a reputation than a dozen glowing reviews in the chief newspapers will do to-day. We must give credit to Henri IV for the promptitude with which he perceived that the cold new poetry, which must have sounded very strangely on his ears accustomed to the lute of Desportes and the trumpet of Du Bartas, was exactly what was wanted in France. He himself had laboured to bring back to this country, distracted as it had been in its late political disorders, the virtues of law, logic, and discipline. He recognized in this grim, middle-aged Norman gentleman the same desires, but directed to the unity and order of literature. A recent French historian has pointed out that ' the very nature of Malherbe's talent, its haughty, solemn, and majestic tone, rendered him peculiarly fitted to become the official and, as it were, the impersonal singer of the King's great exploits, and to engrave in letters of brass, as on a triumphal monument, the expression of public gratitude and admiration'. Malherbe, as has been said, was appointed ' the official poet of the Bourbon dynasty'.

The precious correspondence with his Provençal friend Peiresc, which Malherbe kept up from 1606 till his death in 1628, a correspondence which was still unknown a hundred years ago, throws a good deal of light upon the final years of the poet, and in particular on the favour with which he was entertained at court. There are more than 200 of these letters, which nevertheless, like most such collections at that age, succeed in concealing from us the very facts which we are most anxious to hear about. Thus, while Malherbe expatiates to Peiresc about queens and princes, he tells us nothing, or next to nothing, about the literary life in which we know that he made so disconcerting a figure. But that most enchanting of gossips, Tallemant des Réaux, has preserved for us an anecdote of a highly illuminating nature. We have seen that the supremacy in French poetry had been held for many years by Philippe Desportes, who was now approaching the close of a long life of sumptuous success. It could not be a matter of indifference to the last and most magnificent of the Ronsardists that an upstart, till now unheard of, should suddenly be welcomed at court. He desired his nephew, Mathurin Régnier—himself a man of genius, but not in our picture to-day—he desired Régnier to bring this M. de Malherbe to dinner. They arrived, but were late, and dinner stood already on the table. The old Desportes received Malherbe with all the politeness conceivable, and said that he wished to give him a copy of the new edition of his 'Psalms', in which he had made many corrections and additions. Such a compliment from the acknowledged head of French poetry was extreme, but Malherbe had already made up his mind to bring down the reputation of Desportes with a crash, as Samson destroyed the gates of Dagon in Gaza. Desportes was starting to go upstairs to fetch the book, when Malherbe in rough country fashion (*rustiquement*) told him he had seen it already, that it was not worth while to let his soup grow cold, for it was likely to be better than his 'Psalms' were. Upon this they sat down to dinner at once, but Malherbe said nothing more, and when dinner was done he went away, leaving the host heart-broken and young Régnier furious. This must have been very soon after Malherbe's arrival in Paris, for Desportes died in 1606.

All that has been recorded of the manners and conversation of Malherbe tends to explain this story. He could be courtly and even magnificent, and he had a bluff kind of concentrated politeness, when he chose to exercise it, which was much appreciated by the royal family. He was a tall, handsome man, with keen eyes, authoritative and even domineering, generally silent in society, but ready to break in with a brusque contradiction of what somebody else was saying. He was ?

scorner of human frailty, believing himself to be above
the reach of all emotional weakness. The violent force,
which burned arrogantly in his spirit, comes out in
everything which is preserved about him, in his verses,
in his letters, in the anecdotes of friends and enemies.
His retorts were like those of Dr. Samuel Johnson, but
without the healing balsam of Johnson's tenderness.
There was nothing tender about Malherbe, and we may
admit that he could not have carried out his work if
there had been. His intellectual conscience was implacable; he allowed nothing in the world to come
between him and his inexorable doctrine. When he
learned that the Vicomtesse d'Auchy (Charlotte des
Ursins), the 'Caliste' of his own verses, had been encouraging a poet of the old school, he went to her house,
pushed into her bedroom, and slapped her face as she
lay upon her bed.

Tallemant tells us that 'meditation and art made a
poet' of Malherbe, *non nascitur sed fit*. At no time did
he learn to write with ease, and after so many years
spent in the passionate cultivation of the Muse, his
poetical writings are contained in as narrow a compass
as those of Gray, who confessed that his 'works' were
so small that they might be mistaken for those of a
pismire. Malherbe had long pauses during which he
seemed to do nothing at all except meditate and lay
down the law. Balzac, who was one of those young
men in whose company he delighted, declares that
whenever Malherbe had written a thousand verses he
rested for ten years. All this was part of a studied
frugality. The Ronsardists and their followers had
been lavish in everything; they had poured out floods of
slack verse, loose in construction, faulty in grammar. If
a slight difficulty presented itself to them, they evaded

it, they leaped over it. Having no reverence for the
French language, they invented hideous and reckless
words, they stretched or curtailed syllables, in order to
fit the scansion. There is recorded a saying of Malherbe
which is infinitely characteristic. When he was asked
what, in fact, was his object in all he was doing, he
replied that he proposed 'to rescue French poetry from
the hands of the little monsters who were dishonouring
it'. The glorious Desportes, the sublime Du Bartas,
the rest of the glittering and fashionable Petrarchists of
Paris, what were they in the eyes of this implacable
despot of the new intellectual order? They were simply
'little monsters' who were 'dishonouring' what he
worshipped with a fanatic zeal, the language of France.

When we turn to his own poetry, we see what there
was in it which fascinated the opening seventeenth
century. After all the tortures and the spasms, the
quietude of it was delicious. If you go to Malherbe
now, you must learn to put aside all your romantic preoccupations. His verse is very largely concerned with
negations : it is *not* ornamented, it is not preposterous, it
is not pedantic. It swept away all the insincere imagery
and all the violent oddities of the earlier school. For
example, Bertaut had written, wishing to explain his
tears :

> By the hydraulic of mine eyes
> The humid vapours of my grief are drawn
> Through vacuums of my sighs.

Desportes had talked of a lover who was 'intoxicated
by the delectation of the concert of the divine harmony'
of his mistress. All this preciousness, all this affectation
of the use of scientific terms in describing simple
emotions, was the object of Malherbe's ruthless disdain.
Ronsard had said, 'The more words we have in our

language, the more perfect it will be '. Malherbe replied,
' No, certainly not, if they are useless and grotesque
words, dragged by the hair of their heads out of Greek
and Latin, an outrage on the purity of French grammar '.
He advised his disciples to eject the monstrous creations
of the neo-Hellenes, and to go down to the quays of
Paris and listen to the dock-labourers. They used
genuine French words which ought to be redeemed
from vulgar use, and brought back to literary service.

The existing poems of Malherbe, written at intervals
during the last twenty years of his life, are largely
pieces of circumstance. They are odes on public events,
such as the retaking of Marseilles, the official journeys
of the King, the regency of the Queen Mother, and the
alliance between France and Spain. They are elegies
on the deaths of private persons, a subject on which
Malherbe expatiates with the utmost dignity and
solemnity. They are sonnets, very unlike the glittering
rosy gimcracks of the preceding generation, but stiff
with stately compliment and colourless art. There is
no exact English analogue to the poetry of Malherbe,
because in the seventeenth century whenever English
verse, except in the hands of Milton, aimed at an effect
of rhetorical majesty, its stream became clouded. We
may observe the case of Cowley, who, I think, had
certainly read Malherbe and was influenced by him, in
spite of the diametrical views they nourished with regard
to the merit of Pindar. Cowley, at his rare and occasional best, has the same serious music, the same clear
roll of uplifted enthusiasm, the same absolute assurance
as Malherbe. He has the same felicity in his sudden
and effective openings. But there is too frequently
confusion, artifice, and negligence in Cowley. In
Malherbe all is perfectly translucent, nothing turbid is

allowed to confuse the vision, no abuse of wit is left to
dazzle the attention or trip up steadily advancing progress of thought. It is not easy to give an impression in
English of the movement of this clear and untrammelled
advance. But here are a couple of stanzas from the 1611
Ode to the Queen Regent on occasion of the King's
Mediterranean expedition:

Ah! may beneath thy son's proud arm down fall
    The bastions of the Memphian wall,
And from Marseilles to Tyre itself extend
    His empire without end.

My wishes, p'rhaps, are wild; but—by your leave—
    What cannot ardent prayer achieve?
And if the gods reward your service so
    They'll pay but what they owe.

By general consent the crown of Malherbe's poetic
genius is the famous 'Consolation to Monsieur Du
Périer on the death of his daughter'. It contains the
best-known line of Malherbe—

Et, Rose, elle a vécu ce que vivent les roses,

about which I would merely say that it is one of those
accidental romantic verses which occur here and there
in all the great classical poets. There are several in
Pope, where they are no more characteristic of his
general style than is this of Malherbe's. So far from
being the chief line in the poem, it is, in spite of its
beauty, the least important to us in our present inquiry.
The 'Consolation' consists of twenty-one stanzas, written
long after the sad event of the death of the young lady,
whose name, by the way, was not Rose, but Marguerite.
The advice which the poet gives to the stricken father is
stoical and Roman. Weary yourself no more with
these useless and prolonged lamentations; but hence-

forth be wise, and love a shadow as a shadow, and extinguish the memory of extinguished ashes. The instances of Priam and Alcides may seem to have little in them to cheer Du Périer, but we must remember that antiquity was held a more sacred authority three hundred years ago than it is now. Malherbe, with great decorum, recalls to Du Périer the fact that he himself has lost two beloved children. The poor man under his thatched roof is subject to the laws of death, nor can the guard on watch at the gates of the Louvre protect our kings against it. To complain of the inevitable sacrifice, and to lose patience with Providence, is to lack wisdom. The only philosophy which can bring repose to a heart bereaved is implicit submission to the will of God.

All this may not seem very original, but it is exquisitely phrased, and it is sensible, dignified, and wholesome. There is in it a complete absence of the ornament and circumstance of death which had taken so preposterous a place in the abundant elegiac poetry of the sixteenth century. We are familiar with the grotesque and sumptuous appeals to the *macabre* which we meet with in Raleigh, in Donne, in Quarles, all the dismal trappings of the tomb and embroideries of the winding-sheet. They are wholly set aside by Malherbe, whose sonnet on the death of his son is worthy of special study. This young man, who was the pride of the poet's life, was killed in a duel, or, as the father vociferously insisted, murdered by a treacherous ruffian. Malherbe made the courts ring with his appeals, but he also composed a sonnet, which is a typical example of his work. It is not what we should call 'poetical', but in clearness, in force, in full capacity to express exactly what the author had in mind to say, it is perfect. We seem to hear the very cry of the fierce old man shrieking for revenge on the slayer of his son. The sonnet was composed some time after the event, for the whole art of Malherbe was the opposite of improvisation. One amusing instance of his deliberate method is to be found in the history of his ode to console President Nicolas de Verdun on the death of his wife. Malherbe composed his poem so slowly, that while he was writing it the President widower not merely married a second time, but died. The poet, with consummate gravity, persisted in his task, and was able to present the widow with the consolation which her late husband should have received after the death of her predecessor.

During thirty years of growing celebrity, Malherbe fought for his doctrine. He had but slowly become a convert to his own laws, but when once they were clearly set out in his brain, he followed them scrupulously, and he insisted that the world should obey them too. It seems a strange thing that it was the young men who followed him first and with most enthusiasm, until the fashionable ladies of Paris began to compete with one another in support of the classical doctrine, and in repudiation of their old favourite Desportes, whose fame came down clattering in a single night, like Beckford's tower at Fonthill. Malherbe brought poetry into line with the Court and the Church, in a decent formality. Largely, as is always the case in the history of literature, the question was one more of language than of substance. Take, for example, the 'Stanzas to Alcandre on the Return of Oranthe to Fontainebleau', and you will find them as preposterous in sentiment, as pretentious and affected in conception, as any sonnet of Desportes, perhaps more so, but their diction is perfectly simple and graceful, and they are composed in faultless modern French. Long before Molière was born Malherbe was in the habit of reading his verses to an old servant, and if there was a single phrase which gave her difficulty, he would scrupulously revise it.

He was supported by a sublime conviction of his own value. It was a commonplace in all the poetical literature of the sixteenth century to claim immortality. Desportes had told his mistress that she would live for ever like the Phoenix, in the flame of his sonnets. We all remember Shakespeare's boast that 'not marble, nor the gilded monuments of princes shall outlive this powerful rhyme'. But no one was ever more certain of leaving behind him a lasting monument than Malherbe. He said, addressing the King :

All pour their praise on you, but not with equal hand,
For while a common work survives one year or two,
What Malherbe writes is stamped with immortality.

The self-gratulation at the close of the noble ' Île de Ré ' ode is quite disconcerting. In this case, also, he reminds the King that

The great Amphion, he whose voice was nonpareil,
    Amazed the universe by fanes it lifted high;
Yet he with all his art has builded not so well
    As by my verse have I.

His boast, extravagant as it sounds, was partly justified. Not in his own verse, but in that which his doctrine encouraged others to write—and not in verse only, but in prose, and in the very arrangement and attitude of the French intellect—Malherbe's influence was wide-spreading, was potent, and will never be wholly superseded. He found French, as a literary language, confused, chaotic, no longer in the stream of sound tradition. He cleared out the channel, he dredged

away the mud and cut down the weeds ; and he brought
the pure water back to its proper course. Let us not
suppose that he did this completely, or that his authority
was not challenged. It was, and Malherbe did not live
to see the victory of his ideas. He did not survive
long enough to found the Académie, or to welcome
Vaugelas, the great grammarian who would have been
the solace of his old age. There were still many men
of talent, such as Pélisson and Agrippa d'Aubigné, who
resisted his doctrine. But he had made his great appeal
for order and regularity ; he had wound his slug-horn in
the forest. He had poured his ideas into the fertile brain
of Richelieu ; he had started the momentous discussions
of the Hôtel Rambouillet. He had taught a new generation to describe objects in general terms, to express
natural ideas with simplicity, to select with scrupulous
care such words as were purely French and no others,
to eschew hiatus and inversion and to purify rhyme, to
read the ancients with sympathetic attention but not to
pillage them. His own limitations were marked. He
seems to have had no sense whatever for external nature ;
while he overvalued a mathematical exactitude of balance
in versification and a grandiose severity in rhetoric.

But we are not attempting this afternoon to define the
French Classic School, but merely to comprehend how
and when it came into being. It preceded our own
Classic School by the fifty years which divide Malherbe
from Dryden, who, in like manner, but with far less
originality, freed poetry from distortion, prolixity, and
artifice. Whe Malherbe died no one could guess how
prodigious would be the effect of his teaching. Indeed,
at that moment, October 6, 1628, there might even seem
to be a certain retrogression to the old methods, a
certain neglect of the new doctrine, which seemed to

have been faintly taken up. But, looking back, we now see that at the moment of Malherbe's death, Corneille was on the point of appearing, while there were children in the nurseries who were to be La Fontaine, Pascal, Molière, Mme de Sévigné, Bossuet. Boileau and Racine were not even born, for Malherbe sowed early and the harvest came late.

The ruling passion accompanied this resolute reformer to the very close of his career. His faithful disciple, Racan, his Boswell, has drawn for us the last scene :

> One hour before he died, M. de Malherbe woke with a start out of a deep slumber, to rebuke his hostess, who was also his nurse, for using an expression which he did not consider to be correct French. When his confessor ventured to chide him, he replied that he could not help it, and that he wished to preserve up to the moment of his death the purity of the French language.

NOTE

The passage on p. 8 is quoted from Josuah Sylvister's version of 'Les Semaines'. For all the other translations the lecturer is responsible.

The Taylorian Lecture

1921

RACINE IN ENGLAND

By

F. Y. ECCLES.

RACINE IN ENGLAND

I TRUST the title ' Racine in England' has led no one
to expect a startling discovery in the biographical sphere.
I have none to offer. It has not yet been suggested that
Jean Racine ever set foot upon our shores, or that he
was tempted at any moment in his career (as his friend
the Fabulist undoubtedly was tempted) to cross the
Channel and join the little group of French gentlemen in
London whose exile was cheered by the wisdom of
Saint-Évremond and the grace of Madame Mazarin. My
subject is the reception which the tragedies of Racine
met with among our ancestors, and the reputation they
have borne during the seven or eight generations which
have passed since they were first brought to the notice
of English people. It would be strange if it had always
stood at a dead level, and in any fair account of the
matter several phases ought to be distinguished; but upon
the whole, let it be said at once, the fluctuations of favour
and disfavour do not seem to have been considerable.
It is known that Racine was read from the first, in the
original, by the small class of English people who, in
the age of Dryden, looked eagerly to France for novelties
in literature. A much wider public saw English translations or imitations of his plays performed upon our
stage in the last quarter of the seventeenth century and
the first of the eighteenth. Similar experiments had
been made much earlier, and continued to be made,
with Corneille. The *Cid* had been played in English
before Charles I and his French queen ; and, in the first
years of the Restoration, versions of *La Mort de Pompée*,
Horace, Héraclius, Nicomède, and *Le Menteur* had been

produced with more or less applause. The most famous of these is the *Pompey* of Katherine Philips, 'the matchless Orinda', a faithful and spirited translation brilliantly presented in Dublin and hyperbolically praised by her elegant and learned circle ; the most popular was probably *Heraclius, Emperor of the East*, which Pepys saw several times with much satisfaction. The first attempt to acclimatize, or to exploit, Racine was made in 1675, when an *Andromache* was produced at the Duke's Theatre in London and published by the prolific playwright John Crowne, with a preface in which he disclaimed the authorship. The translator, 'a young gentleman, who has a great esteem of all French plays, and particularly of this', had asked him to revise for the stage a version of *Andromaque* in English rhyming couplets. Crowne thought the verse poor, and turned nearly four acts into prose, but left the rest as it was. This hybrid seems to have had very little success, in spite of an improvement on the original in the last act, where (says Crowne) ' what was only dully recited in the French Playe, is represented '. This is, of course, the assassination of Pyrrhus.

Two years later appeared the *Titus and Berenice* of Thomas Otway. It has three acts for Racine's five, and there are some important differences in the affabulation. Otway makes Antiochus confide his love for Berenice to the Emperor before he is entrusted with the message which is to destroy the Queen's hopes ; and the play ends upon a note of savage despair, very different from the sorrowful acquiescence which is that of *Berenice*. We are unprepared for the final tirade in which Titus threatens to avenge his private wound by becoming the tyrant of his people. Throughout, the logic of passion is merely obscured by merciless excisions. With all this, the English play is a translation, and in many parts a close one, and it is not true that nothing of Racine's spirit has passed into the verse of Otway. We miss, indeed, at many turns, the pregnancy and the reticence of the French. When Berenice, in her first confident mood, learns that Antiochus is leaving Rome, she asks, with ingenuous cruelty:

> What pleasure in my greatness can I find,
> When I shall want my best and truest friend?

Antiochus answers:

> I reach your Púrpose; you would have me there,
> That you might see the worst of my Despair.
> I know it, the Ambition of your Soul;
> 'Tis true, I've been a fond obedient Fool.
> Yet came this to me but to new-freight my heart,
> And, with more love possest than ever, part.

Here is the corresponding passage of Racine:

> *Bérénice.*   A regret je reçois vos adieux.
> Le Ciel fait qu'au milieu des honneurs qu'il m'envoie
> Je n'attendois que vous pour témoin de ma joie ...
> Cent fois je me suis fait une douceur extrême
> D'entretenir Titus dans un autre moi-même.
>   *Titus.* Et c'est ce que je fais. J'évite, mais trop tard,
> Ces cruels entretiens où je n'ai point de part.
> Je fuis Titus. Je fuis ce nom qui m'inquiète,
> Ce nom qu'à tous moments votre bouche répète.
> Que vous dirai-je enfin? Je fuis des yeux distraits,
> Qui, me voyant toujours, ne me voyoient jamais.
> Adieu. Je vais, le cœur tout plein de votre image,
> Attendre, en vous aimant, la mort pour mon partage.

On the other hand, exact and satisfying equivalents are not rare: this, for instance—

> Oh! give me more Content, and less of State,

for:

> Hélas! plus de repos, Seigneur, et moins d'éclat.

Above all, that grandiloquence, which is the common vice of Otway's contemporaries in serious drama, and disfigures almost all imitations of Racine, is wholly absent. If this early effort does not promise *The Orphan* or *Venice Preserv'd*, it shows already something of that power in him which Dryden called nature. The characters here, as in the French, talk simply. Yet it must be owned that Otway, more than once, in seeking simplicity achieves flatness, as when his confidant calls Antiochus

> One of the greatest of our Eastern Kings,

and Titus confesses :

> The loose wild Paths of Pleasure I pursu'd
> Till *Berenice* first taught me to be good.

On the whole, this version is not too much to be despised. Though Betterton and Mrs. Lee appeared in the chief characters, it never became a favourite with the Restoration public, and the translator was not tempted to repeat his venture. For the sake of Racine, we may regret it. The mature art of Otway has no analogy, whatever may be said, with the Frenchman's : yet in temperament—in the union of tenderness and devouring passion—they were not, perhaps, so unlike, but that he, if any one, might have succeeded in the delicate task of transplantation.

In the year 1699 a Huguenot refugee, Abel Boyer, put forth an adaptation of *Iphigénie* under the title of *Achilles, or Iphigenia in Aulis*. Boyer was known in London as a French tutor and an industrious translator, and was shortly to publish the great dictionary of the two languages which had no serious rival for upwards of a century. Later on, he won a kind of celebrity as a pamphleteer, as the editor of *The Post-Boy*

and the historian of the reigns of King William and
Queen Anne. He knew English intimately and wrote
it as easily as his countryman Motteux. Nothing in
Achilles betrays the foreigner, and its blank verse (barring
some dubious stresses) is pretty tolerable. There are
some alexandrines, and occasional short lines. He said
long afterwards that Dryden himself had looked through
his manuscript. A great part of the play is a free but
most distinct rendering of the French : but the longer
speeches are divided, and there is a great deal of mere
'padding'.

Four lines are enough to illustrate his manner :
You may securely tire the Gods with Prayers,
And load their Altars with tame Offerings ;
You may consult the panting Victim's Breast,
And search the Cause of the Wind's tedious silence . . .
There is nothing to be said against these lines as a
translation, except that the words 'tame', 'panting', and
'tedious' are superfluous. But it is not until the final
act that he gives rein to his constructive talents. This
is how he understood the process of accommodating
Racine to the English taste. The moment is arrived
at which the awful sacrifice is to be consummated.
After a last passionate outburst, Clytemnestra 'runs off
with her maids' and the stage is left empty for a
moment. Then (I am quoting the stage directions),

> *while a symphony is playing, an Altar is rais'd near
> the sea-shore. Enter King* Agamemnon *weeping;*
> Menelaus, Nestor, Ulysses, Aeneas, etc.; Calchas
> *the High Priest;* Iphigenia *between two Priests;*
> Eriphile, Doris.

A chorus of priests sings the invocation to Diana 'set by
Mr. Finger'.

> *As Iphigenia is leading to be sacrific'd, the Sun is
> eclips'd; Shrieks in the Air; subterranean Groans
> and Howlings; Thunder.*

Calchas asks, 'What mean these Horrors?', and
Eriphile whispers: 'Oh! Doris, how I tremble!'

(*Clashing of Swords within.*) *Enter* Achilles, Patroclus,
and Followers.
Achilles. Where! Where's my Iphigenia?
Hold, Murderers, hold!
Calchas. My Lord, constrain your Passion; I bid
you hold.
The Gods themselves are angry—They must first be
heard.   (*Thunder.*)

The High Priest having consulted the Oracle returns
with all the signs of terror and delivers it.   He ends by
pointing to Eriphile: 'The Gods demand'——

(*As* Calchas *is going to lay hold on* Eriphile, *she
snatches the Knife.*)
Butcher, avaunt! . . .
I fall a Victim to a greater Power.
Almighty Love now strikes the fatal Blow.
                                                (*Stabs herself.*)
Achilles, dear—Achilles . . (*Dies.*)
Iphigenia. Unhappy Maid!
(*Thunder and Lightning.* . . . *Diana, in a Machine,
crosses the Stage.*)
Calchas. Great sir, the gods are satisfied;
And Iphigenia is yours again!
Agamemnon. Must I believe my Eyes! Oh! Sir!
Oh! Daughter!

In spite of (I fear we must not say because of) these
spectacular condiments, Boyer's play was a failure.
His own account of the matter is that it was prejudiced
by the recent appearance of a classical tragedy by John
Dennis on the subject of *Iphigenia in Tauris*, and
also by the ill-acting of Eriphile.   He was certainly
unfortunate, for in 1714 another adaptation of Racine's
tragedy, called *The Victim*, by Charles Johnson, was
produced by Wilks at Drury Lane, and pleased the
public better, for reasons I have been unable to discover.

Boyer, accusing Johnson of plagiarism, promptly repub-
lished his own play with Johnson's title. A charge of
this kind brought by one adapter against another will
always be heard sceptically. I have had the patience to
compare them, and I conclude that as far as the main
body of Johnson's play goes, Boyer has little to complain of. The second version is more distant from
Racine, and in some things follows Euripides : Menelaus,
who is only seen in dumb show in Boyer's play and does
not appear in Racine's, intervenes here, as he does in
Euripides. But it is incredible that Johnson did not
filch his final scene from Boyer. The altar, the procession, the Invocation to Diana, the thunder and lightning,
all are there. The entry of Achilles is a little delayed,
and Eriphile is rather longer dying; the speeches (which
are to the same effect) are a little more substantial and
the Invocation somewhat shorter ; nor does Diana
appear in a Machine : that is the whole difference. As
for the relative merit of the two plays, it may be said
that Johnson's lines are smoother and his style upon the
whole less vigorous. A last distinction must be added :
he does not name Racine ; Boyer does, and handsomely.

Between these two adaptations, in 1706 and 1712
respectively, appeared the two most famous English plays
which are connected with the name of Racine. The
first is *Phaedra and Hippolytus*, by Mr. Edmund Neale or
Smith, of Christ Church, known sometimes as 'the handsome sloven', and sometimes as 'Captain Rag'. This
tragedy is only in part a paraphrase of *Phèdre*. Smith
went directly to Euripides and to Seneca for a great
part of his material ; apart from a number of particular
passages, he got from Racine the idea of Hippolytus in
love; the unravelling is entirely his own. Some characteristic differences in the affabulation are these : Phaedra, in

the first act, confesses her passion before Ismena (the
Aricie of Racine), who is already known to be beloved by
Hippolytus ; in the scene in which Hippolytus learns her
guilty secret (in which the author follows Racine pretty
closely), the Queen endeavours to reassure him by protesting that she has been only in name a wife to Theseus ;
Ismena reproaches her lover at first with infidelity, but
is convinced of his innocence, and they plan to escape
together, but are arrested by the Queen's orders ; the
return of Theseus is delayed until this point. As for
the catastrophe, Phaedra kills herself on hearing that
Hippolytus has died by his own act, but the news was
false, and at the end he reappears to receive Ismena
from the hand of his father. The play has little to
recommend it, being as poor in characterization as it is
inflated in language. When it was first put upon the
stage, it ran for four nights only, the rival attraction of
the Italian opera being too strong for it, if we may trust
Addison, who, in a well-known essay attacking that kind
of entertainment, asked indignantly :

' Would one think it was possible (at a time when an
author lived that was able to write the *Phaedra and
Hippolytus*) for a people to be so stupidly fond of the
Italian opera, as scarce to give a third day's hearing to
that admirable tragedy ? '

Something must be allowed to private friendship and
something to a sincere dislike of a foreign fashion.
Addison repeated the attack in a prologue with which
he consoled the author of the slighted tragedy. Smith,
however, did not need consolation long. *Phaedra and
Hippolytus* was revived and soon became almost popular ;
it was played at intervals until near the end of the
century, and the book was certainly much read : a
fourth edition appeared in 1729. But a more immediate

triumph and a more durable reputation was won by *The Distrest Mother* of Ambrose Philips, the author of the Pastorals, the client of Steele and Addison and the victim of Alexander Pope. It is not necessary to say much of the circumstances which attended the production of this tragedy, or of the quarrel which followed it: they belong at most to the suburbs of my subject. Every reader of the *Spectator* knows how Steele prepared his public 'to see truth and human life represented in the incidents which concern heroes and heroines', in a play of which the style 'is such as becomes those of the first education', and the sentiments are 'worthy of those of the highest figure'; every one who loves Sir Roger has accompanied him, with Captain Sentry, to Drury Lane, and has been diverted with the old Knight's comments on the tragedy: his saying, upon the entering of Pyrrhus, 'that he did not believe the King of France himself had a better strut', and of Andromache's obstinacy: 'You can't imagine, Sir, what it is to have to do with a widow', and of Hermione: 'On my word, a notable young baggage', and the anxious question: 'Should your people in tragedy always talk to be understood?' The piece appeared on March 17, 1711, before a house packed, according to Pope, with the author's friends. The prologue was written by Steele. It is (like the preface with which Philips introduced the published play) mainly a vindication of what was understood to be the grand characteristic of classical drama:

Since Fancy of itself is loose and vain,
The wise by Rules that airy Power restrain.

The genius of Shakespeare might be suffered to laugh at distance; but

Our Author does his feeble force confess . . .
And therefore makes propriety his aim . . .

Not only Rules of Time and Place preserves,
But strives to keep his Characters entire,
With French Correctness and with British Fire.
This Piece presented in a foreign Tongue
When France was glorious and her Monarch young
A hundred times a crowded Audience drew,
A hundred times repeated, still 'twas new.

The Distrest Mother is written in blank verse of mid-
dling quality, with the usual tail-pieces in rhyme, and in
a style not indeed inflated, but thoroughly conventional.
The heroine is ' Hector's afflicted widow' and even
'*bright* Andromache', Hermione is an 'inhuman fair';
and such lines as

> Will you refuse me a propitious smile?
> I have determined to espouse Hermione.
> O charming princess! O transcendent maid!
> This violence of temper may prove fatal,
> The court of Pyrrhus has no room for me.

are by no means exceptionally insipid. To establish the
exact relation of this paraphrase, which every now and
then becomes an almost literal translation, would be a
tedious task. In general I would say that Philips
follows his author scene by scene, and most often
speech by speech, is commendably anxious to let
nothing drop, and sometimes shows himself skilfully
concise; but that his whole tendency is to be explicit
where Racine was reserved, and that this result is
obtained chiefly by a deplorable prodigality of epithet,
but also by the systematic addition of moralizing tirades
at the end of every act. One example will suffice. The
second act closes with this speech of Pyrrhus:

> Oh 'tis a heavy task to conquer love,
> And wean the soul from her accustom'd fondness!
> But come—A long farewell to Hector's widow!
> 'Tis with a secret pleasure I look back,
> And see the many dangers I have pass'd.

The merchant, thus, in dreadful tempests toss'd,
Thrown by the waves on some unlook'd-for coast,
Oft turns, and sees, with a delighted eye,
Midst rocks and shelves, the broken billows fly;
And, while the outrageous winds the deep deform,
Smiles on the tumult, and enjoys the storm.

It is, I suppose, creditable to the courage of Ambrose
Philips that he ventured to deprive his audience of a
bloody scene. Except for a 'flourish within' which
provokes Andromache, preparing to meet the King of
Epirus in the temple, to exclaim:

Hark how the trumpet, with its sprightly notes,
Proclaims th' appointed hour, and calls me hence!

he abstains from scenic effects until near the end. Then,
however, he cannot resist the temptation to prolong the
delirium of Orestes—for the edification of such spec-
tators as Sir Roger de Coverley, who, you may
remember, 'grew more than ordinarily serious, and took
occasion to moralize, in his way, upon an evil conscience', adding, that Orestes in his madness looked as
if he saw something. Nor can he forbear to give a last
sight of Andromache, who comes on processionally,
with 'a dead march behind', to vituperate the Greeks,
praise Pyrrhus, and justify the title:

O, Cephisa!
A springing joy, mix'd with a soft concern,
A pleasure which no language can express,
An ecstasy that mothers only feel,
Plays round my heart, and heightens up my sorrow,
Like gleams of sunshine in a low'ring sky.
Though plunged in ills, and exercised in care,
Yet never let the noble mind despair.
When press'd by dangers, and beset with foes,
The gods their timely succour interpose;
And when our virtue sinks, o'erwhelm'd with grief,
By unforeseen expedients brings relief?

Of the immense success achieved by this tragedy at its first appearance there seems to be no doubt. It was withdrawn after nine representations, however, to be revived only in 1735; but until the end of the century it remained in the repertory of the British stage, and among the famous actors who have appeared in the leading parts are Kean, the two Kembles, Mrs. West, Mrs. Siddons, and Mrs. Litchfield. The book ran through ten editions between 1712 and 1777.

Charles Johnson, the second adapter of *Iphigénie*, brought out a paraphrase of *Bajazet* at Drury Lane in 1717 under the title of *The Sultaness*. With Booth to represent Bajazet, Mrs. Porter as Roxana, and Mrs. Oldfield as Atalida, it was at first applauded, but pretty soon forgotten. Johnson, in his prologue, did not forget to name Racine, nor to repeat, from Racine's preface, the French poet's justification for so modern a subject:

A thousand leagues are like a thousand years.

An allusion to the recent fiasco of *Three Hours after Marriage*,

Such wags have been, who boldly durst adventure,
To club a farce by Tripartite indenture,

secured him a place in the *Dunciad*. This piece is not an adaptation; but it is as distant a copy of Racine as a translator, who has no notion of altering his text substantially, could execute. One quotation will, I believe, make it evident that Johnson understood neither the relations of the principal personages nor their characters. This is how Roxana speaks in that wonderful first interview with the Prince:

Oh! Bajazet, I feel, I feel I love thee!
Do not destroy us both! Let me not go,
Drive me not out to rage, to wild despair!
If one rash word or signal shou'd escape me,
Urged by thy cruel usage, thou art lost.

The French is:

Bajazet, écoutez, je sens que je vous aime.
Vous vous perdez. Gardez de me laisser sortir.
Le chemin est encore ouvert au repentir.
Ne désespérez point une amante en furie.
S'il m'échappoit un mot, c'est fait de votre vie.

Who does not feel that the tone of supplication in the English conflicts with the poet's conception of an appetite too peremptory to be pitiful, and a resentment that wastes no words? But the truth is that Johnson knew French too superficially for his task. On the impulse of her first disappointment, Roxana countermands the revolution in the palace, and says to Acomat:

Que le sérail soit désormais fermé,
Et que tout rentre ici dans l'ordre accoutumé!

This becomes in Johnson's version:

And on your life let none presume to enter
Without the *accustom'd orders!*

And, in the fourth act, when her confidant bids the Sultaness reflect that she has gone too far in treason to purchase forgiveness at any price, she is made to say:

Shou'd some unfaithful tongue, as such there are,
Disclose this fatal story to the Sultan;
Alas! you know too well, that hearts like his
Can never be regain'd, when once offended:
His sudden death, and at this very moment,
Wou'd prove your passion, not your duty, mov'd you!

What Racine wrote is this:

Et qui sait si déjà quelque bouche infidèle
Ne l'a point averti de votre amour nouvelle?
Des cœurs comme le sien, vous le savez assez,
Ne se regagnent plus quand ils sont offensés;
Et la plus prompte mort, dans ce moment sévère,
Devient de leur amour la marque la plus chère.

It did not occur to Johnson apparently that any life but Bajazet's could be at stake, or that any other passion than Roxana's could write itself in blood. In short, *The Sultaness*, considered as a translation, is inadequate ; and, considered as English poetry, contemptible.

These experiments, on which you will feel, perhaps, that I have spent too much time, are only a selection from the considerable number of English plays founded on Racine which belong to this period ;[1] but I will mention two more, which were never intended, it seems, for the regular stage. One is Thomas Brereton's *Esther, or Faith Triumphant ; a Sacred Drama*, published in 1715, with a letter of dedication to the Archbishop of York, in which the translator approves the example of ' the Virgins of Saint-Cyr ', and though he dare not suggest ' that the Maids of the Retinue of our Queens (one Apartment of whose Palace, if I mistake not, is allotted to *Theatrical* Representations) might be not unsuitably exercised in such sort of Performances ', recommends them as a recreation for ' chearfully Christian Families '. The version, in rhyming couplets, is fairly close, but colourless. The other is William Duncomb's *Athaliah*. Duncomb was himself a playwright, and was later to adapt to our stage the *Brutus* of Voltaire, when the tragedies of that author had their momentary vogue in England. His version of *Athalie* is competent and scrupulous, as may be judged from this rendering of a famed passage, ' Celui qui met un frein à la fureur des flots ' :

The Pow'r, which curbs the proudly-swollen Waves,
Can also blast the Plottings of the Wicked :
Humbly resign'd to his most holy Will.
Abner, 'tis God I fear, and Nought beside him.
Yet am I bound to thank that friendly zeal,
Which makes thee watchful to preserve my Life.

[1] The list may be completed by reference to : L. Charlanne, *L'Influence française en Angleterre au 17ᵉ Siècle* 1906). pp. 369-386 ; and to Miss D. F. Canfield's essay. *Corneille and Racine in England* 1904'.

I see, Injustice grieves thy secret Soul,
And that thou'rt still, in Heart, an *Israelite*.
Thanks be to Heav'n! but wilt thou be content
With such Tame Anger, and such slothful Virtue?
Can Faith, which does not act, be thought sincere?

This is unpretentious, but faithful and not too creeping: the lyrical passages are less adequate, to say the least:

> With lavish Hand, his Bounties He
> Diffuses all around,
> Let us adore his Deity,
> His endless Praise resound.
> Ere unborn Time had yet a Name,
> He was Eternal King:
> Let us his Benefits proclaim,
> His boundless Glories sing.

This tripping rhythm has, I know, been frequently chosen for devotional exercises. To no one who knows the last drama of Racine will it recall the sweetness and amplitude of the choric interludes in *Athalie*.

*　　*　　*　　*　　*

It may be thought that a survey of English plays derived from one or other of Racine's can throw little light upon the general subject of his reputation in England. The multitude of these attempts shows at least that his prestige was already high enough to commend them to English playwrights as a likely foundation for new pieces. It is certain that not one of these gave London playgoers the opportunity of judging Racine upon his merits as a dramatist. We may take it for granted that in the most faithful and scholarly translation the peculiar essence of his poetry must evaporate. But how is it that his presentment of character and passion, his conception of dramatic economy, were invariably disfigured? How is it that hardly one of his imitators dreamed of presenting him untravestied? The ill success of many does not furnish a presumption that

an ingenuous transposition would have served the turn
any better.   If they missed the mark of public approval,
it is likely that they aimed at least in the right direction.
The fact is that, with an English audience, popular or
cultivated, no serious story had then—or perhaps has
ever had—a chance of pleasing, which did not kindle
intense and instant emotion by vehement language
supported or not by external means.   Of that essential
need the liking for a drama of complex incident and
alternating moods, for pageantry, for bloodshed, was the
superficial symptom, sometimes kept under by a theory :
the need was constant.   Too evidently Racine does not
supply it.   The interest of his tragedies lies not primarily
in the intensity of suffering represented, but in the
anxiety of spiritual conflicts.   The 'improvements' practised upon them by our romantic cobblers, however
clumsily executed, are an indication of what was thought
wanting in him to satisfy a general taste.   But their
excisions are not less significant than what they added.
In every version, in every adaptation I have seen, the
speeches which exceed some dozen lines are interrupted, when they are not actually curtailed.   This impatience, no doubt, proceeds from an idea of dramatic
action which excludes, not analysis (for Racine does not
suffer his characters to dissect themselves), but the active
reasoning of contrary motives, and narrative designed
not merely to illuminate the past but to prepare the
future.   In a word, in our classical period, Racine was
acceptable in a travesty, or not acceptable at all, upon
the English stage..

I find no trace of his influence on original drama in
England, except in so far as his example, after that of
Corneille, may have reinforced a spontaneous, or at least
a homebred, tendency towards concentration and sim-

plicity of structure. He has no share in the vehemence
of Lee or the placidity of Rowe. Nothing in *The
Mourning Bride* recalls him ; and if Addison's rigid
and emphatic Cato has any prototype in the French
Theatre, he has none in any tragedy of Racine.

That Racine was read in French by the polite and
the judicious among our countrymen, in his own lifetime and increasingly through the next century, appears
certain ; but deliberate judgements upon his works are
scarce. Dryden, who is well known to have admired
Corneille, with reservations, as a fellow craftsman and
as a dramatic theorist, had little to say of his successor.
There is, however, one passage in which he delivers
himself of some vigorous strictures upon *Phèdre*, and,
though it is probably familiar to you, I will quote most
of it, as a sort of pattern of much later criticism. It
occurs in the preface to *All for Love*, where Dryden
justifies the encounter between the wife and the mistress
of Mark Antony :

'The French poets, I confess, are strict observers of
these punctilios. They would not, for example, have
suffered Cleopatra and Octavia to have met ; or, if they
had met, there must have only passed betwixt them
some cold civilities, but no eagerness of repartee, for
fear of offending against the greatness of their characters,
and the modesty of their sex. This objection I
foresaw.'

And, after quoting Montaigne on ceremony, its impor-
tunity and deceitfulness, he continues :

'But while they affect to shine in trifles, they are
often careless in essentials. Thus, their Hippolitus is
so scrupulous in point of decency, that he will rather
expose himself to death, than accuse his step-mother to
his father ; and my critics I am sure will commend him
for it : But we of grosser apprehension are apt to think,
that this excess of generosity is not practicable, but with

fools and madmen. This was good manners with a
vengeance ; and the audience is like to be much concerned at the misfortunes of this admirable hero. But
take Hippolitus out of his poetic fit, and I suppose he
would think it a wiser part, to set the saddle on the
right horse, and chuse rather to live with the reputation
of a plain-spoken honest man, than to die with the
infamy of an incestuous villain. In the meantime we
may take notice, that where the poet ought to have
preserved the character as it was delivered to us by
antiquity, when he should have given us the picture of
a rough young man, of the Amazonian strain, a jolly
huntsman, and both by his profession and his early
rising a mortal enemy to love, he has chosen to give
him the turn of gallantry, sent him to travel from Athens
to Paris, taught him to make love, and transformed the
Hippolitus of Euripides into *Monsieur* Hippolite.'

The notion that Hippolytus keeps silent from no other
motive than good breeding could not, you would suppose, have been entertained by any one who had read
Racine's tragedy all through. But the other head of
this hearty and amusing indictment—that Racine has
turned 'a rough young man of the Amazonian strain'
into a French courtier—is more serious. In a more
general shape the charge of gallicizing the ancients had
already been brought against him by critics of his own
nation, notably by Saint-Évremond : indeed, I am not
sure that these thrusts owe nothing to the suggestion of
the old sceptic, whom Dryden knew and respected,
especially as an authority on the limits of the French
genius for poetry. The larger question involved is,
whether the personages of antiquity, if they are to come
alive again in modern works, must not be brought into
the circle of our habits and credited with the manners
we know. And the answer Shakespeare gives to the
question in his Roman plays is the same, only more
decidedly affirmative, as Racine's. But Dryden, pre-

possessed with the idea that *Phèdre* is an attempt to imitate Euripides, resented the alteration of a legendary character. And 'Monsieur Hippolite' has stuck.

Addison, in the next generation, passed for an admirer of the French classical tragedy; we know what he thought of the sensationalism of the English stage, and how he objected to tragicomedy that 'it breaks the tide of the passions while they are yet flowing'. Doubtless he valued many qualities in Racine, especially the natural tone, the single theme, the contempt for mechanical accessories; but I do not know where to look in his writings for an appreciation of the French poet. It is possible that Addison sincerely admired the *Phaedra and Hippolytus* of Edmund Smith: but could he at the same time have appreciated *Phèdre*?

In such a dearth of recorded opinions, an adjective might have its value:

Exact Racine, and Corneille's noble fire
Show'd us that France had something to admire,

wrote Pope in an imitation of Horace. And it is true that Racine is exact, and that Shakespeare, as Pope told his readers a few lines later, was fluent. The former of these epithets is not much more distinctive than the second. Another English poet, Thomas Gray, is among the few who are known to have enjoyed Racine, at least in the playhouse. Norton Nicholls, in his memorials of Gray, tells us that 'he admired Racine, particularly the *Britannicus*', but 'disliked French poetry in general', though he made exception in favour of La Fontaine and (of all poets!) the author of *Vert-Vert*. Gray and Walpole saw several of the classical masterpieces played in Paris in 1739: the *Cid*, Molière's *Avare* (of which Gray, writing to West, 'cannot at all commend the performance'), and *Phèdre*, besides *Britan-*

nicus. 'All the characters, particularly Agrippina and Nero, done to perfection,' he writes. Agrippina was most probably Mlle Dumesnil, of whose talent Mme du Deffand, against Walpole's judgement, thought poorly. It was the pleasure he took in this performance, apparently, which set him thinking of a tragedy to be called 'Agrippina', of which in 1741 he wrote a scene and the beginning of a second. West poured cold water on his friend's enthusiasm, and we have no more than a fragment in rather stately verse.

The greatest English critic of the eighteenth century hardly mentions Racine. He did indeed observe to Boswell, when they were sitting in the inn on the island of Mull, that 'as for original composition, the French have two tragic poets, Racine and Corneille, who go round the world ; and one comic poet, Molière'. That Racine 'went round the world' nobody in that age could doubt : in England, his eminence was taken for granted, and gave no offence : a little of Racine perhaps was read by every one who read anything in French besides novels and memoirs : this is not to say that his works were often studied, discussed, or enjoyed in the eighteenth century.

A faithful but not otherwise remarkable verse translation of *Britannicus*, by Sir Brooke Boothby, published in 1803, is worth mentioning for its 'initial preface'. The translator's excuse is that 'the only pieces of Racine which remain on the English theatre, *Phèdre* and *Andromache*, are so much altered by their English dress as scarcely to afford any idea of the manner of the original'. He offers Racine as he is, but he is aware that there is less room than ever for 'so chaste and simple a tragedy' on a stage where the love of senseless show and sentimental extravagance is grown so universal that 'Shake-

speare and Congreve must retire for *Ballets of Action*, as
Accius and Pacurius made way, in the days of Horace,
for a camelopardus or a white elephant '.

' The characteristic of Racine', he continues, ' is purity
of taste. He seldom attempts to create, but is content
to imitate, and this he always does with great force and
infinite propriety and art. His versification is generally
agreed to have attained the summit of perfection, in a
language the least of all others formed either for melody
or figurative expression ; and when it is remembered
that he has restrained himself to the difficult unities of
time and place, suited to the regular and simple construction of his plans, the best performances of Racine
will always be considered as masterpieces of dramatic
art.'

I will spare you Sir Brooke Boothby's remarks on
the decay of declamatory skill among our actors, and on
the demoralizing effect of a new kind of romantic play
imported from Germany. The romantic battle is but
opening ; but you may observe that the position which
the English admirer of Racine is ready to defend is
nearly desperate already. His poet is an imitator of
rare skill ; his lines are wonderfully good, for French
lines ; and he deserves credit for having ' restrained
himself to the difficult unities of time and place '.

At the moment of our imaginative revival, when 'the
school of Pope' and 'the French school of poetry ' were
convertible terms, the tolerance of our neighbours fell
into contempt with the leading critics of this nation.
The bias of opinion which has nothing to do with literature sometimes may be observed in the expression of
this general disesteem. 'France is my Babylon ',
avowed Coleridge. 'The impudence, even of a Frenchman,' cries De Quincey, 'would not dare to connect the
sanctities of religious feeling with any book written in

his language.' It was natural that the French theatre
should receive particular attention at this juncture.
While scholars and poets were refreshing the study of
Shakespeare and rediscovering Shakespeare's comrades
and rivals, the comparison of the English poetical drama
with that of other peoples, ancient and modern, became
a favourite exercise of criticism.   Racine was singled
out to be confronted with Shakespeare ; and so it
happens that at the only period when his name occurs
pretty often in English critical writings, he is never
produced but as a foil.

The common attitude of English critics towards
Racine in the early part of the nineteenth century could
be illustrated out of many authors : but one must do ;
and I choose the most tolerant and the least pedantic,
William Hazlitt.   There is a passage which, as it does
infinite credit to Hazlitt's candour, ought to be quoted
first in this connexion :

'Neither can the disagreement between the French
and English school of tragedy ever be reconciled, till
the French become English, or the English, French.
Both are right in what they admire, both are wrong in
condemning the others for what they admire.   We see
the defects of Racine, they see the faults of Shakespeare, probably in an exaggerated point of view.   But
we may be sure of this, that when we see nothing but
grossness and barbarism, or insipidity and verbiage, in
a writer that is the God of a nation's idolatry, it is we
and not they who want true taste and feeling.'

This is handsomely said, though as a fact Racine, so
far from being 'the God of a nation's idolatry', has
never been an object of unanimous veneration, beyond
the reach of eminent detractors, in his own country.
But the tone of Hazlitt's actual criticism is very different.   In *The Plain Speaker*, he compares Scott,

Racine, and Shakespeare: here is a paragraph which sums up the parallel:

'The genius of Shakespeare is dramatic, that of Scott narrative or descriptive, that of Racine is didactic. He gives, as I conceive, the *commonplaces* of the human heart better than any one, but nothing, or very little more. He enlarges on a set of obvious sentiments and well-known topics with considerable elegance of language and copiousness of declamation, but there is scarcely one stroke of original genius nor anything like imagination in his writings. He strings together a number of moral reflections, and instead of reciting them himself, puts them into the mouths of his *dramatis personae*, who talk well about their own situations and the general relations of human life. Instead of laying bare the heart of the sufferer with all its bleeding wounds and palpitating fibres, he puts into his hand a commonplace book, and he reads us a lecture from this. This is not the essence of the drama, whose object and privilege it is to give us the extreme and subtle workings of the human mind in individual circumstances, to make us sympathize with the sufferer, or feel as we should feel in his circumstances, not to tell the indifferent spectator what the indifferent spectator could just as well tell him. Tragedy is human nature tried in the crucible of affliction, not exhibited in the vague theorems of speculation. The poet's pen that paints all this in words of fire and images of gold is totally wanting in Racine. He gives neither external images nor the internal and secret workings of the human breast. Sir W. Scott gives the external imagery or machinery of passion; Shakespeare the soul; and Racine the moral or argument of it.'

I have often wondered whether, as a fact, Hazlitt had ever read through one whole act of any tragedy of Racine, with or without a dictionary. Racine didactic? Racine reading us a lecture from a commonplace book? This should be the character of a poet from whom we could easily glean an anthology of maxims. Where are the well-known topics, the vague theorems of specu-

lation in Racine ?   For there must be instances.   Is it
Roxana's ' Sortez ', or Hermione's ' Qui te l'a dit ? , or
Phaedra's ' Ils s'aimeront toujours ' ?

  Hazlitt continues :

  ' The French object to Shakespeare for his breach of
the Unities, and hold up Racine as a model of classical
propriety, who makes a Greek hero address a Grecian
heroine as *Madame*.'

And yet Hazlitt had certainly read Shakespeare, and
was familiar with Sir Diomed and Lady Cressid.   But
there are other examples of his inattention.

  ' The finest line in Racine, that is, in French poetry,
is by common consent understood to be the following :

  *Craignez Dieu, mon cher Abner, et ne craignez que
      Dieu !*'

And for a striking instance of *pathos* in Racine he
quotes Agamemnon : *Tu y seras, ma fille !*

But I will not insist on Hazlitt's incompetence.   It is,
after all, less presumptuous than that of Landor, who,
in an Imaginary Conversation, undertakes to show that
Racine's ear was defective.   Hazlitt's opinion of French
poetry, and of the dramatic poetry of Racine in particular, is a type of the opinion held by cultured Englishmen in the Romantic age.   And, if it had been only his,
it has had an influence, and has helped to diffuse a
prejudice.

  A generation later, Macaulay, who was not a Romantic
critic, writes thus :

  ' We are sure that the Greeks of Shakespeare [he is
speaking of *Troilus and Cressida*] bear a far greater
resemblance than the Greeks of Racine to the Greeks
who besieged Troy '

and I dare say he is right ; but why is he so sure ?

' for this reason, that the Greeks of Shakespeare are
human beings, and the Greeks of Racine mere names,

mere words painted in capitals at the head of paragraphs of declamation. Racine, it is true, would have shuddered at the thought of making a warrior at the siege of Troy quote Aristotle. But of what use is it to ,avoid a single anachronism, when the whole play is one anachronism, the sentiments and phrases of Versailles in the Camp of Aulis ?'

The comment which suggests itself, even if one had never read *Iphigénie*, is this : If the personages gathered at the camp of Aulis express the sentiments of Versailles in the phrases of Versailles, though they do not talk like ancient Greeks, is there not a presumption that they talk at least like human beings ? But, illogism apart, there is in Macaulay's tone, when he writes about Racine, an unmistakable antipathy which, as far as I can discover, was not at all exceptional in the middle of the last century.

Has that attitude become less common—I do not say among serious students of French Literature, who until quite recently were extremely few in England—but among well-educated Englishmen who in their general reading give some place to the French tragic poets ? I might take such a book as Henry Trollope's *Corneille and Racine*, which forms part of a series of ' Foreign Classics for English Readers ' and was evidently designed to be appreciative, and infer from some of the judgements it contains the persistence of an inveterate detraction. Or I might quote Mr. John Bailey's spirited endorsement of the traditional verdict on the extravagant claims which, as he supposes, are advanced by Frenchmen on behalf of Racine. To balance the weight of even the most recent testimony in this sense, it would need something more substantial and authoritative than an occasional expression of praise, such as might be discovered perhaps in the obscurer paths of contemporary English criticism. But, indeed, the general conclusion, in regard to the reputation of Racine in England, is irresistible. It is recorded of very few Englishmen that they have read him with delight; and of many that his tragedies have been to them a stumbling-block upon the threshold (for it is there they meet him) of French literature. Those famous works, when most favourably judged, have been considered as accomplished examples of an unvalued kind, and credited with such merits of composition as are held irrelevant to the noblest ends of poetry.

In a case so notorious, it may seem idle to look for reasons. A genuine dislike owes none, and is intangible so long as it forbears to justify itself. Taste is not a matter of persuasion, and no man can be proved to have so written that he ought to please us better than he does. Yet no critic, and few ordinary readers, are content to register without comment the uncorrupted verdict of their palate. Deliberate judgements have, as a fact, been passed upon Racine. What they point to, when we have discounted the inattention, the inconsequence, or the mere prepossessions of the writers, is a conflict of traditions. Difficulties of a kind that may fairly be called national stand in the light of English readers when they turn from their own dramatic poets to explore that other continent of French tragedy. They may bring perhaps an open mind to the discovery, but not a vacant memory nor an unprejudiced ear. They are bred to a habit of poetical speech which the French manner contradicts at many points ; which governs their expectation, and may easily prepare their disappointment. Their own playwrights of the great period have accustomed them to a higher temperature of language and to a freer solicitation of the senses. They are apt

to think feverish and coloured words essential to any
poetry which deals with human passion; nor do they
readily imagine mortal issues cramped within the walls
of an antechamber that seems to open no windows on
the world. It is besides for many an English reader
a disillusion to find in Racine no sublime irrelevance,
no fantasy, no pathetic symptoms of metaphysical incer-
titude.

Where these differences and others no less traditional
are felt, there may be no positive aversion, but there
will always be at first an estrangement, for which there
is no help but through a patient initiation. Few Englishmen are ready to taste the excellence of Racine before
they have learned at least that the drama which he
brought to its perfection is not a parody of the Greek,
but one of the great autonomous types of Western art,
developed gradually in an indissoluble collaboration of
theory and accident, of genius with the social sense. To
trace French tragedy to its national origin is to find the
starting-point of the divergence between us and our
neighbours in dramatic ideals; and to trace it only as far
back as Schelandre or Rotrou or Tristan is to be startled
very often by a romantic luxuriance of invention that
reminds us of the Jacobeans. But undoubtedly the most
precious part of Racine escapes any analysis of his ante-
cedents. He is, for one thing, a musician; and the apti-
tude and the familiarity are usually wanting which make
it possible to hear with intimate pleasure the music of a
foreign verse. And his rarest virtue of expression is
not exactness, nor propriety, but an ardour robed in
discretion which most foreigners perhaps, and some of
his own countrymen, do not distinguish from frigidity
and 'rhetoric'. He is not what is sometimes called 'a
world-poet', but peculiarly a poet of his own soil, the

flower of a certain civilization ; nor do those who love him best in France seek to impose their admiration on the world at large. They know how little of him is fit for export—far less than of Shakespeare, though there is a part of Shakespeare too which Englishmen reserve tacitly out of the universal gift as being inaccessible to strangers : but when Racine is transplanted, he loses not only what is most exquisite but much that is really essential. And that, more than all the accidents of mis-translation, hasty reading, incompetent criticism, and illiberal prejudice, is the reason why the fortunes of Racine in England have been so little prosperous.

The Taylorian Lecture

1922

SHAKESPEARE

AND

SPAIN

By

H. THOMAS

The Taylorian Lecture

1922

SHAKESPEARE

AND

SPAIN

By

H. THOMAS

SHAKESPEARE AND SPAIN

I HAVE entitled this lecture 'Shakespeare and Spain', but I shall deal with one side only of the suggested subject, Spain's influence in Shakespeare, leaving to others the question of Shakespeare's influence in Spain. I am conscious that I have chosen the lesser part, and in the end I shall concur with your criticism that a more fitting title would have been one which Shakespeare himself has provided ready to hand—Much Ado about Nothing—for I am on the side of those who think that Spain's direct influence in Shakespeare is small.

That is perhaps the general view among such as have given no special consideration to the matter. Eminent scholars hold widely differing opinions. On the one hand, Mr. Aubrey Bell boldly speaks of the Spanish language 'which Shakespeare seems to have known well', and he continues: 'Several Shakespeare plays were derived from Spanish sources, and one, *The Tempest*, followed very closely on the publication of its Spanish source. Shakespeare's allusions to Spain are very numerous, he uses Spanish phrases and gives an English garb to others.' On the other hand, Professor Fitzmaurice-Kelly cautiously admits: 'There are in Shakespeare a few touches which, with a little goodwill, may be taken as implying some acquaintance, however slight, with Spanish. It is conceivable that Shakespeare contrived to plod through some of the Spanish books which were reprinted in the Netherlands and brought thence to England; some such supposition is almost unavoidable if we choose to accept Dorer's well-known theory that *The Tempest* derives from Antonio de Eslava's *Noches de Invierno*. Were this so— the theory is not received with universal favour—we should have to assume either that Shakespeare knew enough Spanish to pick out the plot of a story from a Spanish work, or that there existed in Shakespeare's time some French or English version, no longer known, of Eslava's dreary book.'

Those quotations represent very divergent views; but however opinions may differ, it is common ground that Shakespeare had some knowledge of Spain and the Spaniards, that a few Spanish words were among his stock-in-trade, and that he incurred certain small obligations to Spanish literature. These topics I propose to examine, with special reference to recent investigations which would make Shakespeare's knowledge of and indebtedness to Spain far greater than even Mr. Bell allows. The temporary lull in Shakespeare study due to the war affords an opportunity to review suggestions and theories which have not yet had a chance of passing through the gateway of general criticism into the realm of accepted doctrine or the limbo of rejection.

The extent of an author's acquaintance with the language of a foreign country is obviously an important factor in considering the possible influences exercised upon him by that country's literature. None of the known facts of Shakespeare's life would lead us to suppose that he had natural opportunities of acquiring Spanish, as he certainly had of acquiring French. We must turn for information to the evidence of his literary work.

As Mr. Bell says, Shakespeare 'uses Spanish phrases I have carefully read through Shakespeare's works in recent years, and I only find two such phrases, both of a popular character. As to the Spanish phrases to which he 'gives an English garb', I confess that I have recognized none of them, and I await enlightenment. I have, however, noted three or four words which are or may be Spanish, and which must have been on most men's lips in Shakespeare's day. I have also collected several instances of words derived from the Spanish or showing Spanish influence; but these are not of Shakespeare's own coining: they were current in the language of the time, and no one man's property more than another's.

The linguistic evidence, at any rate, hardly supports Mr. Bell's statement that Spanish was a language 'which Shakespeare seems to have known well'. How far is the further statement justified, that 'Shakespeare's allusions to Spain are very numerous'? If we were to understand Spain here simply in a geographical sense, it would be easy to prove the exact opposite; but no doubt the word is used to cover Spanish characters and Spanish commodities as well. The latter may be considered first. Falstaff's 'good bilbo' is just a variant of the 'sword of Spain', the 'Spanish sword', and the 'Spanish blade', met with elsewhere; all of which merely show that the Spanish sword had penetrated the English as well as the other markets of the world. So too had the wines of the Peninsula: the nondescript bastard, besides the canaries, charneco, and sherris, or sherris-sack, or simple ubiquitous sack, which produced the comfortable 'Spanish pouch', as Prince Henry calls it. But Shakespeare knew more about the properties of these wines than about their place of origin. Mistress Quickly was not alone in thinking canaries 'a marvellous searching wine', that 'perfumes the blood ere one can say "What's this?"' Nor is it a second-hand panegyric of sherris-sack that is put into Falstaff's mouth:

'A good sherris-sack hath a two-fold operation in it. It ascends me into the brain; dries me there all the foolish and dull and crudy vapours which environ it; makes it apprehensive, quick, forgetive, full of nimble fiery and delectable shapes; which, delivered o'er to the voice, the tongue, which is the birth, becomes excellent wit. The second property of your excellent sherris is, the warming of the blood; which, before cold and settled, left the liver white and pale, which is the badge of pusillanimity and cowardice; but the sherris warms it and makes it course from the inwards to the parts extreme: it illumineth the face, which as a beacon gives warning to all the rest of this little kingdom, man, to arm; and then the vital commoners and inland petty spirits muster me all to their captain, the heart, who, great and puffed up with this retinue, doth any deed of courage; and this valour comes

of sherris. So that skill in the weapon is nothing without
sack, for that sets it a-work ; and learning a mere hoard of
gold kept by a devil, till sack commences it and sets it in
act and use. Hereof comes it that Prince Harry is valiant;
for the cold blood he did naturally inherit of his father, he
hath, like lean, sterile and bare land, manured, husbanded
and tilled with excellent endeavour of drinking good and
good store of fertile sherris, that he is become very hot
and valiant. If I had a thousand sons, the first humane
principle I would teach them should be, to forswear
thin potations and to addict themselves to sack.'

A strong personal note rings in the finale.

In addition to these swords and wines, another Spanish
product is alluded to in Beatrice's remark 'civil as an
orange', and the mere possibility of this pun on Seville
being made from the stage shows that the Spanish fruit
was as well known in England as the Spanish wines—then
as now. In short, Shakespeare reveals the knowledge of
Spanish commodities that one would expect of the average
Englishman ; he is only above the average in his power of
expressing his appreciation of them.

We shall find that Shakespeare's references to the
country itself reveal a similar state of knowledge. The
members of his audiences who did not know that Julius
Caesar 'had a fever when he was in Spain' were not
necessarily ignorant of Spain ; they simply had not read
or misread or enlarged on Plutarch. And those who were
unaware that John of Gaunt 'did subdue the greatest part
of Spain' were better informed than they perhaps imagined.
These statements, however, occur in historical plays, and,
in the sphere of history, imagination and patriotism tradi-
tionally enjoy great licence. It is to the comedies that we
look for real evidence as to Shakespeare's knowledge of
the Peninsula.

No one has suggested that Shakespeare ever went to
Spain, and it is simply the general verdict of travellers that
is crystallized in his description 'tawny Spain'. He displays indeed a greater knowledge of Spain than some
of his modern editors, when he makes Helena a 'Saint

Jacques' pilgrim ', 'to great Saint Jacques bound'; but no one in his day would fail to take the reference to the great mediaeval pilgrimage to the shrine of the apostle Saint James in Santiago de Compostela. It is certainly less Shakespeare's interest in the neighbouring country of Portugal than his memory of recent events and his familiarity with seafaring men that is responsible for Beatrice's simile: 'My affection hath an unknown bottom, like the bay of Portugal.' The apparently unusual expression 'the bay of Portugal' is said to be still current among sailors to denote the deep waters that wash the nose and brow of Portugal, while a disastrous English expedition to that country, the year after the Armada, may have made the allusion worth while. Shakespeare's acquaintance with the affairs of the sea, again, no doubt leads to the bare inclusion of Lisbon among the places whither Antonio has ventured his argosies; while this short list gains nothing from the mention of Aragon in *Much Ado about Nothing*, for it is simply due to the fact that Don Pedro of Aragon is one of the principal characters in the play, and he, with the whole plot, was taken over by Shakespeare from a source which goes back to Bandello.

As far as he reveals himself in his geographical references, then, Shakespeare has no special knowledge of the Peninsula; but the evidence by which we have to judge him is limited, and we may be allowed to extend it by including his references to Spanish characters.

We may ignore three unnamed Spanish characters introduced merely to add local colour or to appeal to national prejudice. Such touches show that Shakespeare knew, not so much the Peninsula, as his audiences. Yet he came into contact with real Spanish personages in two of his historical plays. The Lady Blanch of Spain, daughter of Alphonso VIII of Castile by Eleanor, sister of King John of England, figures in *King John*; but in this play Shakespeare was simply revising the work of an anonymous predecessor. In *King Henry VIII* several Spanish characters are mentioned: Queen Katharine, her father Ferdinand the Catholic, and her 'royal nephew' the emperor Charles V, whose abdication is thought by some to have revived an interest in the story of King Lear in England. These characters, however, only enter into *King Henry VIII* through the medium of the English chronicles on which the play is based; they imply no special interest in Spanish history. Moreover, Shakespeare is only partly responsible for *King Henry VIII*. No doubt he was attracted by the moving story of Queen Katharine, but in view of the usual division of the play among possible collaborators, it would be going too far to attribute the sympathetic treatment of this stranger queen to him, uninfluenced by the aftermath of war ; otherwise we might have conceived Shakespeare as working here on the same serene level as Cervantes, who drew so friendly a picture of Queen Elizabeth in *La Española Inglesa*, and we might have contrasted both with the intensely patriotic Lope de Vega, who paints the virgin queen in his *Dragontea* as 'the Scarlet Lady of Babylon'.

At the best, *King John* and *King Henry VIII* only throw light on the information respecting historic Spanish characters which Shakespeare derived from books. We must turn to the comedies if we wish to discover anything concerning his personal knowledge of Spaniards, whom he had no lack of opportunity to study in London itself. The expression ' a Spaniard from the hip upward, no doublet,' was doubtless based on personal observation of cloaked figures in the capital, and he may have drawn inspiration from one or two prominent Spaniards resident there in his day. The incentive to write *The Merchant of Venice* was perhaps provided by the anti-semitic wave that followed the sensational case of the court physician, Rodrigo Lopez, a Portuguese Jew by birth, though nominally a Christian, who was suspected of attempting to poison Queen Elizabeth. Political bias and religious prejudice amply confirming this suspicion, the unhappy man was hanged at Tyburn, where he had the additional misfortune of earning the derision of the mob by protesting that 'he loved the queen as well as he loved Jesus Christ', which, as Camden tells us, 'from a man of the Jewish profession moved no small laughter in the standers-by'. To Mr. Martin Hume indeed, amongst other possible hints from Lopez's case, his 'sanctimonious expressions during his trial and execution would seem to suggest Antonio's words of Shylock—"the devil can cite Scripture for his purpose".' But Antonio's comment follows as naturally on Shylock's Old Testament illustration, ' When Jacob grazed his uncle Laban's sheep', as that illustration arises in the context; and Mr. Hume himself would not carry the parallel too far. Shakespeare, being an artist, certainly left any direct suggestion of a particular figure to the cruder capacities of the actors.

Rodrigo Lopez had served as interpreter to Antonio Perez, formerly Secretary of State to Philip II, and afterwards his enemy. Perez had been brought to England in 1593 by Lord Essex, and utilized to counter Spanish influences, and the court physician was suspected of conspiring to poison Perez, as well as the queen, as part of a Spanish intrigue. It seems probable that Shakespeare had Perez in his mind's eye when remodelling the Braggart of the earlier *Love's Labour's Lost* as the fantastical Spaniard Don Adriano de Armado. Mr. Hume finds confirmation of this in the correspondence in styles between Perez's letters and Armado's speeches, and he calls attention to Perez's favourite pseudonym 'el peregrino' and that most singular and choice epithet 'too peregrinate', applied to Don Adriano by Holofernes. Don Adriano's style, both in his speeches and in his letters, is at the most a very free parody of Perez's, and it is doubtfully that, for any hints taken from Perez would be superimposed on the original sketch of the Braggart, and this clearly owed something to an eccentric Italian well known in London for his strange talk some years before, the 'Phantasticall Monarke' whose 'epitaphe' appears in Churchyard's *Chance* (1580).

But we are not called upon to test the precise degree of

truth underlying these possible reflexions of contemporary figures in Shakespeare's plays. However interesting in themselves, they do not point to his having enjoyed any personal intimacy with Spaniards in London, and discussion of them is only necessary in order to avoid overlooking any evidence as to his knowledge of Spain and of Spanish.

We may summarize the results of the evidence so far collected, before passing on to the question of Shakespeare's literary borrowings from the Peninsula. Shakespeare's knowledge of Spain seems to have been that of the intelligent London citizen. He was vaguely familiar with a few historic Spanish figures, but his information concerning them was derived from English chronicles, and in itself did not particularly interest him. If he suggests acquaintance with living Spaniards, it is apparently a distant one, and throws no light on the possibility of his naturally acquiring Spanish ; and the knowledge he displays of that tongue is no more than we should expect if he had ' been at a great feast of languages, and stolen the scraps '.

We can now consider without prejudice Shakespeare's literary indebtedness to the Peninsula. What we have seen above merely warns us not to assume that Shakespeare was so familiar with Spanish that he would regularly turn to Spanish books and read them fluently and freely. We must be on our guard too against drawing rash conclusions from similarities of plot, incident, thought, or expression in Shakespeare and in Spanish literature. The great defect of the diligent source-hunter is that he so often finds what he looks for, and Shakespeare's versatile mind and fertile imagination have provided abundant scope for his activities.

It has for some time been on record that Shakespeare's *Cymbeline* and *Twelfth Night* deal respectively with the same subjects as Lope de Rueda's *Comedia Eufemia* and *Comedia de los Engañados*, and his *Romeo and Juliet* with the same theme as Lope de Vega's *Castelvines y Monteses*.

Recently *Pericles*, which is partly Shakespeare's work, has been similarly brought into line with Gil Vicente's *Comedia de Rubena*. These are isolated facts. Shakespeare drew from the same sources as the Spanish dramatists ; it is not suggested that he utilized their plays.

But there are subtler parallels between Shakespeare and Spanish literature, which, from the fact that no conscious relationship is claimed for the authors in question, serve to emphasize the danger of inferring too much from such resemblances. Professor Fitzmaurice-Kelly, besides quoting the familiar coincidence of expression whereby both Hamlet and Don Quixote state that the purpose of the drama is 'to hold, as 'twere, the mirror up to Nature', gives a more illuminating instance of his own : the picture of two parallel creations, Falstaff and Sancho, pursuing similar thoughts to the same conclusion, Falstaff by the King's camp near Shrewsbury soliloquizing on honour and deciding 'I'll have none of it', and Sancho under a tree outside El Toboso, reflecting on the doubtful advantages of faithful service, and concluding that 'the devil, the devil, and no one else, dragged me into this affair'. These are chance resemblances of thought and expression arising out of analogous situations, such as will frequently be found in writers like Shakespeare and Cervantes, whose minds range widely over life's activities. Christopher Sly's sudden elevation to the peerage—though the theme is not developed—recalls Sancho Panza's promotion to be governor of Barataria, and Petruchio and his horse on their way to the wedding suggest Don Quixote and Rozinante prepared for equally perilous adventures. Falstaff's threat to toss the rogue Pistol in a blanket shows that Sancho's unlucky experience might have befallen him just as easily in an English inn as in a Spanish one. Polonius in proverbial mood is reminiscent of Sancho, while Edgar, the fool, and King Lear, and Hamlet himself, vie with the Licenciado Vidriera for 'matter and impertinency mixed, reason in madness'.

But we are not limited to Cervantes, nor to situation,

thought, and expression, for parallels. In method, too, Shakespeare has Spanish counterparts. The picture of Launcelot Gobbo, holding the balance between the fiend and his conscience as to whether he shall run away from the Jew his master, has its exact parallel in the *Celestina*, though in this case Sempronio decides to remain with the love-struck Calisto. Shakespeare and the unknown author of the *Celestina* had unerring instincts for the drama of irresolution, which is almost the very negation of drama, and so one of its subtlest forms.

In style, too, Shakespeare strangely recalls past vogues in Spanish literature. Don Quixote delighted in Feliciano de Silva's long-winded romances of chivalry for their lucidity of style, and especially for such complicated conceits as 'the reason of the unreason with which my reason is afflicted so weakens my reason that with reason I murmur at your beauty', which were as pearls in his sight. He would have been equally dazzled by Romeo's 'O single-soled jest, solely singular for thy singleness!' and Richard the Second's

> Your cares set up do not pluck my cares down.
> My care is loss of care, by old care done;
> Your care is gain of care, by new care won.
> The cares I give I have, though given away;
> They tend the crown, yet still with me they stay;

while the poor gentleman might well have lain awake trying to unravel the carefully plaited reasoning of Cardinal Pandulph in *King John*. In spite of the warning against affectation which he puts in Hamlet's mouth, Shakespeare could serve 'a very fantastical banquet' of words, 'just so many strange dishes' as there were tastes, with the result that critics have recognized his gongorism before ever gongorism was.

All parallels between Shakespeare and Spanish romances of chivalry are particularly instructive in view of recent attempts to increase the English dramatist's indebtedness to these generally tedious books. As we shall see shortly, Shakespeare gives apparent evidence of knowing two of them. At present, however, I wish to emphasize how easy it was for parallels to exist, without his having any acquaintance with the Spanish romances themselves. By his day, these books had been extensively printed in the Peninsula for nearly a century; through the medium of translations they had exercised a considerable influence elsewhere in Europe for half a century; and after such a lapse of time whatever was digestible in them had been absorbed and was circulating unidentified and unidentifiable in the general organization. Moreover they brought back to England little that had not come out of the country. England had its own romances of chivalry of older date; English history had been moulded by their spirit, and in many ways the native chronicles approximated all too closely to the romances. When Shakespeare quotes a hero of chivalry, he chooses an English one: Sir Guy or Sir Colbrand or Sir Bevis. Chivalry had become an essential part of English life; its themes and terms had saturated through to the lower classes. After the ignominious rout of himself and his companions by the phantom host whose nucleus was the Prince and Poins, Falstaff shelters himself from open shame behind a mediaeval notion vulgarized by the romances of chivalry: 'Was it for me to kill the heir-apparent? Should I turn upon the true prince? Why, thou knowest I am as valiant as Hercules; but beware instinct: *the lion will not touch the true prince.*' And chivalresque remarks are bandied round in Falstaff's rascally circles. To Falstaff, the red-nosed Bardolph is the 'Knight of the Burning Lamp', and Pistol a 'base Assyrian knight', while by a degrading extension Doll Tearsheet is to the beadle a 'she knight-errant'. It need not surprise us therefore to find in Shakespeare things that would be quite in place in a Spanish romance of chivalry, such as the boy that King Henry the Fifth and Katharine are to compound, 'that shall go to Constantinople and take the Turk by the beard', or Othello's bitter cry, 'O the world hath not a sweeter creature; she might lie by an emperor's side, and command him tasks.'

Hector's challenge in *Troilus and Cressida* is pure romantic chivalry : he will make good

> He hath a lady, wiser, fairer, truer,
> Than ever Greek did compass in his arms,

in lists that are frankly mediaeval :

> If any come, Hector shall honour him ;
> If none, he'll say in Troy when he retires,
> The Grecian dames are sunburnt and not worth
> The splinter of a lance.

The mechanism of chivalry is of course present in the historical plays ; it sometimes gives way to that of chivalresque romance. Talbot in battle is a very hero of romance ; but he occurs in a play with which Shakespeare may have had little or no connexion. It is otherwise with *Cymbeline*, which is sprinkled with the commonplaces of chivalresque romance superbly told : the kidnapping of the King's two sons from the nursery ; the unfolding of their royal qualities in spite of their rustic training ; their impatience when danger threatens ; their defeat of the conquering Romans, with their foster-father's help ; their knighthood after the battle, and the subsequent discovery of their royal origin : these were hackneyed themes among the later romance-writers ; they were common property in Shakespeare's time, and we need not try to connect *Cymbeline* with any particular romance of chivalry, though this has recently been attempted. The vague parallels that have been pointed out above will warn us not only to scrutinize narrowly any claims that Shakespeare borrowed incidents or expressions from Spanish literature, but to view them broadly too.

If all the claims could be substantiated which have been made in the present century alone, then Shakespeare was widely read in Spanish literature : he was familiar, through representative books, with the principal developments in early Spanish prose fiction, the didactic anecdote, the chivalresque romance, the sentimental tale, the realistic novel, the pastoral romance, and the picaresque story. The alleged evidence on which these claims are based varies from casual

reminiscences to profuse borrowings. The latter are confined to the pastoral and the chivalresque romances ; the
consideration of them may be deferred while we deal with
the minor cases.

The earliest Spanish work that has been connected with
Shakespeare is the *Conde Lucanor*, the fourteenth-century
collection of apologues by Don Juan Manuel, which was
first published in 1575. One of the stories told in the
Conde Lucanor, obviously taken from an oriental source,
has a similar theme to *The Taming of the Shrew*, and as
late as 1909 Mr. Martin Hume was still claiming that the
Shakespearian play was derived from the Spanish story.
Those who have not his reason for bias will recognize the
theme of both as a widespread folk-lore motive, and will
simply regard the Spanish story as an interesting Shakespeare parallel. We do seem to be remotely indebted to
a Spaniard for the induction to the play, a European variant
—since it is based on intoxication—of another oriental
motive : in whatever way the jest of 'the waking man's
dream' came to be utilized on the English stage, its
appearance in Europe has been traced to a letter of
Juan Luis Vives, who reports it as having been practised
on a drunken artisan by Philip the Good of Burgundy.
Shakespeare, however, is as distantly related to Vives as
he is to Don Juan Manuel, for in the induction, as in the
play itself, he was merely retouching an already existing
Pleasant Conceited Historie, based on versions of the two
themes involved which were already current in this
country.

It is but a vague suggestion that would bring Shakespeare into relationship with a more famous example of
early Spanish fiction, the *Comedia de Calisto y Melibea*,
usually known as the *Celestina*. Professor Fitzmaurice-
Kelly, who cannot be accused of rashness in these matters,
thinks that the English version of the first four acts of this
realistic novel in dialogue, made by Sir Thomas More's
brother-in-law John Rastell, and printed by him about
1530, may have contributed something to the conception

of the two immortal lovers Romeo and Juliet, and he stresses the fact that, according to the *Stationers' Register*, there was projected a London edition of the *Celestina* in Spanish about the time when Shakespeare was preparing his play. Shakespeare may have known of the project, and something of the nature of the book, from those interested; but he had ample sources of inspiration for Romeo and Juliet in his English predecessors in the same field, Brooke and Painter. The suggested influence of the *Celestina*, while unnecessary and unprovable, remains within the realm of possibility. It involves no knowledge of Spanish on Shakespeare's part. Not so a rash attempt recently made to connect Shakespeare with Feliciano de Silva's *Segunda Celestina*, in which Dr. Joseph de Perott, a scholar in the United States, finds a parallel to the hiding of Falstaff in a buck-basket at Mistress Ford's house in *The Merry Wives of Windsor*. A Portuguese girl in the Celestina's house receives a visit by appointment from a Trinitarian friar whom she has captivated by her beauty; they are interrupted by the girl's jealous and ferocious lover, and the friar is only saved from destruction by being concealed in a huge pitcher of water. Dr. Perott convinces himself that Shakespeare copied this incident, because he also finds in the *Segunda Celestina* the original of Falstaff, a serving-man equally boastful, equally white-livered in the presence of danger, and equally facile in converting a taunt to his credit; one of whose speeches might be headed, in Falstaff's words, 'the better part of valour is discretion'. Dr. Perott also sees in this man's master, a young lordling of affected speech, the germ of Don Adriano de Armado. Those who are not intent on finding a Spanish source for everything Shakespeare wrote will not readily share Dr. Perott's conviction. As we have seen, Shakespeare had models for Don Adriano in London itself. Further, *The Merry Wives of Windsor* was made for Falstaff, and not Falstaff for *The Merry Wives*; he developed in the historical dramas, and is just a supreme example of an ancient literary type. Again, the concealment of the clan-

destine lover nowhere depends on written authority, and
the creator of Falstaff had no need to look to Spain for
the simple practical jokes played on his hero; if he had
been under any such necessity, popular Spanish literature
would have provided him with something much nearer to
the buck-basket incident than the *Segunda Celestina* offers.

Dr. Perott is almost as reckless in trying to bring
Shakespeare into association with Juan de Flores' *Historia
de Grisel y Mirabella*, a representative of the sentimental
tales that developed in Spain about the time the *Celestina*
was written and printed.   Published in English abroad in
1556, and at home thirty years later, as *The History of
Aurelio and Isabella*, this story may well have been known
to Shakespeare—it is known to Shakespearians as having
been at one time, under a complete misapprehension, regarded as the source of *The Tempest*.   Briefly, it relates
the secret love-intrigue of the knight Grisel and the princess
Mirabella, revealed by a servant to her father, the King of
Scotland.   According to the law of the country, whichever
of the pair gave the other the greatest cause for love was
to suffer death, and this other lifelong banishment.   The
difficult question as to which was the guiltier party was
argued at great length, and the lady finally condemned.
Dr. Perott regards this story as having influenced Shakespeare in *Measure for Measure*, because here the same
law prevails in Vienna, and he is absolutely convinced by
the Duke's remark to Juliet in prison:

Then was your sin of heavier kind than his.

Not being bound to find Spanish influence in *Measure
for Measure*, we may treat the Duke's remark in relation
to its context.   In his pretended character of a friar, the
Duke tells the penitent Juliet:

I'll teach you how you shall arraign your conscience,
And try your penitence, if it be sound,
Or hollowly put on.

He then brings her to confess she loves the man who
wronged her, so that their 'most offenceful act was

mutually committed'. It is robbing Shakespeare of his insight, and the Duke's remark of its subtlety, to pretend that the conclusion, 'Then was your sin of heavier kind than his', was inspired by the *Historia de Grisel y Mirabella*. But Dr. Perott had already blinded himself by identifying the ordinary law of Vienna, by which the man forfeited his life for immorality, while the woman was let off lightly, with the exceptional law of Scotland, by which the guilty woman died. As a matter of fact, neither the general plot nor the particular situations of *Measure for Measure* bear any relation to the *Historia de Grisel y Mirabella* ; as is well known, Shakespeare followed closely George Whetstone's play *Promos and Cassandra* of 1578.

After these strained comparisons, it is a relief to return to a modest suggestion that Shakespeare may have known the anonymous *Lazarillo de Tormes*, with which the picaresque story began in Spain about the middle of the sixteenth century, and of which two or three editions appeared in English during the last quarter of that century. A passage in *Much Ado about Nothing*, 'Ho! now you strike like the blind man : 'twas the boy that stole your meat, and you'll beat the post,' is said to recall the incident in *Lazarillo de Tormes* which terminated the youthful hero's service with his first master. He stole a piece of sausage from the blind man, and was well beaten for the offence. In revenge, he induced his master to jump across a stream head first into a stone pillar. The master is stunned, and the boy runs away from him for good. The main elements in these two cases are so similar that the above passage in Shakespeare will certainly recall the incident in *Lazarillo de Tormes* to those who have read the Spanish story. These elements, however, must formerly have occurred in conjunction often enough in real life, and the circumstances in the two cases we are considering are so different that it is reasonably certain Shakespeare was not alluding to *Lazarillo de Tormes*, but to some anecdote or incident better known to his audiences.

We reach the literature of Shakespeare's own time in

Mr. Martin Hume's claim that the dramatist was indebted to Juan Huarte's *Examen de Ingenios*, which appeared in English in 1594 and at later dates. We are told that 'this book was a very remarkable one, for it formulated a new theory of sanity, talent and madness'—sanity being the result of an equilibrium of the four humours. Of this new theory, however, Mr. Hume finds 'no traces in Shakespeare's studies of mental alienation, but that the great dramatist must have read Huarte in the translation of his friend, Carew, is obvious to any one who will read Nym's quaint talk about "humours" in "The Merry Wives of Windsor" and the speech of the bastard, Edmund, in "King Lear", where he states the reasons for the mental and physical superiority of illegitimately-born children over those born in wedlock.' 'As the speech and Huarte's original are somewhat coarse', Mr. Hume refrained from quoting, and he was as discreet as he was delicate, for quotation would have revealed the fact that the indignant protest of one who 'stood in the plague of custom' had nothing in common with the cold reasoning of the scientist, except the commonplace error concerning the superiority of the love-child. As to Nym's 'quaint talk about humours', Mr. Hume must have forgotten Ben Jonson's *Every Man in his Humour*, in which Shakespeare had acted; he certainly overlooked the induction to *Every Man out of his Humour*, or he would have realized that Nym's nonsensical remarks had nothing to do with Juan Huarte, but were simply another attempt

> To give these ignorant well-spoken days
> Some taste of their abuse of this word humour.

The last of these minor cases—minor only because of the obscurity that surrounds it—is the most interesting of all, for it involves the possibility of Shakespeare having come under the influence of Cervantes. Parallels between the two we have already seen, but they remain parallels and nothing more. The one chance of connecting them more closely depends on the evidence of a lost play, *The*

History of Cardenio, mentioned in the *Stationers' Register*
under the late date 1653, though perhaps identical with
a play performed forty years earlier.   If the *Stationers'
Register* is correct in ascribing this play to ' Mr. Fletcher
and Shakespeare', then the latter must have known and used
Don Quixote—which he might have read in Shelton's version
—for *The History of Cardenio* could hardly fail to unfold the
entangled love-stories of Cardenio and the Lady Luscinda,
and Don Fernando and the fair Dorothea, whom the
Knight met in the Sierra Morena.   We have no means
of judging the question, and so we cannot definitely say
that Shakespeare knew Cervantes, yet he supplemented,
unconsciously and not unworthily, the portrait which Cervantes drew of himself in the preface to his *Novelas
Exemplares*, and certainly more than one Spanish Desde-
mona was captivated by the tale

> of most disastrous chances,
> Of moving accidents by flood and field,
> Of hair-breadth 'scapes i' the imminent deadly breach,
> Of being taken by the insolent foe
> And sold to slavery.

In the above chronological *résumé* the discussion of
Shakespeare's relationship to the Spanish pastoral and
chivalresque romances has been deferred, because in both
cases we are on firmer ground.   The pastoral romance
was of course not originally Spanish, but it was popularized
in the Peninsula and elsewhere by Jorge de Montemôr's
Diana.   It has long been acknowledged that Shakespeare
was in some way indebted to the *Diana* for part of the plot
of *The Two Gentlemen of Verona* : Proteus' wooing of Julia
by letter, with the maid Lucetta as intermediary ; Julia's
coquetting with the letter; Proteus' departure for the
Court, followed by Julia in male attire ; Julia's stay at the
inn, and overhearing Proteus serenade another mistress ;
her service with him as a page, and employment to further
his new suit ; the recognition in a forest, after a scene
of combat.   All this is simply the story of Felix and
Felismena in the second book of the *Diana*.   Shakespeare

may have taken it from a lost play, *The History of Felix
and Philismena*, acted at Court in 1584 ; but there are points
which suggest that he may have known the romance: the
outlaw Valerius may be called after Valerio, the name adopted
by Felismena when she turned page ; and the magic juice
which Puck sprinkled on his victims' eyes in the *Midsummer Night's Dream* may have been suggested by the
Diana.   Even so, Shakespeare need not have had to read
the romance in the original Spanish.   The book seems to
have been popular with translators since Barnaby Googe
published a fragment from the Felix and Felismena episode
in English verse three years after the appearance of the
original.   Bartholomew Young translated the whole work
by 1582, though his version was not printed till 1598, after
the date assigned to *The Two Gentlemen of Verona*, and
Shakespeare may have known the story from a manuscript
copy, or from accounts given him by friends.   We know,
however, from Bartholomew Young himself, that others
had translated the *Diana*.   Among them was Sir Thomas
Wilson, who translated the work in 1596, dedicating it to
Shakespeare's patron, the Earl of Southampton.   Later he
could only find his copy of the first book, and it would be
tempting to think that Shakespeare used, and retained, the
second and later books, if the critics were not fairly well
agreed that *The Two Gentlemen of Verona* belonged to the
earlier nineties.   In any case, there seems to have been
material enough in English on which Shakespeare could
draw.

The case is different with regard to some of the Spanish
romances of chivalry which have recently been much
advertised as sources of Shakespeare's plays.   Over a
century ago, Robert Southey, fixing on the name Florizel
in *The Winter's Tale*, observed that Shakespeare in this
play imitated *Amadis de Grecia*—one of Feliciano de
Silva's continuations of the famous romance *Amadis de
Gaula*—which was not translated into English till 1693.
Southey had in mind those scenes in which Prince
Florizel, 'obscured with a swain's wearing', woos Perdita,
just as his namesake in *Amadis de Grecia* turns shepherd

to court the temporary shepherdess Silvia. The general plot of *The Winter's Tale*, including the pastoral scenes in question, was taken over bodily by Shakespeare from Greene's romance *Dorastus and Fawnia*; but as in these pastoral scenes Greene was clearly inspired by Feliciano de Silva, Shakespeare incurs at least a second-hand indebtedness to *Amadis de Grecia*. There the matter might have been allowed to rest if Shakespeare, in altering the names of Greene's characters, had not reverted to the Spanish original (Florisel) in the case of Prince Florizel. Shakespeare must have known something about the relationship of Greene's *Dorastus and Fawnia* to *Amadis de Grecia*. Did he learn the name of Dorastus' prototype from better informed friends, or had he himself read *Amadis de Grecia*, which he might have done in the French version? In the latter case, did he confine himself to the change in the name, or did he borrow further from the Spanish romance? Southey prudently spoke of nothing more than imitation. Later writers have followed up the clue, none with greater zeal than Dr. Perott, who examined not only the few end-chapters of *Amadis de Grecia* devoted to Prince Florizel's birth and pastoral adventures, but also all the books of the *Amadis* series written by Feliciano de Silva. Besides the name Florisel, Dr. Perott points out that these books contain a bear-hunt, a genial thieving rascal, and statues called to life, all missing in Greene's romance, and he concludes that the conjunction of these in *The Winter's Tale* must be attributed to the direct influence of Feliciano de Silva. His conclusion is convincing; but the conviction is almost completely destroyed by the proofs on which the conclusion is based. Let us examine them briefly.

The bear-hunt selected by Dr. Perott is to be found in *Lisuarte de Grecia*, the seventh book of the *Amadis* romances. The Florisel episode occurs in the final chapters of the ninth book, *Amadis de Grecia*, and assuming that Shakespeare was incapable of deciding how to get rid of Antigonus without some literary precedent, he might have found it in the bear-hunt which is described in these very chapters. Dr. Perott convinces himself that the bear-hunt in *Lisuarte de Grecia* inspired Shakespeare, because in this case the hunters in their pursuit hear 'a sad lament from a part of the mountain side washed by the sea', which is reproduced in the clown's 'O, the most piteous cry of the poor souls!' in *The Winter's Tale.* Shakespeare apparently would never have thought of making his clown utter a human cry of sympathy with shipwrecked souls unless he had read of a distressed damsel's cry for help under totally different circumstances in a chivalresque romance.

The incident of the 'statues called to life' which Dr. Perott finds 'united with' the pastoral motive also occurs in *Lisuarte de Grecia.* A princely pair were suddenly turned to marble by enchantment. A few years later they were just as suddenly restored to life, with the drawback that they could neither eat nor talk. These disadvantages could only be removed by two perfectly faithful lovers, which leads to numerous 'adventures' in a society that had departed from the high moral standard set by Amadis of Gaul. It is only by obscuring the details that this incident can be passed off as having inspired the method of Hermione's restoration in *The Winter's Tale.*

The case of the thieving rascal is somewhat different. It is not altogether impossible that Shakespeare should have taken the barest of hints for his Autolycus from Feliciano de Silva. The rascal in question, known as El Fraudador, is indeed a mounted horse-thief by profession, but he is somewhat similar in conception to Autolycus. Dr. Perott, however, is not content with vague resemblances, and strains proofs to the breaking-point to establish a close relationship between the two. He retells one of El Fraudador's tricks which Autolycus is said to have copied. A noble damsel tells a knight she meets that her brother is wounded, and begs for his help. The knight follows her to the wounded man, sets him on his horse, and gets on a tree-stump to mount behind him; but the wounded man, who is El Fraudador, and not wounded at all, rides away with the knight's horse, exhorting him to preach

a sermon from the improvised pulpit. Autolycus, it will
be remembered, pretends that he has been beaten and
robbed, and picks the pocket of the clown that helps him
up. The pick-pocket pedlar is the more natural of the
two rogues. Shakespeare may well have met him and his
tricks at Stratford fairs and Warwickshire harvest-wakes;
he is the less likely to have copied this incident from the
Spanish romance as the book in which it is told was
written out of the proper sequence, and apparently for
that reason was not translated into any language. We
should have to assume that Shakespeare read it in the
original. This presents no difficulty to Dr. Perott, who
supplies from it further convincing details: El Fraudador
plays tricks on emperors and queens, yet regards himself
as a true vassal, and helps on the occasion of a war, just as
Autolycus, a former servant of Florizel, helps him later;
both El Fraudador and Autolycus change their dress;
each swindles people after warning them against himself.
A single example will discover how Dr. Perott achieves
this close and unnecessary parallel. On one occasion, El
Fraudador, being pursued by his victims, changes dress to
avoid discovery. Autolycus is persuaded to change clothes
with Florizel in order that the latter may escape in dis-
guise. The circumstances are entirely different; the only
thing in common is the mere changing dress. Dr. Perott,
by stripping off their leaves, would persuade us that an
English oak were own brother to a Lombardy poplar.
He realizes that isolated incidents which have little or no
evidential value in themselves may acquire a convincing
force in accumulation; he has not realized that there is all
the difference in the world between the corresponding sequence of parallel events, essential and unessential, in two
similar stories, which proves the relationship of *The Two
Gentlemen of Verona* to Montemôr's *Diana*, and the fortuitous gathering of scattered incidents torn from their con-
texts in the different books of a long series for comparison
with isolated incidents in a totally different story. The
very accumulation of proof which convinces Dr. Perott
will tempt others impatiently to reject his thesis. Yet one

point has escaped him which, had he noticed it, he would regard as proving that thesis beyond all doubt. Shakespeare's prince bears the same name as the hero of one of these *Amadis* romances; the hero of a later romance, in which El Fraudador occurs, is Rogel de Grecia. It may be mere coincidence that the gentleman in *The Winter's Tale* who brings the news that 'the oracle is fulfilled, the king's daughter is found', is called Rogero; but the fact is disconcerting to those who would reject Shakespeare's direct indebtedness to Feliciano de Silva.

Dr. Perott would even increase this indebtedness. He thinks that Shakespeare took the plot of *Love's Labour's Lost* from the last of Feliciano de Silva's romances, which was never translated. His abridged version stresses the points which prove Shakespeare's borrowing: an academy; an embassy; the parting of the sexes; a queen accused of violating this (caricatured by Shakespeare in the Armado-Costard-Jaquenetta episode); encounters of knights with masked ladies, and surprises on unmasking; changing of clothes; music played by Ethiopian girls; famous worthies, such as Hector, Achilles, Helen, and Polyxena, called up by magicians for the diversion of the princes. Even the abridgement of the suggested source makes it clear that if Shakespeare extracted *Love's Labour's Lost* from this entangled story of knights and magicians, he deserves greater credit than if he drew it from his own imagination. But Dr. Perott convinces himself by a subtle test, which shows that he has entered into the spirit of the play, and is young enough to 'climb over the house to unlock the little gate'. In the Spanish romance the sexes are kept a third of an hour apart; in *Love's Labour's Lost*, one mile apart. Dr. Perott soberly consulted Minsheu's Dictionary 's.v. *legua*' to discover that 'an English mile is the equivalent of one-third of an hour'! After this, it need surprise no one to find him suggesting that Shakespeare possibly utilized phrases from two of Feliciano de Silva's romances in *The Tempest* and *King Lear*.

The question of Shakespeare's borrowing from Feliciano de Silva perhaps hardly merits such a lengthy discussion, for at the most it is only pretended that he took but a few hints from the Spanish writer. Attempts have recently been made to show that he was more deeply indebted to a smaller series of these Spanish romances, the *Espejo de Principes y Cavalleros*, a late and handy compendium of sixteenth-century chivalresque nonsense, which was translated into English as *The Mirror of Princely Deeds and Knighthood*. The early books appeared when Shakespeare was a young man, and may have formed part of his youthful reading; the later books, with reprints of the earlier ones, came out during the period of his literary activity. The series was popular in England, and Shakespeare seems to have been familiar with it, for there is an apparent allusion to its principal hero, the Cavallero del Febo, in Falstaff's reproach of the prince: 'Indeed, you come near me now, Hal; for we that take purses go by the moon, and not by Phoebus, he "that wandering knight so fair".'

Following no doubt the clue afforded by this allusion, Dr. Perott set out to find the original from which Shakespeare drew the plot of *The Tempest*. Hitherto the honour of providing this source had been doubtfully conceded, since Edmund Dorer's time, to Antonio de Eslava's *Noches de Invierno*, a collection of tales published only a year or so before *The Tempest* was written, and not then available in any known translation. For this and other reasons scholars have sought a common source for *The Tempest* and the story from the *Noches de Invierno* that has been associated with it. Dr. Perott discovered this common source in *The Mirror of Knighthood*. I have printed elsewhere a summary of the main theme from this romance, 'ending with two happy marriages', which he published in 1905 as 'the probable source of the plot of Shakespeare's Tempest', and I described it as not very convincing. On reconsideration, I am as willing to accept it for the original plot of *Much Ado about Nothing*, which also 'ends with two happy marriages', as of *The Tempest*, and I need not burden you with it here. But Dr. Perott supplemented this main theme with two other matters more suggestive of *The Tempest*. The first is the story of a prince who devoted himself to magic instead of to government, and after his wife's death retired to an island with his two children, a boy and a girl; the latter when grown up falls in love with the picture of a renowned knight whom the father kidnaps to keep her company. The second is the description of the island of Artimaga, named after its mistress, an old witch who worshipped the devil, and through his agency had a son, her successor from birth; the hero of the romance reaches this island after a dreadful storm, and has adventures which need not be recounted, as they bear no relationship to *The Tempest*. There are, however, precedents for other Shakespearian details. 'To the magician disarming there is an approach in *The Mirror of Knighthood*', and there are besides 'boats (often moved by magic power); storms (often conjured up by magicians); taking away a book from a magician in order to deprive him of his power; phantoms; mighty structures swallowed up; buffetting against the waves; Milon caught by a split oak; the sage waiting on people without being seen.'

Dr. Perott subsequently realized that the princely magician in *The Mirror of Knighthood* was not the elder son driven from his kingdom by a usurping younger brother, but himself a younger son who retired from public life as having no interest in the succession. The story summarized above hereby loses much of its resemblance to *The Tempest*, but Dr. Perott felt adequately compensated for this by a truly remarkable parallel: just as the kidnapped knight—who is really an emperor—stays twenty years in the magic island, so Prospero reveals his story to Miranda after a lapse of twelve years. And there are equally convincing parallels connected with the Devil's Island, which was uninhabited, but full of mysterious fires and smoke and noises: just as in *The Mirror of Knighthood* the monster Fauno was brought there from Mount Atlas, so Sycorax was transported from Algiers to the island in *The Tempest*; and just as a Spanish ship in *The Mirror of Knighthood* has a captain, so the English ship in *The Tempest* has a boatswain.

And if these parallels are not sufficient evidence of
Shakespeare's borrowings, there are linguistic proofs to
support them.   Dr. Perott had already claimed in 1905
that 'two of the finest flowers in Miranda's wreath' had
been 'culled in a Spanish garden', by which he meant that
prosaic phrases in *The Mirror of Knighthood* blossomed
forth into the well-known passages in *The Tempest* beginning: 'O, I have suffer'd with those I saw suffer', and
'For several virtues have I liked several women'.   To
these he added later the even better known passage:

> We are such stuff
> As dreams are made on, and our little life
> Is rounded with a sleep;

and about the same time he printed a list of thirteen
parallel passages which reveal Shakespeare's 'verbal
borrowings' from *The Mirror of Knighthood* 'in the
protasis-scene of *The Tempest*'.   From the suggested
original 'the chariot took landing', the verbal borrowing
in Ariel's 'the king's son have I landed by himself' is
limited, if I am not mistaken, to the word 'the', probably as
common in Shakespeare's time as now; but it is perhaps
uncharitable to assume that Dr. Perott means what he
says, and we should no doubt understand that Shakespeare in such cases only borrowed the general idea.   Yet
what idea was it that he borrowed in the above, or in the
following typical examples?

The forward ship arrived in a faire and delectable island.	Here in this island we arrived.
The Emperor's ship rushed on the shore.	How came we ashore?

Shakespeare's language could not be simpler, and the
entire absence of any characteristic words or phrases
proves exactly the opposite of what Dr. Perott would have
us believe.   We are simply dealing with two authors who
describe in their own words the commonplace events of
the same simple theme—in this case the arrival of a ship at
an island.   With such 'verbal borrowings' as Dr. Perott
adduces, aided by his method of selecting and piecing

together scattered incidents for comparison, one could just as easily prove that *Robinson Crusoe* or *Treasure Island*, for instance, was derived from *The Mirror of Knighthood*.

It is pleasant to turn from the scholar's reconstruction of the workings of a great creator's mind to Mr. Kipling's brilliant theory of *How Shakespeare came to write The Tempest*—and Mr. Kipling, though he modestly proclaims himself no Shakespeare scholar, has some title to speak on the point. Here we see *The Tempest* brewing from such a small beginning as the chatter of a half-tipsy sailor. Shakespeare overhears him discoursing to his neighbour in the theatre of a grievous wreck in the Bermudas. A hint from the distressed mariner is followed by a drink in an adjacent tavern and a more minute description of the island scene of the wreck, so faithfully reproduced in *The Tempest* that Mr. Kipling at once recognized the very spot three hundred years afterwards. With the sailor dipping to a deeper drunkenness, the story became more graphic : discipline had melted under the strain, and some of the revolted crew learned what it meant to wander without officers on a devil-haunted beach of noises. By the time the sailor was without reservation drunk, Shakespeare had quite sanely and normally come by the setting and some of the incidents of *The Tempest,* and his informant was ripe for immortalization as the drunken butler Stephano. Some vaguely remembered story of Italy was encased in the setting so naturally acquired ; and in this connexion it is curious to find Mr. Kipling reviving the old heresy of *The History of Aurelio and Isabella* : his library was not sufficiently up to date to suggest Eslava's *Noches de Invierno*, much less *The Mirror of Knighthood*.

Dr. Perott is not content merely to refer *The Tempest* to this latter. He finds in it the inspiration for ideas and incidents in several other plays. In some cases indeed he appears to offer us nothing more than parallels, but we feel all the time that he implies more than he actually states. The most plausible of his suggestions—though I can accept none of them—is that Margaret's impersonation

of Hero in *Much Ado about Nothing* was copied directly
from *The Mirror of Knighthood*, rather than from other
available sources; but I have dealt with this elsewhere,
and need not trouble you with it here.   Nor is it necessary
for me at this stage to do more than enumerate the other
supposed borrowings from this romance: the pursuit of
their lovers by ladies disguised as pages in *Twelfth Night*;
the kidnapping of the children and their training as
warriors in *Cymbeline*; the dagger-incident in the wooing-
scene in *King Richard III*; the drowning-scene, and even
the phrase 'the adventurous knight', in *Hamlet*; the brook-
simile in *The Two Gentlemen of Verona*.

The very number of these suggested borrowings, com-
bined with their distribution, is against them.   If they
were individually true, their collective value would be
sufficient to disprove their individual truth, which is
absurd, but not more so than the picture of Shakespeare
which Dr. Perott suggests to us.   Here the great philosophical dramatist appears little better than a scissors-and-
paste artist.   Like Don Quixote in his study, Shakespeare
is surrounded by Spanish romances of chivalry; some of
them are constantly open on his table throughout his
literary career, and he dips into them for inspiration when
at a loss for a plot, an incident, a phrase, or even an
epithet.   The most confirmed Hispanophile will hardly
welcome this ponderous portrait, and will turn with relief
to Mr. Kipling's quick sketch of a human Shakespeare
wheedling information from a drunken sailor.   Mr. Kipling
at least sees his subject in proper focus.

Source-hunting is a necessary evil: some of my own
worst moments have been devoted to this degrading sport,
with insignificant and, I trust, harmless results.   The discovery of literary sources may alter our estimate of an
author, and where more than one country is involved, any
ascertained facts are of interest for the interrelation of
literatures.   It can hardly be claimed that our estimate of
Shakespeare will be affected by new discoveries as to his
sources; his indebtedness—both actual and possible—to
his predecessors in one country or another has already

been fully discounted; any new facts will derive their importance mainly from their exalted association. Of late years Shakespeare's possible Spanish sources have been diligently investigated, with but little result; indeed, many of the 'discoveries' dealt with above may seem hardly worthy of serious treatment. Yet they were made by responsible people in reputable publications. Most of them are stated as unquestionable facts, with proofs often depending on very rare—to most people inaccessible—books. Some which are merely put forward as suggestions have been taken over in abstract by other publications and represented as facts. Readers who have not access to the originals quoted, or who have not the arguments before them, are likely to accept the 'discoveries' as proved facts, on the authority of the persons and the periodicals that print them. It was in the interests of such readers, among others, that the present examination of the results of recent investigations was developed.

It would have been gratifying to Spaniards and to Hispanophiles to find that Shakespeare incurred a heavier debt to Spain than we are warranted in acknowledging. It would have been a pleasure to me to enhance, rather than to depreciate, his indebtedness; yet a vain pleasure may be sacrificed without regret for the satisfaction of being on the side of truth. And after all, we. have little reason to be dissatisfied with the truth in this matter. The sixteenth century was a period of Italian and French influence in England: Shakespeare himself illustrates this fact. The period of Spanish influence in England, especially in the drama, was still to come. Yet at various points we can bring Shakespeare into relationship, direct or indirect, with Spanish literature. *The Two Gentlemen of Verona* owes something to Montemôr's *Diana*, and *The Winter's Tale* to *Amadis de Grecia*. *The Tempest* is at any rate related to Eslava's *Noches de Invierno*, even if Shakespeare knew nothing of the Spanish book. His apparent allusion to *The Mirror of Knighthood* may warrant the suspicion that he read, and perhaps utilized, that romance; and we may at least speculate as to whether he

came under the influence of Cervantes and the *Celestina*.
Some may entertain favourably a few more of the suggestions discussed above. But our speculations must be
controlled by common sense. We must not consider
supposed Spanish originals so closely that we fail to see
their relation to general literature. We must not rashly
detect a borrowing when we find two writers using a
commonplace idea in different (or even in similar) surroundings. We must not all too hastily conclude that
a creative artist is incapable of creating. The proverb
'there is nothing new under the sun' is to be interpreted as meaning that the same idea often occurs inde-
pendently to different people at different times; we must
not assume that, because we find it in a great writer's
work, this great writer necessarily took it from an earlier
(and usually very inferior) writer, simply because we can
trace it back so far, and no farther. In short, we must
obey a code of rules which can easily be compiled by
observing those broken in most of the assertions or suggestions of literary borrowing we have been discussing.

Guided by such rules, we may expect small and indeci-
sive results, where in any case the field is limited. Even
as a snapper-up of unconsidered trifles, Shakespeare was
usually artistic enough to cover up his tracks, and while
we may frequently suspect, we cannot often bring his
borrowings home to him. He himself warns us that it is
useless to pry too curiously. Like his own creation Holofernes, he has an 'extravagant spirit, full of forms, figures,
shapes, objects, ideas, apprehensions, motions, revolutions:
these are begot in the ventricle of memory, nourished in
the womb of *pia mater*, and delivered upon the mellowing
of occasion'.

We may well be content to praise the Lord for men in
whom these gifts are acute, even as Nathaniel did. Certainly those who have gone out of their way to tamper
indiscreetly with Shakespeare's intellectual remains seem
justly to have fallen under the curse he laid on such as
should move his bones.

The Taylorian Lecture

1923

TOMMASO CAMPANELLA

AND HIS POETRY

By

EDMUND G. GARDNER

TOMMASO CAMPANELLA AND HIS POETRY.

THE end of the sixteenth century saw the political independence of Italy crushed beneath the domination of Spain, her intellectual freedom fettered by the contemporaneous triumph of the Counter-Reformation. Her national and social life was overshadowed by the Spanish predominance, her religious and philosophical thought by the presence of the Inquisition. Although no one to-day would accept the once traditional view that the period immediately following the Renaissance was an epoch of mere decadence, nevertheless *Secentismo*—the tendency that manifested itself in the latter years of the sixteenth and came to fulfilment in the first part of the seventeenth century—has become synonymous with the false and pretentious in art and in literature. It has been defined as ' the assiduous endeavour to conceal poverty of imagination under the mask of emphasis and artifice, and to simulate the movement and the heat of passion where the breath of life is absolutely wanting '.[1]

But this tendency—represented in particular by the Neapolitan poet, Giovanni Battista Marino, and his followers—is not the most significant aspect of the epoch. In spite of the Inquisition, Italy was preparing triumphs in the field of natural science and philosophical speculation. The spirit of philosophical investigation, independent of Aristotelian tradition, had already appeared with Pietro Pomponazzi in the early years of the sixteenth century, and Leonardo da Vinci, subscribing

[1] A. Belloni, *Il Seicento*, p. 457. But cf. Croce, *Saggi sulla letteratura italiana del Seicento*, preface.

himself 'discepolo della sperienza', had attempted to
discover the laws of nature by the observation of phenomena.   In the latter part of the century this spirit
possesses itself of a Calabrian, Bernardino Telesio of
Cosenza, whom Francis Bacon was to acclaim as 'a
lover of truth' and 'the first of the new men'.   The first
and second books of his great work, *De rerum natura
iuxta propria principia*, were printed at Rome in 1565;
the complete edition, in nine books, appeared at Naples
in 1587. Telesio describes himself as one who is attempting to introduce a new doctrine: 'not content with the
doctrine of Aristotle, whom now for so many centuries
the whole race of men venerates like a deity, and, as
though he were taught by God Himself and the interpreter of very God, hears with supreme admiration
and even with supreme religious observance.'[1]   For the
Aristotelian conception of the actualizing of matter by
form, Telesio strove to substitute that of the unity of
nature in which matter and form are inherent, the
contending principles—upon which the *natura rerum*
depends—being heat and cold.   But his hypothesis
itself is less significant than his norm of investigating
natural phenomena, the consideration and questioning
of nature herself rather than accepting the authority of
her commentators: 'Allured solely by love of truth, and
venerating this alone, unable to acquiesce in what was
handed down by those who have gone before, we looked
for long into the nature of things, and wished at last to
reveal to men what, if we mistake not, we had seen;
deeming that we should not fulfil the duty of a free or
upright man, if—because we grudged this to the human
race or feared hostility from men—we were to keep it
hidden.'[2]

[1] Proem to the 1565 edition.   [1] *De rerum natura* (1587), iii. 1.

Telesio died in 1588. Though his work had excited hostility and censure, he had not been personally molested. In 1600 Giordano Bruno—with his ideal of philosophical liberty—perished at the stake in Rome. Midway between the two centuries we meet three very great men, in their various fields champions of freedom in an age of servitude, men of extraordinary virility of character (that *virilità* which is typically Italian): Galileo Galilei, Paolo Sarpi, Tommaso Campanella. Campanella stands apart from the others in that he is a type that Italy has produced at intervals through the centuries —from Joachim of Flora to Giuseppe Mazzini—the prophet of humanity.

Like Joachim of Flora, he was a Calabrian. Born at Stilo in 1568, Gian Domenico Campanella entered the order of Friars Preachers in 1582 as Fra Tommaso.[1] Dissatisfaction with the current philosophy of the cloister and a casual taunt of a fellow Dominican drew him to the work of Telesio: 'Telesio delighted me; both on account of the liberty of his philosophy, and because he depended on the nature of things, not on the sayings of men.'[2] Debarred from personal acquaintance, he looked upon his dead body on the bier in 1588, and felt himself his spiritual heir. His own first work—the *Philosophia sensibus demonstrata*, published in 1591—is a defence of

[1] The study of Campanella, especially on the biographical side, was put upon a new basis by the various publications of Luigi Amabile in the eighties of the nineteenth century. Recently we have two most admirable monographs: Léon Blanchet, *Campanella* (Paris, 1920), and C. Dentice di Accadia, *Tommaso Campanella* (Florence, 1921). There are important studies by Croce, *Materialismo storico ed economia marxistica* (Bari, 1918), and G. Gentile, *Giordano Bruno e il pensiero del Rinascimento* (Florence, 1920), and *Studi sul Rinascimento* (Florence, 1923).

[2] *De libris propriis et recta ratione studendi* (Paris, 1642), i. 1, pp. 5-6.

Telesio, 'philosophorum maximus'. But Telesio seemed to restrict his researches to physical science; whereas Campanella yearned for a complete philosophy based on nature, which should cover every field of human thought and activity, and should be recognized as Italian. The Inquisition seized his manuscripts; but three successive processes, and some months in the prison of the Holy Office at Rome, resulted in his absolution and release in 1595. A vision of the unification of nations and peoples now occupied his mind. Professedly he looked to its fulfilment by the universal monarchy of Spain as the arm of the spiritual monarchy of the Papacy, and rejected the Protestant reformation as a movement of disgregation; Lutheranism being especially distasteful to him on account of its doctrine of justification by faith and repudiation of free will. But his real thought went farther. Joachim of Flora had foretold the advent of the epoch of the Holy Ghost, in which the Everlasting Gospel, the spiritual interpretation of the Gospel of Christ, would be the only law and norm of life, and spiritual men would be the rulers. Campanella dreams of a new age, a universal brotherhood of humanity, with a universal religion and laws in accordance with natural principles, to be inaugurated in a sacred theocratic republic based upon nature and worshipping God under the image of the Sun, and he himself is the man of destiny, born to be the regenerator of the world. Initiated into occult science and necromancy by a young Jew at Cosenza, he becomes convinced that great mutations, announced by astrology for the end of the century, will give the opportunity. From his convent at Stilo he secretly promulgates his doctrines, urging that the world should recover the state of liberty in which man was created; he gains adherents, and prepares an extensive conspiracy which, with the promised aid of the Turks, should establish this City of the Sun among those mountains of Calabria from which, four centuries before, Joachim of Flora had proclaimed the advent of the Kingdom of the Spirit.

The conspiracy was discovered, and Campanella betrayed into the hands of the Spanish authorities in September 1599. He is at first calmly defiant. 'You have taken a man,' he said to his captors, 'but nevertheless what further is to happen shall not remain unfulfilled.' Heretics, ancient or modern, could merely gloss or pervert a text of Scripture, whereas he, one of those great men who ordained new modes of life, 'like a new Messiah, had come to the world for the salvation of men'.[1] Threats of death left him unmoved; there is no death, but only mutation of being. But, brought to Naples, subjected to a double process for attempted rebellion and heresy, repeatedly and horribly tortured, he resolves to preserve that being for the accomplishment of his mission; he saves his life by persisting in feigning madness, and is consigned to an indefinite imprisonment which, under varying conditions, was to last for more than a quarter of a century.

In the early days of his captivity, in 1602, Campanella wrote in Italian the best known of his works, the *Città del Sole*, or, as he called it later when translated into Latin, *Idea reipublicae philosophicae*.[2] In the form of a

[1] *Ragguaglio de' movimenti suscitati in Calabria da F. Tomasso Campanella*, a contemporary account of the conspiracy, dated Reggio, October 8, 1599, published by J. Kvačala, *Thomas Campanella und Ferdinand II*, in *Sitzungsberichte der philosophisch-historischen Klasse der k. Akademie der Wissenschaften*, Band clix (Vienna, 1908), pp. 29-32.

[2] In 1612 Campanella translated it into Latin and consigned it

dialogue, a Genoese sailor describes the ideal state of
the City of the Sun, ruled over in spiritual and temporal
things alike by a Prince Priest, with three collateral
princes: Power, concerned with war and peace; Wisdom,
with science and art; Love, with generation, education,
and the like. The life of the citizens is based on
communism and what we should now call eugenics.
All things are in common, in the hands of officials who
dispense them. There is no private property, no family,
and no heritage. Education is the perfect training of
mind and body, the objects of study being things, not
books. The young serve the old. There is no marriage, generation and all sexual relations being strictly
regulated for the general good of the state. No servile work is reputed base, but all are called 'learning'.
Military, agricultural, and pastoral duties are obligatory
on all, and each citizen is ruled by the head of his own
art. The penalty of death is inflicted by all the people,
the accused being first convinced and brought to accept
his sentence as just. All officials are priests, and there
is a remarkable system of confessions and continual
sacrifice of prayer. One God is worshipped under the
image of the Sun; they adore God as Trinity, but do
not know of distinction of Persons. Men merit by
power, wisdom, and love, and sin by deficiency in these
principles. They believe in the immortality of the soul,
and hold that after death they will associate with good

to his German disciple, Tobia Adami, who published it at Frankfort
in 1623. After his liberation, Campanella made a third version,
also in Latin, at Paris (published 1637). These Latin versions
show an attempt to conform more closely with orthodoxy, and it
is from them that the current Italian versions were taken. The
original Italian text was first published by E. Solmi (Modena,
1904), and recently a *testo critico* has been edited by G. Paladino
(Naples, 1920).

or bad spirits according to their merits. The other interlocutor in the dialogue remarks that, if those who follow only the law of nature are so near to Christianity, which adds nothing to the natural law save the Sacraments, he gathers that the 'true law' is the Christian; when abuses are taken away, Christianity will rule the world, and the Spaniards have discovered a new hemisphere to unite all in one law. We know not what we do, but are instruments of God: 'They go through greed of wealth to seek new lands, but God intends higher ends.' The Genoese, however, does not commit himself to this, but declares that the citizens of the Sun hold that the wonderful inventions of the century point to the reunion of the world, and that astrology indicates that a great new monarchy and a complete renovation of all things is at hand: 'They say that this will bring great utility to Christians, but first comes uprooting and cleansing, then building and planting.'

The City of the Sun is no doubt the idealized image of that fantastic state which Campanella and his strange fellow conspirators—outlaws and friars aided by the arm of the Turk—had thought to realize in Calabria. There are traces of it in the confessions, whether spontaneous or wrung from them by torture, of his accomplices during the trials. But Croce has observed: 'It is not Campanella the reformer and communist who still lives for us, but Campanella the poet of reform and communism. The lofty ideal of justice and of human felicity cherished by him confronts us with the force of an aspiration and poetic vision.'[1]

We know from Campanella's own statements that his extant poems represent only a portion of what he

[1] *Il Comunismo di Tommaso Campanella*, in the volume *Materialismo storico*, &c., cited above.

composed. They have come down to us from two
sources. During his long imprisonment he put together
seven books of *Cantici*, 'on the Primal Wisdom and
Power, the Primal Love, the Good, the Beautiful, and
like themes', of which a selection was given to Tobia
Adami, together with annotations written in 1613, and
published by him in Germany nine years later, as *Scelta
d'alcune poesie filosofiche di Settimontano Squilla*. But
also, Campanella says: 'I sang elegies concerning my
own sufferings and those of my friends, prophetical
rhythms, and a fourfold psalmody concerning God and
all His works, and with this poetical discourse I fortified
my friends lest they should succumb in their torments.'[1]
A number of these latter, with other poems (probably
not all by Campanella) and including some of the *Scelta*,
were collected by one of his fellow prisoners, Fra Pietro
Ponzio, in 1601, and discovered by Luigi Amabile. An
admirable critical edition has been published by Gentile.[2]

These poems give lyrical utterance to the doctrines
set forth in Campanella's prose works, to which the
accompanying annotations (now recognized as his own)
frequently refer the reader: his metaphysical creed of
God, his conception of nature, his hatred of the corruption of the age in religion and literature alike, his
detestation of tyranny, his utopian and messianic dreams
for the coming renovation of mankind; mingling with
the cries that are wrung from him by his torments and

---

[1] *De propriis libris*, i. 2, i. 3, pp. 13–15.

[2] Tommaso Campanella, *Poesie*, a cura di Giovanni Gentile, in
the *Scrittori d'Italia* (Bari, 1915). John Addington Symonds (*The
Sonnets of Michael Angelo Buonarroti and Tommaso Campanella*,
London, 1878) translated sixty sonnets and one canzone; he
naturally only knew the *Scelta*, and wrote before the researches
of Amabile had revealed the facts of Campanella's life and imprisonment.

those of his companions. A few pieces—notably love sonnets—are unworthy; they are in the debased style of the age, with the repulsive conceits which the Marinisti affected, and even the mythological imagery which Campanella ruthlessly condemned in others. But the majority, though frequently uncouth and harsh, unpolished and abrupt, have an intensity of feeling, a rugged power and sublimity which takes us back to Michelangelo, reminding us how Berni, rebuking his contemporary Petrarchists, said of the great Florentine: 'Ei dice cose, e voi dite parole.' At times they suggest a greater name. Croce remarks that the verses of Campanella, 'per la semplicità vigorosa delle immagini e delle espressioni, hanno proprio quel carattere che noi siamo soliti di chiamare dantesco'.

Here and there poems are evidently earlier than the conspiracy of 1599: the sonnet to Telesio, 'ch'uccide Aristotile, tiranno degli ingegni umani'; another rebuking Cesare d'Este for opposing the papal occupation of Ferrara; a powerful and noble sonnet, written during Campanella's previous imprisonment at Rome, on one who had died in the dungeon of the Holy Office:

'Soul, that now hast left the dark prison of this world, of Italy and of Rome, of the Holy Office and of the mortal load, soar hence to heaven, for we shall follow thee.

'There shalt thou set forth with mournful strains the harsh severity that weighs us down from golden curls to hair of eld, so that in thought I am pierced in heart and turn to stone.

'Say that if soon to send the succour of the awaited new redemption is not Heaven's will, from torment so bitter let it in mercy take our persons to itself, or re-create and arm us for the destined course which eternal reason has decreed.'[1]

---

[1] *Poesie*, ed. Gentile, p. 211. The sonnet on Italy (ibid., p. 89) was perhaps (as Amabile suggested) written in 1599.

Campanella tells us that, while he was at Rome, he began 'to compose Tuscan verses in Latin metre'. In an elegy, *Al senno latino*, he gives to this kind of vernacular verse the title which—with Carducci—it bears in our own day: 'Musa latina, è forza che prendi la barbara lingua.' This short piece, inspired by that sense of *italianità* in which Campanella surpasses his contemporaries, may perhaps have been written at the time (as Gentile holds); but the chief of these quantitative elegies, *Al Sole*, was written from the dark and frigid Neapolitan dungeon of Sant' Elmo, 'nella primavera per desio di caldo'. In its way, it is a lyrical masterpiece; the hymn which priests and people might have raised in that Solar City for the sake of which, this Easter day, while all things else are called to a new life, the poet though living is buried like a corpse in his rigid tomb.[1]

Most of Campanella's poetry falls between the years 1600 and 1613. Pomponazzi had written: 'Prometheus is the philosopher who, whilst he strives to know the mysteries of God, is gnawed with perpetual cares and thoughts, mocked by all, held as foolish and sacrilegious, persecuted by inquisitors, a spectacle to the vulgar herd.'[2] This image Campanella adopts as his own. He is the new Prometheus, who has robbed fire from the Sun, the fire of the knowledge of nature in which the ignorance of men may be burned away.[3] The subterranean dungeon of Sant' Elmo is Caucasus, and his meditations find words curiously resembling those which Shakespeare, almost contemporaneously, was placing on the lips of Hamlet:

---

[1] *Poesie*, ed. cit., pp. 188-92.   [2] *De Fato*, iii. 7.
[3] *Poesie*, p. 7 (*Proemio*).

'I fear that through dying man's state is not bettered;
therefore I slay not myself; for so wide is the nest of
misery that, by changing place, one leaves it not.

'By changing ills, oft-times we fare worse; sense is
everywhere, and I could forget my present cry as I have
a thousand others too.

'But who knows what will be with me, if the Omni-
potent is silent? And if I know not whether I had war
or peace when I was another being?

'Philip shuts me in a worse prison to-day than yester-
day; nor without God doth he do this. Let us abide as
God wills, for He errs not.' [1]

Per tutto è senso! In one of his earliest works, re-
written in prison, Campanella claims to prove that 'the
world is the living and conscious statue of God, and
all its parts and particles have sense, some more clear,
others more dim, as far as suffices for their conservation
and that of the whole in which they harmonize'. He
has four canzoni on the contempt of death, *Dispregio
della morte*:

'My soul, why such dismay? Dost fear perchance
to perish amidst boundless woes? Let the vulgar herd
fear. Thou knowest he is said to die who lies outside
his good. If nought is ever doomed to nought, he who
is not first dead to himself cannot suffer death or wrong,
nor he who in himself has peace fear war.' [2]

And he adds in a note: 'If no being is annihilated,
we must say that death is mutation; and that he in
truth is dead who abides outside the good that befits
him, not he who is changed into another being.' Campanella does not usually push this doctrine to its logical
conclusion, and deny individual immortality save as a
part of the soul of the universe in which 'per tutto è
senso'. He believes in the transcendent immortality
of the soul and the immanent divinity of man. In any
case, pursuing a thesis already insisted upon by Pom-

[1] *Poesie*, p. 113 (*Sonetto nel Caucaso*).   [2] Ibid., p. 139.

ponazzi, he maintains that sin is its own penalty, virtue its own reward, even here and now, sin being punished in its consequences by nature, of whose laws it is a violation, and, like virtue, realized in the will.[1]

A sublime sonnet, entitled *modo di filosofare*, may be taken as setting forth the syllabus of his philosophical teaching:

'The world is the book where the eternal Wisdom wrote its own concepts, and the living temple where, depicting its deeds and own example, it adorned the depth and the height with statues;
'that every spirit here may learn and contemplate art and law, lest it become impious, and can say: I fulfil the universe, by contemplating God within all things.
'But we, souls fettered to books and dead temples, copied from the truth with many errors, place them above such teaching.
'O suffering, discord, ignorance, labour, grief, make us aware of our mistake. Ah, by God, let us return to the original.'[2]

L'original libro della natura! To this the sufferings of the human race, through studying by preference 'the books and dead temples of men', should make us at length return. Campanella cites the lines of Dante:

E se 'l mondo là giù ponesse mente
al fondamento che natura pone,
seguendo lui, avria buona la gente;[3]

but he would extend this principle to every sphere of

---

[1] Sonnet, *Seco ogni colpa è doglia* (*Poesie*, p. 83). Cf. Gentile, *Il concetto dell' uomo nel Rinascimento*, in the volume *Giordano Bruno e il pensiero del Rinascimento*, pp. 114-26.

[2] *Poesie*, p. 16.

[3] *Par.* viii. 142-4. Another sentence of Dante's which he makes his own is *Inf.* xi. 105: 'sì che vostr' arte a Dio quasi è nepote.'

human thought and activity, as others of his poems show :
poetry, philosophy, religion, politics, and daily life must
all be based upon nature. Those who in politics would
substitute the accursed 'ragione di stato' are Machia-
vellians; Campanella happily not anticipating that the
English version of one of his books, the *Monarchia
hispanica*, would be announced as the work of a 'second
Machiavel'.

Throughout the poems runs Campanella's metaphysical doctrine of what he calls the three pro-principles
or primalities of Being: Power, Wisdom, and Love ;
from which every power and knowledge and desire
comes. Against them rise the three extreme evils
from which all the suffering of the world depends:
tyranny, sophistry, hypocrisy. These have their root
in blind self-love, the child of ignorance: 'Dunque a
diveller l'ignoranza io vegno.'[1] The three primalities
at times tend to become identified with the orthodox
doctrine of the attributes of the three Persons of the
Blessed Trinity ; but this is not what they originally
meant for Campanella; indeed, he represents his acceptance of the Catholic dogma on the subject as an
illumination which came to him later in prison.

He is not always a visionary. A noble canzone,
celebrating Christopher Columbus and Amerigo Ves-
pucci, bidding Italy remember her own glories and
celebrate these in song rather than the fables of Greek
mythology, is followed by a series of sonnets which
inevitably suggest to English readers a comparison with
Wordsworth's sonnets dedicated to Liberty. Venice,
'nuova arca di Noè' in the flood of foreign domination
that has swept over Italy, preserves her freedom in an

---

[1] *Poesie*, p. 18. For the doctrine of the 'primalities', cf. Blanchet,
op. cit., pp. 310–14.

age of servitude; Genoa, by her mighty memories of old and the more recent glory of Columbus, is exhorted to rise to a new life; Switzerland has the divine gift of liberty, but her sons are rebuked for supporting tyranny in other lands with their mercenary arms; Poland is praised above all other kingdoms because of the elective principle of her monarchy, but urged to seek her rulers, not among princes, but in the lowly dwellings of the people.[1]

Campanella's more elaborate poems are canzoni composed in sequence, or take a form of prolonged sapphic ode with linked stanzas and internal rhymes which metrically seems at the same time to suggest the mediaeval *serventese incatenato*. Among these latter is one lyrical masterpiece, *Della possanza dell' uomo*. The conception of the worth and dignity of man, which Burckhardt regarded as the great conquest of the Italian Renaissance, finds its supreme expression in this poem, which harks back to Pico della Mirandola and Marsilio Ficino, reminds us that its writer was the contemporary of Shakespeare, and anticipates the lyrics of the fourth act of Shelley's *Prometheus Unbound*.

'Glory to Him who knows and can do all! O my art, grandchild to the Primal Wisdom, give some hint of his beauteous image which is called "man".

'"Man" is he called who is born of clay, witless he lies low, unarmed and nude; a harsh stepfather seemed to him the Primal Being, though father of others.

'Father of others, to whom at birth He gave the strength they need, industry, bark, hide, scales. They conquer hunger; they have speed, claws, and horns, against every affront.

'But at every affront man yields and weeps; till of

---

[1] *Poesie*, pp. 85-93. Campanella's admiration for Poland is shared by his contemporary, Traiano Boccalini.

his wisdom comes the hour, late indeed, but so mighty that in the world below he seems a second God.

'A second God, the First's own miracle, he commands the depths; he mounts to Heaven without wings, and counts its motions and measures and its natures.

'The natures of the stars he knows and their names, why one is tressed with light, another bare. . . .

'The wind and the sea he has mastered, and the earthly globe with pooped ship he encircles, conquers and beholds, barters and makes his prey. . . .

'He sets laws, like a God. In his craft he has given to silent parchment and to paper the art of speech, and, to distinguish time, he gives tongue to brass. . . .

'O hidden virtue, of Thine own glory Thou art bounteous to him.

'Thou art bounteous to him, if one revives the dead; another passes the Red Sea, and is not drowned; Eliseus sings the future; Elias soars hence unto Thy school.

'Unto Thy school Paul ascends, and finds, with manifest proof, Christ on the right of the immense ruling Power. Think, man, think!

'Think, man, think; rejoice and praise the high First Cause, and do Him reverence; that every other thing He made may serve thee, let pure and gentle faith unite thee to Him, and thy song soar to greater height than theirs.'[1]

It is obvious that Christ is here, not the second Person of the Trinity of the Catholic creed, but the image of the immortality and the Divinity of man, united to God the First Cause.

One of Campanella's most remarkable poems is the *Salmodia metafisicale*, composed of three canzoni united together. It surveys his own life as expounded by his metaphysical creed. In the darkness in which mankind lay he kindled a light; his consequent sufferings and persecutions are in accordance with the law of the universe, in which the mutation which we call 'evil and

---

[1] *Poesie*, pp. 170-3. Cf. Gentile, *Il concetto de' uomo*, pp. 127-33.

death', and in which nature consists, may be the life and joy of the whole,—though he can pray to have his bitter torment lessened or be delivered from 'il dolce crudo amor di vita'. If this mutation were painless, things would be without sense and without pleasure, and, unless beings struggled for existence and preservation, there would be no generation, and the world would return to chaos: 'e'l caos immenso la bella distinzione assorbirebbe.' The third of these canzoni is an impassioned appeal to God—invoked by all the principles of Campanella's metaphysical creed—for man to return to that natural law on behalf of which he himself lies entombed. To this new life of the world God has given him the key, but he is helpless and cannot use it:

If Thou dost free me, I promise to make a school of all nations to God the liberator, true and living, if to so great a thought is not denied the end to which Thou urgest me; to cast down the idols, to strip of worship every false god, and him who makes God his means and serves God not; to raise the throne and standard of reason against coward vice; to summon enslaved souls to liberty, to humble the oppressor. Nor under built roofs, which lightning or beast degrades, shall I utter the new songs for which Sion craves; but I shall make heaven my temple, my altar the stars.

There is a characteristic note at the end. A certain promise has been made to him in visions. Let these three canzoni go to the Lord, craving pity for their maker's torment: 'Nor let one return to give me other news from the Ruler of the spheres save the promised end of the goodly story (whether the messenger was false or true), singing: *Viva, viva Campanella.*'[1]

At times Campanella's megalomania, his conviction that he is a superman of intellect with a supreme destiny,

---

[1] *Poesie*, pp. 119, 126-7, 135, 138.

somewhat reminds us of the heroes of D'Annunzio's romances: Claudio Cantelmo looking to be the father of the superman of his race, 'Colui che doveva venire', as a dominator over men and the incarnation of aristocracy of blood; Stelio Èffrena aspiring to be superhuman in the triumphs of art, manifesting and concentrating his vision of the universe in the living forms of poetry. At times, in the notes to his poems, this tendency in Campanella finds the most naïve utterance: 'sonetto stupendo', 'mirabile sonetto', 'mira qual voto d'animo divinissimo'. Here, however, he admits 'ch' e' fu deluso dal diavolo', and refers the reader to another poem: the *Canzone a Berillo*.

This is a singularly beautiful lyric, the *canzone di pentimento*, in which Campanella professes to abjure his past, to repudiate his old effort to realize his messianic dream as impious human presumption, when, deeming that he held God in his hand, he sought to 'migliorar la comun sorte' without a mandate from Him. He appears in the guise of a penitent sinner, and this repentance finds the most impassioned and convincing accents. He describes the poem as 'fatta nel Caucaso', that is, composed in the dungeon of Sant' Elmo before being transferred to a less harsh prison in 1608.[1] It does not stand alone. A Latin prayer of his has been preserved, written in 1618, in which he depicts himself as a mighty genius, to whom no branch of knowledge was hidden, who had thrown away the shield of God's protection and the sword of His word, and given himself up to serve the Evil One with tumid desires and impure lusts. For this God had humbled him by the torments he had undergone; but, when thinking to be soon restored to liberty (an evident allusion to his being

---

[1] *Poesie*, pp. 157–63.

removed from Sant' Elmo in 1608), he had returned to his former thoughts. Now he has been humbled again, he is convinced of the truth of the Catholic doctrines, and he prays that God may make him His ambassador to arouse the remembrance of Him in all the human race: 'Thou hast put into my mind that I, who wished to become the lord of all, should become the servant of all unto salvation, and should stir them to the remembrance of Thee, even as I too am stirred.'[1]

The real significance of this phase in Campanella has been disputed. Some have held that, since the friar justifies the use of dissimulation by philosophers 'per schifar la morte', he was adopting the attitude most likely to induce papal intervention for his liberation; others, that it was a genuine case of conversion in the confessional sense. A similar problem confronts us with his prose works written in prison: a vast treatise on Metaphysics, which he called *biblia philosophorum*, designed to embrace all sciences, attempting to harmonize the naturalism of Telesio with the orthodox scholasticism of Aquinas; the *Atheismus triumphatus*, which by means of the truths of science would convert all unbelievers to religion; the *Monarchia Messiae*, a demonstration of the rightfulness of the universal sway of the Papacy. The truth seems to lie between these two views. On the one hand, in these works, under their frequently traditional orthodox expression, there is a sincere attempt to conciliate his own religious naturalism with the Catholic faith, to construct a naturalistic theology that will be crowned with orthodox conclusions.[2] And, on

---

[1] *Oratio ad Deum Deorum pro legatione sua ad excitandam Reminiscentiam Dei toto in genere humano*, ed. Kvačala, op. cit., pp. 33-6. Cf. Blanchet, op. cit., pp. 90-3.

[2] See in particular the treatment of this phase of Campanella in,

the other, his experiences have given a new colour to his messianic dream. Still looking forward to the regeneration of mankind and its unification in a philosophical religion, a universal theocratic monarchy, he has become convinced of the impossibility of that City of the Sun for which he had striven and suffered ; he will make his dream a reality through the medium of the Papacy. Should he gain his liberation, he will impress his personality upon the Church, and lead her to triumph along his own lines. He will conquer the Church and, with her universality as weapon, conquer the world. We may accept this view, and yet believe that both the *canzone di pentimento* and the *Oratio ad Deum Deorum* are absolutely sincere utterances, even if they do not reveal the whole of the friar's thought.

Something of Campanella's mentality is revealed in his attitude towards his two great contemporaries : Sarpi and Galileo. He hears, in 1606, of the conflict between Paul V and the Venetians, in which the Servite is the spokesman of the Republic. Promptly he transforms his former sonnet of praise into one of bitter denunciation, and addresses Venice with an impassioned prose invective in which his worship of the great republic is mingled with the fiercest rebuke of her present line of policy. Sarpi for him is merely ' un teologo venduto ' ; while, as for himself, ' I do not speak for my own interest, nor for friendship and love of the clergy, who in all my life have afflicted me with such unspeakable woes that few martyrs surpass me in torments.'[1] The motive is clear ; the principle of unity has been attacked, and in earlier days Campanella had taken a similar line in the question of

C. Dentice di Accadia, op. cit., vi and vii. I am much indebted to her work.

[1] *Poesie*, pp. 251-4.

the devolution of the duchy of Ferrara to the Holy See.
But it is another matter when 'libertas philosophandi'
is involved.   Into his prison—brought probably by
Manso, the friend of Tasso and Milton—came tidings of
the discoveries of Galileo and the *Sidereus nuncius.*   To
adopt a phrase of De Sanctis, the 'immaginazione napole-
tana' is brought face to face with the 'saviezza fioren-
tina'.   Campanella writes enthusiastically to the great
Florentine, who as the glory of Italy is to surpass all the
astronomers of the world as Virgil and Dante had
eclipsed Homer: 'Amerigo gave his name to a new
earthly world, thou wilt give thine to a new celestial
one.'   He urges Galileo not to confine himself to physical
science, but to reveal a universal philosophy which shall
be known as Italian: 'Scriva nel principio che questa
filosofia è d'Italia.'[1]   In February 1616 came the first
condemnation of the Florentine's propositions by the
Holy Office, and the injunction upon him of silence.
Campanella at once produces a vigorous defence of his
method, the *Apologia pro Galileo*, written in the same
year and published in Germany in 1622.   Neither Moses
nor Christ, he declares, revealed physiology and astronomy to us, all such matters being free field for human
investigation: 'Deus tradidit mundum disputationi eorum.'
'He who fears contradiction from things of nature is
conscious of his own falseness. . . . Therefore those
who wish sciences and studies and the investigation of
physical and heavenly things to be condemned by
Christian law, either themselves think badly of Christianity or are the cause of evil suspicions in others.'

[1] Letters of January 13, 1611, and March 8, 1614, in D. Berti,
Lettere inedite di Tommaso Campanella, in *Atti dell' Accademia de'
Lincei* (S. iii, vol. ii, Rome, 1878), no. 1, and L. Amabile, *Fra T. C.
ne' castelli di Napoli, in Roma ed in Parigi* (Naples, 1887), ii, doc. 185.

'Wisdom is read in the whole book of God, which is the world, and more is always found. To that, therefore, not to the codicils of men, the Holy Scriptures refer us.'[1]

Released by the Spanish government in 1626, Campanella was re-arrested by the Inquisition and sent to Rome, where he was finally set at liberty in 1629. For a while, encouraged by the favour of Urban VIII, he aspired to lead the policy and theology of the Church into new paths, as consultor of the Holy Office or even as cardinal. In a remarkable and characteristic letter to the Pope's nephew, Cardinal Francesco Barberini, he suggests the foundation by Calabrian Dominicans under his direction of a college for the propagation of the faith, to be based upon his own writings, of which he proposes the publication of a complete edition.[2] But the final condemnation of Galileo, whom he had offered to defend before the Holy Office, brings new suspicion upon him; a fresh conspiracy in Naples, in which one of his disciples, Fra Tommaso Pignatelli, is involved, leads Spain to demand his extradition. With the connivance of the Pope, he is smuggled out of Rome by the French ambassador, and in October 1634 finds his refuge in France under the protection of Richelieu. Now his dream of the renovation of the world and the unification of mankind takes a new form, with France substituted for Spain as the secular arm of a renovated universal Church. He begins the longed-for publication of his collected works, which is cut short by his death in the Dominican convent at Paris, on May 21, 1639.

Campanella's last utterance is in poetry: a Latin

---

[1] *Apologia pro Galileo* (Frankfort, 1622), pp. 13, 23, 25.
[2] Letter of February 14, 1630. Berti, op. cit., 5.

eclogue written a few months before the end came.[1]
It combines his early dream of the City of the Sun with
his later theocratic doctrine and his ultimate theory of
the destined part of France.   But the detail that the
hero, who is to deliver the world from wrong and build
the City of the Sun, is to be a French prince, is of no
more consequence than the nationality of the ideal
emperor of the *Monarchia* or the identity of the Veltro
in the *Divina Commedia*.   A golden age shall return
and universal peace.   Labour shall become sport when
divided in friendly fashion amongst men, and all acknow-
ledge one Father and God.   The nations will understand each other, and fraternal love will reconcile all
differences: 'Conciliabit amor fraternus cognitus omnes.'
The kings and peoples shall assemble in the City of the
Sun, the sceptres be laid upon the altar, and laws be
given as of old the prophets taught.   But, instead of the
'Viva, viva Campanella' of his earlier dream, the cry of
the exultant peoples, acclaiming their liberation and
universal peace, is now the 'Gloria Patri':

> Unanimes populi cantantes 'Gloria Patri',
> perpetuum alleluia sonent pacemque beatam.

With this poetical image of the future of humanity the
old persecuted friar, martyr to philosophy and what he
deemed the cause of man, closed his days.

---

[1] *Poesie*, pp. 195 et seq. (*Ecloga*).

The Taylorian Lecture

1924

THE GODS OF GREECE
IN GERMAN POETRY

By

J. G. ROBERTSON

Professor of German Language and Literature at the
University of London

THE GODS OF GREECE IN GERMAN POETRY

The theme which I have chosen for the present lecture obviously far transcends the compass of a single hour. Were I to justify the promise of my title, and attempt to deal conscientiously with the changing aspects of the Greek gods as they emerge at various stages in the evolution of northern poetry, not one, but a long series of lectures would be necessary. In fact, it has been a little disheartening to me to review the vast field and realize how very little of it I can afford to cover.[1] For it is a field full of endless unsolved problems, of broken ends which one's fingers itch to try to link up. Were we to begin at the beginning, we might study the bewildered *naïveté*—or rather, a *naïveté* that is hardly self-conscious enough to be bewildered—with which medieval poets like Heinrich von Veldeke and the German chroniclers of the story of Troy present in very human terms the divine personalities of the ancient epics; here the old gods are little more than the knights and ladies of chivalric romance. Or we might watch, in the following centuries, how flashes of southern beauty tingle the northern fantasy, and how the Greek mythology begins to temper with finer nuances the stern dualism of naïve joy and austere asceticism of medieval poetry. It would

---

[1] An old book viewing the theme in its widest aspects, and still not unreadable, is C. L. Cholevius, *Geschichte der deutschen Poesie nach ihren antiken Elementen*, 2 vols., Leipzig, 1854. The modern reader can have no better guide, as far as the important part of the subject is concerned, than F. Strich's admirable work, *Die Mythologie in der deutschen Literatur von Klopstock bis Wagner*, 2 vols., Halle, 1910.

A 2

be interesting, too, had we time, to investigate the fortuitous courses by which this new knowledge trickled into the German mind. You might expect me again— and with more justice—to linger on the Renaissance period, when unequivocal and sometimes even dazzling light spread from the south of Europe; but I doubt whether this would be profitable for the point of view which I particularly wish to lay before you. The Renaissance brought a kind of intoxication to the German mind ; but there was no question of a real assimilation of the spirit of antiquity; else the literature of that age would not so soon have degenerated into dull and lifeless imitation. To the German sixteenth century, intensely preoccupied as it was with its own spiritual problems, the discovery of the ancient world was still a matter of comparative indifference. It might be well enough for humanistic scholars, who had, so to speak, divested themselves of their nationality by writing in Latin, to interest themselves in it ; but Luther's Germany had more immediately vital things to think about. At most, the German poets employed, not very intelligently, and as a kind of stucco ornament, the mythological imagery which the humanists had introduced ; for the serenity of the ancient mind they had, and could have had no comprehension. To Hans Sachs, for instance, the gods of Greece, when he set them on his primitive stage, were just as plain and simple Nuremberg citizens as any other figures in his plays—as our Christian God himself.[1] And think of the Lutheran bigotry with which the old *Faust-book* views its hero's dealings with the heathen

---

[1] e.g. *Comedia, darin die göttin Pallas die tugend und die göttin Venus die wollust verficht* (1530) ; *Ein comedi, das judicium Paridis* (1532) ; *Comedia oder Kampff-gesprech zwischen Juppiter und Juno* (1534); *Ein gesprech der götter*, &c. (1544).

past; to its unknown author Helen of Troy is indeed the Scarlet Woman. When we turn to the real age of Renaissance poetry in Germany, the baroque seventeenth century, we find ourselves no whit nearer an understanding of the beauty of Greece. Opitz may discourse, with an irony born of intimate acquaintance, of the deeds of 'Krieges-Gott Mars', or, in the footsteps of his master Heinsius, sing the praises of Bacchus; but of any real conception of what a later age was to call Hellenism there is nothing. Moreover, in his attitude to the antique, he merely struts a daw in Dutch feathers. It is not easy for us to interest ourselves in the Jupiters and Venuses, who stud so familiarly and with so promiscuous a blending of ancient and Christian morals, the dusty alexandrine verse of the seventeenth century; and we cannot but smile at a zealous linguistic purist like Zesen, who tried to acclimatize the gods of Greece by Germanizing their names. When Mars and Vulcan masquerade as 'Heldreich' and 'Gluhtfang', Juno and Venus as 'Himmelinne' and 'Lachmund', it seems like some grotesque carnival jest. The gods of Greece who were subjected to such indignities had certainly not entered the German soul. Still, if we are to understand the spiritual evolution that was to culminate in the eighteenth century, we must learn to focus our eyes to this old baroque poetry.[1] Once we grasp what its criteria of beauty were—and in all epochs it is not what we moderns regard as beauty that counts, but what the age itself regarded as such—it will be found to be by no means devoid of charm. There is fascination in the songs of Kaspar Stieler's *Geharnschte Venus*, although the deity herself is hardly visible through the

---

[1] Cp. the recent enlightening work of a young Viennese scholar, Herbert Cysarz, *Deutsche Barockdichtung*, Leipzig, 1924.

veils ; her name being, indeed, little more than a catch-penny title.

There is no real understanding, then, in the exotic and artificial movement of the baroque for the beauty and humanity for which Greece and the Olympian guardians of Greek beauty stood. It is not until we reach the eighteenth century that I am tempted to linger; for it was that century which first made Hellenism a living factor in the spiritual evolution of Europe. My friend Mr. Montgomery, in his little book on one of the purest souls that ever fell under the fascination of the Greek gods, the unhappy Hölderlin,[1] has admirably described for us the rising tide of appreciation of antiquity in the eighteenth century, and shown us the concept of Hellenism gradually emerging.

There are three great phases in the classicism of the German eighteenth century, each of which represents a marvellous advance over its predecessor. In the first, Gottsched, the literary dictator of the German literature of his day, sees the ancient world mainly, if not entirely, through the distorting medium of the over-cultured French taste of the *grand siècle*. His earth-born, matter-of-fact mind was frankly intolerant of gods of any kind, whether they happened to be Homer's or Milton's; if the poet could not dispense with them, Gottsched recommended him at least to avoid the supernatural as much as possible. The traditional Plautine gods of the *Amphitryon* were, no doubt, most to his liking. On Gottsched we need not dwell.

The second great phase of eighteenth-century development is represented by Lessing and Winckelmann. Lessing stands for what to our modern minds seems

---

[1] Marshall Montgomery, *Friedrich Hölderlin and the German Neo-Hellenic Movement*, Part I, London, Oxford University Press, 1923.

a rather ungenerous denunciation of the classicism of
the French seventeenth century. This need not, however, be reckoned too seriously against him ; for it is only
by such vehement unjustness that literature progresses.
Lessing's insistence that he who would drink of the
waters of Hippocrene must drink them at the source,
was at least an axiom of real significance for his age.
I do not know of any passage in which Lessing has
given his direct opinion about the gods of Greece; but
they were, no doubt, to him mere 'allegorische Wesen',
if not, indeed, what he called 'personifirte Abstracta'.[1]
His great contemporary Winckelmann has much more
to say that matters. Winckelmann was the discoverer
of ancient beauty for northern Europe ; in his famous
phrase, 'edle Einfalt und stille Grösse', he revealed, as
in a flash, what the whole Renaissance movement had
failed to grasp, that Greek beauty is a serene thing, that
its greatness lies in its simplicity. But there were
limits to Winckelmann's revelation; he had at bottom
an antiquarian type of mind, a mind that rose to mighty
deductions by virtue of a rare faculty of casting itself back
into a remote past; but he lacked the life-giving power
of linking up the past with the present, and thereby
giving the latter greater depth and fullness. He taught
us that the gods of Greece were beautiful *eidola* of humanity; but his gods were, after all, lifeless gods, marble gods,
gods of the museum. He saw them with cold, rational-
istic eyes as symbols of a remote beauty, or even as mere
schematic allegories. Winckelmann and Lessing caught
a glimpse of the promised land, but it was given to neither
of them to take possession of it. They magnificently
prepared the way for the coming of the gods of Greece;
but they were not onlookers at their triumphal entry into

[1] *Laocoon*, x.

German literature; they failed to reconcile the symbols of ancient beauty with the ideals of the modern world.

Meanwhile, side by side with the labours of these great classic minds to force antiquity to give up its secret, we have other evidence that the Greek gods were indispensable for eighteenth-century poetry. There is the gay jingling verse of the anacreonticists in France and in Germany; but the only Olympians these poets cared for were Bacchus and Venus, whom they made the symbols of a light and frivolous criticism of life and its lighter joys. Or again, there are the delicate Dresden-china nymphs and fauns of Gessner's mythological world, strange, sentimental perversions of Theocritus. But these were only little enclaves of artificial dalliance; still the bridge was not cast across the great eighteenth-century cleft between the ideal and the reality. Of greater significance was Wieland's interpretation of antiquity. In his early, pietistic days, that poet had frowned disapprovingly on the Bacchuses and Venuses of the rococo; although he had himself introduced the gods in the traditional way in his youthful epics, *Hermann* and *Cyrus*. But he, too, when his pietistic phase passed and he appeared in his true colours as a laughing Democritos, harked back to the rococo. His Hellas was now a Hellas that revelled in unabashed epicureanism, and jumbled together, with reckless indifference, Christianity, Horace, and the Greeks. There was, in truth, not much Greek blood in Wieland's veins; the gods of Greece with whom he was on most familiar terms were those of his favourite author Lucian. But let us not be unjust to him, and there is a danger of this, for few of us have patience nowadays to read the long and tedious novels of his later life. And yet, books like *Agathodämon* and *Aristipp* do show a finer, more serious conception of the

Greek world, and a better understanding of the share of Greece in modern culture; as he grew older, Wieland was susceptible to the new forces of his age; he had learned not merely from Winckelmann, but also from Herder.

We may, then, scorn the baroque and the rococo as artificial and untrue; we may writhe under the frivolity of the anacreonticists; Winckelmann's Olympos in its remoteness may leave us cold; but we must not forget that the Greek gods these men looked up to provided their imaginations with a refuge from the grey world of every day. Gessner's unwillingness to stand up to the living present may be but a cowardly shirking of the true poet's first duty to his time; we may resent Wieland's acrid, euhemeristic rationalism, which fondles the old gods only to proclaim them impostors; or Winckelmann's view, that they were only eternally beautiful allegories; but to all these men the gods ruled over a world of freer, happier fancy, which was more congenial to them than the world they had to live in.

Suddenly, however, the placidity of this age of Enlightenment was disturbed; a wave of militant individualism spread over Germany from that inexhaustible source of spiritual energy, Rousseau; the era of 'Storm and Stress' opened. One might reasonably expect that this age, with its vituperation of classical regularity, its adoration of Shakespeare, its demand for personality— and again personality—in poetry, would not have much thought to spare for the remote gods of Greece. Yet, paradoxical as it may seem, it was just the 'Storm and Stress' which conferred new life upon the gods, and made their blood run red again. How is it to be explained?

The baroque and the rococo, we have seen, had

hob-nobbed with the Greek gods on the most familiar footing; they were at the beck and call of every poetaster. This happens in every epoch of artificial 'correctness'; the more law-bound a literature is, the more ready it is to summon the gods to its aid, until the appeal ultimately becomes as meaningless as the poet's to his muse. Familiarity of this kind may not always breed contempt; but it brings death and petrifaction to its high patrons; the glib friends of the gods are in the end their worst enemies. Another obstacle the Olympians encountered—and, indeed, it has been so in all ages— was the classical tradition. Every return of the gods into our modern imaginative world is effected in the teeth of opposition from the classicists, who with their ponderous learning encrust them with death-masks. That was the reason why Rousseau and his young German disciples, with their repudiation of tradition and artificiality, pre- pared the way for a deeper and truer appreciation of antiquity than Europe had yet known.

With youthful exuberance Goethe, the ' Stürmer und Dränger', attacked the ironic effigies of Wieland's *Alceste* in his *Götter, Helden und Wieland*; but Goethe is more intent here on ridiculing the ' Prinzen-Hofmeister zu Weimar' than in defending the honour of the gods. His real reply to Wieland, a reply before which Wieland's whole would-be Greek world shrivelled up, was his magnificent *Prometheus*:

> Bedecke deinen Himmel, Zeus,
> Mit Wolkendunst,
> Und übe, dem Knaben gleich,
> Der Disteln köpft,
> An Eichen dich und Bergeshöhn . . .

The gods of Greece this Prometheus defied

> Ich kenne nichts Ärmeres
> Unter der Sonn', als euch, Götter!

Ihr nähret kümmerlich
Von Opfersteuern
Und Gebetshauch
Eure Majestät—

were, in the transient vision Goethe vouchsafes us of
them, more living and majestic and terrible than
Wieland's puppets, although these were more in harmony
with the classical tradition. Here in the fate of Prometheus, as again of Niobe,[1] the 'Storm and Stress' found
a chord in the antique mythology which responded to
their own rebel souls. Themselves young Titans, they
were able, as the *petit-maîtres* and sentimental shepherds
of the rococo age had never been, to appreciate the
Titanic majesty of the Olympians. With its intense
craving for life and reality and personality, the 'Storm
and Stress' first made the return of the Greek gods
into poetry possible again.

For what Goethe achieved in the sovereign irresponsi-
bility of genius Herder had made the preparation. It
was Herder, that most prolific and elusive of all the
northern thinkers and pioneers, that 'Mehrer des
Reiches' of the spirit, as no other German of the
eighteenth century, who revealed the meaning of Greece
to the modern world.[2] Herder learned from Winckelmann ; but he was more deeply in the debt of Hamann ;

[1] Cp. F. Strich, op. cit., i, p. 227.

[2] It would be difficult to bring together from the thirty-two
volumes of Herder's works the many passages which have bearing
on this matter. The reader is especially referred to *Vom neuern
Gebrauch der Mythologie*, in the *Fragmente* (*Werke*, ed. Suphan, i,
pp. 426 ff.) ; the second 'Wäldchen' on Klotz's *Homerische Briefe*
(iii, pp. 195 ff.) ; *Journal meiner Reise* (iv, pp. 462 ff.) ; *Denkmahl
Johann Winckelmanns* (viii, pp. 437 ff.) ; and, above all, the *Briefe
zur Beförderung der Humanität* (xvii, xviii), and the section on the
Greeks in *Ideen zur Philosophie der Geschichte der Menschheit* (xiv,
pp. 92 ff.).

and Hamann had already called for, not imitation of the Greeks, but a tapping of the headsprings of antiquity. Herder sought living gods in Greece, not marble images. All Herder's voyages of discovery into the past of the human spirit—and his whole life was spent in such voyaging—were in search of a key to the present. He was the first German thinker to invest the old gods with a modern ethical ideal. Guardians of the highest beauty they had been ; now they became the champions of a new humanity. Herder combated the age-long antagonism of the Christian faith to the Greek mythology by showing that both had their appointed place in the development of humanity. ' Humanität!' Round this one word all Herder's work ultimately crystallizes.

But there were many obstacles to the return of the Olympians into German poetry. For a time, the sturdier Germanic gods of the North threatened to oust them ; and the sudden rise to favour of the northern mythology —our own poet Gray had, perhaps, some share in it— is one of the most interesting episodes of eighteenth-century development.[1] The German poets for a brief spell donned bardic robes and attuned their verses to northern strains ; the gods of the grove were ranged against the gods of the temple on the hill. With a zeal that almost reminds one of Zesen in the previous century, Klopstock expunged from his poetry the names of the classic gods and put Germanic deities in their places. Jupiter is converted into Wodan, Apollo into Braga, Venus and Ceres become Freya and Hertha. So far, this is comprehensible ; but when Klopstock descends to minor Scandinavian deities we are in the absurd

---

[1] Cp. the series of studies by P. van Tieghem on *La Mythologie et l'ancienne poésie scandinaves dans la littérature européenne au XVIIIᵉ siècle*, in *Edda*, xi-xiii, 1919-20.

position of having to consult a dictionary of Northern mythology to discover what they stand for! This sudden affection for the religion of the North was, however, little more than a retarding moment in the restoration of the Greek gods; perhaps, indeed, it was partly due to a growing discontent with the schematic formulas into which the old gods had degenerated in the previous age.

Let us follow the story further. Goethe and Schiller passed with the maturing years out of their 'Storm and Stress'; they became classic poets, and established the third and culminating phase of German classicism, which developed with such amazing swiftness out of the void. We see these two poets wrestling persistently with the classic idea; their highest energies were, we might say, directed towards bringing the gods of Greece into honour again; to creating, on the foundations of Herder's universalism and humanity, a modern world that would be a fit home for them.

It must not be forgotten—and our literary historians are, I think, inclined to dwell overmuch on the turning-over of a new leaf, when Goethe and Schiller passed from their 'Storm and Stress' to the staider classicism of Weimar—that this last phase of eighteenth-century Hellenism was intimately bound up with the old French culture, the 'Storm and Stress' period itself, and all the turbulent, unantique experiences these poets passed through in their youth. They did not repudiate their splendid beginnings; they rather built upon them; endeavoured to reconcile their new horizons with the old.

Schiller had greater difficulty than Goethe in divesting himself of the French tradition; unversed in Greek, he was never able to see the old world face to face; moreover, his whole mentality compelled him to regard it abstractly. To him Homer's heroic world never was—as to Voss when he translated the *Odyssey* or to Werther in those first idyllic days in Wahlheim—an immediate impression. His Hellenism was a philosophical deduction, an ideal; but just here lay its significance and its virtue. And in the restoration of the old theocracy it was Schiller, not Goethe, who had the 'vision splendid'. There is no more wonderful poem in the whole range of German verse, no poem that has reverberated longer through subsequent ages, than *Die Götter Griechenlands*, which Schiller published in Wieland's *Teutscher Merkur* in 1788. With this great poem, we might say, the doors were flung open, and the gods of Greece passed back at last into modern poetry. Out of the fullness of his heart Schiller voices here the longing of the 'sentimental' poet for the lost 'naïve', or, as he put it later, for that nature which is only our lost childhood. The gods of Greece are again the symbols of an 'età d'oro'; and the eighteenth century looked back to such an age no less passionately than the seventeenth.

> Da ihr noch die schöne Welt regieret,
> An der Freude leichtem Gängelband
> Selige Geschlechter noch geführet,
> Schöne Wesen aus dem Fabelland . . .

> Schöne Welt, wo bist du? Kehre wieder,
> Holdes Blütenalter der Natur!
> Ach, nur in dem Feenland der Lieder
> Lebt noch deine fabelhafte Spur.
> Ausgestorben trauert das Gefilde,
> Keine Gottheit zeigt sich meinem Blick,
> Ach, von jenem lebenswarmen Bilde
> Blieb der Schatten nur zurück.

Without Herder and the 'Storm and Stress' there could have been no *Götter Griechenlands*. Had not, indeed, Herder already said all that was to be said, when, in his essay on Winckelmann, he wrote: 'Wo bist du, geliebtes Griechenland voll schöner Götter und Jugendgestalten, voll Wahrheit im Trug und doch voll schöner Wahrheit? Deine Zeit ist hin.'[1] It is this thought that Schiller crystallizes into undying verse. To him the Greek gods represent an ideal of harmonious beauty which has vanished from the world to give place to an outlook on life in which sense and spirit are implacably at war. Like the poets of the preceding age, Schiller turns to Greece in his flight from the discordant present; his vision, no less than theirs, is born of discontent and disillusionment. We are sometimes apt to forget that Weimar Hellenism, with all its noble achievement, is reared upon an irreconcilable dualism; that its most constant element is no exotic culture, Greek or French, but that all-suffusing pietism which forms the abiding basis in the spiritual life of the German people. Hence the eternal cry of 'Entsagung' that rings through all German poetry; hence, too, that unquenchable thirst of the finer spirits, imprisoned within a harsh reality, for a serener world which knows nothing of such 'Entsagung'. And now, as always, the gods of Greece are the guardians of the ideal for the disillusioned soul; the cry goes forth to them when the spirit is in tribulation, or when the craving for beauty makes itself felt above the demands of the moral life. Thus the significance of Schiller's *Götter Griechenlands* lies, not in its criticism of the present, to which the gods are but a foil, but rather in the foil itself.

[1] *Werke*, viii, p. 481. Or, again, in his *Ideen zu einer Geschichte der Philosophie der Menschheit* (xiv, p. 142): 'Verschwunden sind sie von der Erde. Werden, da diese schönsten Idole der menschlichen Einbildungskraft gefallen sind, auch die minder-schönen wie sie fallen? Und wem werden sie Platz machen, andern Idolen?'

At no period of German history have the gods of Greece played a more positive and harmonious role than now. Schiller's gods may be but 'schöne Wesen aus dem Fabelland', merely shadows adorned with infinite 'Anmut und Würde'; but in the shadow-land of the ideal they reign undisputed and indisputable. Of that religious hostility which had dogged Hellenism in Europe since the Renaissance, there is far less in Schiller than is commonly attributed to him. Schiller's Greek gods are not 'heathen' gods to be relegated to the Christian Hell, as Dante and Milton had relegated them; as Heinsius and Opitz; nay, even as Richard Wagner in his *Tannhäuser*. Nor do they stand for an anti-Christian joy in the material and the unspiritual, as with the anacreonticists and the epicurean Wieland. Schiller holds up the Olympos-governed world as a contrast to the imperfect world of sorrow under Christian monotheism; but the antithesis in his mind is mainly an aesthetic one; antagonism to Christianity was no more in his thought than it had been in Herder's. That was left to his critics from Stolberg onwards to discover; left to the new Romantic School to exploit with ever-increasing virulence. Schiller only demanded justice for the old gods; and in a poem he once planned, the Apostate Julian was to have defended these gods against the encroachments of the new faith. Heir of a century of wide-hearted, tolerant deism, Schiller sought conciliation, not strife; his whole spiritual life was a search for harmony —harmony between sense and spirit, between inclination and duty. Thus he sought to reconcile the gods of Greece with the modern world; to bring them back into a distraught age to rule over a kingdom where beauty and the moral world were one.

But to Schiller it was not given to realize his dream,

to re-establish this kingdom of Apollo upon earth. His was an essentially tragic mind; antitheses were—as with all tragic poets—the breath of his being; and he lived and thought in antitheses to the end: his life went down in the tragedy of broken ends. Goethe, the mature, classic Goethe of the middle and the later years, was the truer Hellenist; for to Goethe's serene mind the world was never a thing of antagonisms. God made the world, 'and behold, it was good'. The created universe— matter and spirit, nature and art, the past and the present—was to him one and indivisible. He lacked— for may we not say that it was a defect?—that divine discontent which lent wings to Schiller's flight into the ideal. He did not need to seek an harmonious solution to the dualism of the world; for to him the harmony was always there. Schiller's penetrating insight already discovered this, when he contemplated what might have been, had Goethe been born into his own world, born an ancient Greek.[1]

Goethe first entered into full possession of antique beauty in Italy, where the last vestiges of his 'Storm and Stress' were stripped from him.

O wie fühl' ich in Rom mich so froh! gedenk' ich der
    Zeiten,
  Da mich ein graulicher Tag hinten im Norden umfing,
Trübe der Himmel und schwer auf meine Scheitel
    sich senkte,
  Farb- und gestaltlos die Welt um den Ermatteten
    lag . . .
Nun umleuchtet der Glanz des helleren Äthers die
    Stirne;
  Phöbus rufet, der Gott, Formen und Farben hervor...
Welche Seligkeit ward mir Sterblichem! Träum' ich?
    Empfänget
  Dein ambrosisches Haus, Jupiter Vater, den Gast?

---

[1] Letter to Goethe of 23 August 1794.

Ach! hier lieg' ich, und strecke nach deinen Knieen
    die Hände
Flehend aus. O vernimm, Jupiter Xenius, mich!...
Bist du der wirtliche Gott? O dann so verstosse den
    Gastfreund
Nicht von deinem Olymp wieder zur Erde hinab![1]

In Rome Goethe received the consecration of Apollo;
and from now on his allegiance to the old gods never
wavered. Both in the letter and in the spirit Goethe
was, indeed, the great Hellenist of his age.[2] But even
he was not immune to the Nemesis that has pursued
Hellenism in our modern time: the Nemesis of the
classical tradition, of estrangement from the present. As
Goethe's life moved to its close, his Hellenism gradually
petrified; his rooms grew more and more crowded with
statuary and plaster casts; his eyes dwelt with increasing
pleasure on cold engravings of antiquities. Thus even
in his resplendent, life-giving imagination the old gods
were surely passing back, with the advancing years, into
cold, white marble again.

To Homer Goethe had returned in his *Hermann und
Dorothea*; with Homer he measured himself in his
Achilleis. The Olympians play a large part in the latter
fragment; but one feels somehow that a veil has
descended; they are Homeric gods, imitated gods, not
the gods whom Prometheus had defied. And again in
Pandora, that great deep poem, suffused with the
subtlest Platonism, a poem in which, I often think, is to
be found the most concentrated essence of Goethe's
Hellenism, does one not sometimes cherish a sacrilegious
longing for the passionate pulse-beat of the 'Storm and

[1] *Römische Elegien*, vi
[2] Cp. E. Maass, *Goethe und die Antike*, Berlin, 1912, p. 646: 'Die
Wahrheit bleibt immer Wahrheit. Und die Wahrheit ist jetzt:
Goethe, der erste Hellenist unseres Volkes.'

Stress', to wish that, just for once, his Prometheus there would take on the colour of the great Titan Goethe had conceived in his youth ? But let me turn rather to the culminating creation of Goethe's poetic life, his *Faust*. Is it too great a flight of symbolizing fancy to see in the union of Faust and Helena the crowning contribution of Germany's classic age to the conciliation of the old gods with the modern world ? The 'Klassische Wal-purgisnacht' of that work is a very wonderful, magical creation ; one might even say it only misses being the last word in the consummation of German humanism. Think what the 'Klassische Walpurgisnacht' might have been, had it not been forcibly linked up with Faust, for whose fate it was of no poetic necessity ; had it not been brought into an unnatural parallelism with the 'Walpurgisnacht' of the First Part, and made to serve, in Goethe's mind, a not unsimilar end. Think if, instead of seeking out the grotesque elements of the Greek mythology, Goethe had made this pagan festival the quintessence of what was most beautiful in it ; if the gods of Olympos had been given their rightful share in it ; if, not Galatea, but Aphrodite herself, had risen resplendent from the waves in that gorgeous 'per-vigilium Veneris' with which the festival culminates. Might it not have been the final transfiguration of Schiller's vision ? The gods of Greece may have no part in the Second *Faust*, but we are always conscious of their aura ; they preside invisibly at the nuptials of Faust and Helena ; and their blessing lies on those idyllic scenes in the vale of Tempe and by the Aegean Sea.

Not, however, to the ageing Goethe, but to the young generation of poets and thinkers, passed, in the first third of the new century, the torch of idealism which

Schiller had lighted. The Romanticists viewed the pageant of literature from a high vantage-ground, and with wide sympathies; they dreamt the great dream of a ' universal poetry' of mankind, as it had not presented itself even to Herder. Surely now, if ever, Zeus and Apollo, Pallas Athene and Aphrodite, could consort in harmony with Wotan, Thor, and Freia; with the Jehovah of the Old Testament and the Christ of the New. And yet this was not so. The atmosphere of romanticism, with all its universalism, was far less favourable for the gods of Greece in German poetry than Weimar humanism had been. The world-literature of the Romantic theorists was only a dream, which the Romantic poetry could not make a reality. For with the intenser individualism of the new epoch there came a searching of the heart which the first theorists had not reckoned with. The old passionate self-abnegation of German mysticism and pietism returned, and with it the revival of an intensely personal Christianity,' a repudiation of the cold deism of the eighteenth century. Indeed, this religious revival led not a few of the gentler souls of the epoch back into the fold of the mother Church. The God of such a faith could no longer live in peace with Zeus and Apollo ; in the new Christian temples the altars set up by eighteenth-century Hellenism could have no place. The classic age had not felt the need of tempering its optimistic Christianity with a renunciatory Nazarenism; deism cherished no antagonism to the joyous serenity of Hellenism. But national adversity and the upset of the order of the world, first by the French Revolution and subsequently by Napoleon, had darkened the souls of the new generation, and given a sombrer colouring to their lives. Something of the hostility of earlier centuries to the Greek ideals returned ;

the old battle-cry of ' Hie Christian, hie heathen!' was revived ; the gods of Greece became once more the gods of heathendom.

On the very threshold of this new era stood one whose devotion to the gods of Greece—learned, in the first instance, from his master Schiller—had an intensity beside which Schiller's seems dispassionate indeed: Friedrich Hölderlin. Hölderlin clung to Hellenism with every fibre of his passionate, unbalanced soul; to him it did not represent, as to Schiller, a golden age to look back upon in elegiac retrospect; it was an intense reality, a sheet-anchor—the only sheet-anchor—in his storm-tossed life. Hölderlin's Hellenism was not a thing of a remote past ; the gods of Greece he worshipped were still living gods ; they spoke to him from lake and forest, in the storm and in the sunshine. They lived in the nature around him, or they did not live—had never lived for him—at all. There is no Hellenist among the German poets who was less affected by the dead hand of the classic tradition than Hölderlin. So intense, indeed, was his Hellenism that it led to his ostracism from the great movement of the time ; and yet none was a truer Romanticist than he. Hölderlin's Hellenism was no joyful possession; but a faith which the dark powers in his soul were constantly endeavouring to dispossess. Most distraught of poets—and his distraught-ness ultimately passed over into insanity—Hölderlin lived in a distraught age. Schiller had the advantage of being older, more firmly rooted in the pre-revolutionary eighteenth century; and he might well cherish his placid vision of Olympos. For Hölderlin, on the other hand, the gods of Greece were no unperturbed rulers over a kingdom of beauty ; but rather gods shuddering unceasingly under the Damocles-sword of a soulless

Nemesis, a Schicksal. That there was a pessimistic
foil to the Hellenism of the classic age I have already
tried to show; but it was as nothing compared with the
sinister pessimism in Hölderlin's soul, a pessimism which
was ultimately to destroy his faith in Greek beauty and
in life itself; to drive his Empedocles to immolate himself
in Etna. Eighteenth-century Hellenism was still an
Apollo-governed Hellenism; but the Romanticists had
dethroned Apollo and set the tragic Dionysos in his
place.

The Romantic age was always stronger in theory
than in practice; and it would be profitable, had we
time, to study the attitude of the Romantic thinkers to
the Greek gods, from the penetrating Greek studies of
the great ideologue of Romanticism, Friedrich Schlegel,
to the philosophy of Schelling, and in the Romantic
mythologists from Creuzer onwards. They all deal,
explicitly or implicitly, with the problem that interests us.
It may seem more reprehensible that I have not found
time to dwell upon the attitude to our question of Hegel,
this great Romantic thinker, part of whose mission
would seem to have been to destroy Romanticism: one
after the other he drew the veils of his metaphysical
abstractions across the Romantic firmament, and the
light of its stars went out. Can it be wondered that on
the gods of Greece he had a peculiarly stultifying effect?
They fade away under his scrutiny into abstractions; or rather, let us say, they retire from a conflict
not of their seeking into their museum recluse; they
become marble gods once more. Indeed, this was
literally true; for when the Greek gods do appear in the
Romantic literature, it is either as denizens of a grotesque
underworld of popular fable, or as marble effigies. I
think of Eichendorff, of Diana in Heine's *Atta Troll*:

Auch das Antlitz weiss wie Marmor,
Und wie Marmor kalt;

or that terrible marble Sphinx in the old ' Märchenwald ',
who held the tragic secret of the *Buch der Lieder* in her
keeping.

Thus the religious zeal of the Romantic age either
banished the gods of Greece to the limbo of super-
stitions, or regarded them in the light of the classical
tradition. But there was a difference between the
classical interpretation now and that of Winckelmann's
time: the Romantic marble gods were no longer
invested with the 'edle Einfalt und stille Grösse'; now
under the gentler, mellower light of Romanticism, the
marble glowed. Not Winckelmann or Goethe, but the
Danish sculptor, Thorvaldsen, was, it seems to me, the
real interpreter of these marble gods after the Romantic
heart.

In no poet of the early nineteenth century is the conflict of the Olympians with the spirit of Romanticism
clearer and more acute than in that great renegade of
the Romantic faith, Heine.[1]

There is a wonderful passage in Heine's *Reisebilder*,
which no one who ever reads can forget. After quoting
from the ninth book of the *Iliad* the description of the
gods holding high festival in Olympos:

Also den ganzen Tag bis spät zur sinkenden Sonne
Schmausten sie; und nicht mangelt' ihr Herz des
   gemeinsamen Mahles,
Nicht des Saitengetöns von der lieblichen Leier
   Apollons,
Noch des Gesangs der Musen mit holdantwortender
   Stimme—

---

[1] There is a Berlin dissertation of 1905 by H. Friedemann on *Die
Götter Griechenlands von Schiller bis Heine*; although not as help-
ful as its title might lead us to expect, it is suggestive on Heine's
Hellenism.

Heine continues:

Da plötzlich keuchte heran ein bleicher, bluttrie-
fender Jude, mit einer Dornenkrone auf dem Haupte
und mit einem grossen Holzkreuz auf der Schulter;
und er warf das Kreuz auf den hohen Göttertisch, dass
die goldnen Pokale zitterten und die Götter verstummten
und erblichen und immer bleicher wurden, bis sie end-
lich ganz in Nebel zerrannen.[1]

In this wonderful vision is concentrated all the em-
bittered hostility that had sprung up in the Romantic
mind between Christianity and the old gods.[2] And
indeed, the terrible spiritual conflict in Heine's soul
between Nazarenism and Hellenism is, to my thinking,
the most significant spiritual happening in the period of
declining Romanticism. It has been dwelt upon amongst
us in England by Matthew Arnold, who felt its significance; but he failed to penetrate all that it stood for in
its time. It is usually interpreted—very crudely, I think
—as a mere antithesis of spirituality and sensuality, a
degradation of the gods of Greece into patrons of Heine's
own trivial sensualism. Nothing could be falser. The
conflict is, as much else that made Heine's life the
terribly tragic thing it was, a Romantic heritage, to
which no full-blood Romanticist ever gave acuter expression than he. The sensitive temperament of this

---

[1] *Die Stadt Lucca*, vi.

[2] How Romantic this conception of the fading of the old gods
before the Cross is, is seen in the fact that it is foreshadowed in
Novalis's *Hymnen an die Nacht*:

> Nur Ein Gedanke wars,
> Der furchtbar zu den frohen Tischen trat
> Und das Gemüt in wilde Schrecken hüllte.
> Hier wussten selbst die Götter keinen Rat,
> Der das Gemüt mit süssem Troste füllte;
> Geheimnisvoll war dieses Unholds Pfad,
> Des Wut kein Flehn und keine Gabe stillte —
> Es war der Tod, der dieses Lustgelag
> Mit Angst und Schmerz und Tränen unterbrach.

outcast of Romanticism was tossed helplessly between the two poles of the joy of life and asceticism. His first love had been the Greek Eros—his first love and his last. There is surely no more pathetic scene in all literary history than that where this poor paralysed German poet drags himself from what was so soon to be his 'mattress-grave' to the feet of our lady of Milo in the Louvre, and there weeps the bitterest tears of his life. And she could only look down compassionately on him; she could neither console him nor help him, for she had no arms.[1] Is it not true of all Heine's Greek gods that they have no arms? They are powerless to help him. But Eros played only one part in Heine's life, and that not, I think, the greater. The intense religious emotionalism of Romanticism was deeply engraved on his fervid Jewish soul, and he passed through a renunciation and abnegation of life bitterer than any ever known in the Romantic 'Sanctuary of Sorrows'. Goethe's 'kummervolle Nächte' spent in tears are but a pale initiation into the mysterious ways of God to man, by the side of the excruciating sufferings of the long Paris death-agony.

I should like to have said more of Heine's religious life; for it is not foreign to our theme; I should like to have shown you how the Romantic way of thinking, and, with it, the Romantic attitude to the Greek gods, assumed a new and strange form under the influence of the fantastic—unromantic, and yet of romantic provenance— religion of Saint-Simon. What Saint-Simonism meant for Heine's spiritual life has yet to be fully gauged;[2]

[1] *Nachwort zum Romanzero.*

[2] See an article on *Heine and the Saint-Simonians* by Miss E. M. Butler, in the *Modern Language Review*, xviii, 1923, pp. 68 ff., a forerunner, I hope, of a larger study of the significance of Saint-Simonianism for German thought and literature.

and still more, what it meant for the undermining of the great Romantic movement in Germany. Not Hegel himself did so much to shake German poetry in its allegiance to the Romantic idealism, and sweep it into the arms of a prosaic-minded Young Germany. But these considerations would take us too far afield. Let me only ask you to look for a moment at the gulf that separates these Greek gods of Heine from those of Schiller's vision.

It is not merely that an intense religious antagonism now disturbs the harmony, so dear to Schiller's soul, between the old Hellenism and the new; but the gods themselves have undergone a change. In the disillusioning light of scientific progress, Heine's gods, when they are not mere marble effigies, have become shadowy abstractions. Not the Aphrodite that rose from the Greek sea is Heine's bitter-sweet passion; but the Venus of the Louvre, the Venus who has no arms. The gods of Greece that reigned when Goethe and Schiller dwelt in Arcadia were still living gods; it is only pale ghosts of them that fade away before the Cross in Heine's vision.

> Das sind sie selber, die Götter von Hellas,
> Die einst so freudig die Welt beherrschten,
> Doch jetzt, verdrängt und verstorben,
> Als ungeheure Gespenster dahinziehen
> Am mitternächtlichen Himmel . . .
>
> Doch heil'ges Erbarmen und schauriges Mitleid
> Durchströmt mein Herz,
> Wenn ich euch jetzt da droben schaue,
> Verlassene Götter,
> Tote, nachtwandelnde Schatten,
> Nebelschwache, die der Wind verscheucht —
> Und wenn ich bedenke, wie feig und windig
> Die Götter sind, die euch besiegten,
> Die neuen, herrschenden, tristen Götter,

Die schadenfrohen im Schafspelz der Demut —
O, da fasst mich ein düsterer Groll,
Und brechen möcht' ich die neuen Tempel,
Und kämpfen für euch, ihr alten Götter,
Für euch und eu'r gutes ambrosisches Recht,
Und vor euren hohen Altären,
Den wiedergebauten, den opferdampfenden,
Möcht' ich selber knieen und beten,
Und flehend die Arme erheben.[1]

Yes, ghosts they are all, these gods of Heine's. There is not even a glimpse in this ' Götterdämmerung' of that inspiring hope that lay behind all the elegiac pessimism of Schiller's soul, that the golden age would some day and somehow return again, and the kingdom of Apollo once more be established upon this earth.

In very truth, the gods of Greece now fade out of German poetry. One might perhaps have expected that, with the metamorphosis of Hegelianism into a more positive philosophy under Feuerbach, the old eighteenth-century freedom from spiritual shackles would, as in ' Storm and Stress' days, have been restored, and the conditions be more favourable for a return of the old gods into poetry. But this was not to be. The factors that made for spiritual enfranchisement in the nineteenth century were of a different kind: a scientific materialism on the one hand, a belief in the salving virtues of the historic method on the other. Now, if anything is poison to the gods of Greece in poetry, it is the historical attitude of mind. The old gods can only live their full, rich life in a world where time is not, where past and present are one. No one felt this better than Goethe; his poetic world was timeless, and in its timelessness complete and perfect; while to the Romantic mind the world was one of unending change and evolu-

[1] *Die Nordsee*, II.

tion.[1] To the Romanticists the gods of Greece were
only the historical figments of a primitive imagination,
something that pertained to the youth of our race. Even
more effectually the way was barred for their return
by a new force unknown to the great classical age:
pessimism. In the atmosphere of this modern pessimism
the gods of Greece could not live. Fatalism they knew;
indeed, fatalism was a condition of their existence. But
what a serene and beautiful thing Greek fatalism is,
compared with the pessimism of the modern soul! It
is the linking up of fatalism with the tragic Christian
faith that converts it into a thing of evil. In the age of
dissension and disillusionment between 1830 and 1848
there was no room for the 'schönen Wesen aus dem
Fabelland'; and when that political age fell together
like a house of cards at the Revolution of 1848, and
when its failure besmirched and disheartened all that
was best and noblest in the mind of Northern Europe,
the Germans did not—could not—turn back to the gods
of Greece for consolation. The age of pessimism broke
in in grim earnest; the gods that appealed to this hope-
less Europe were not Zeus and Apollo, not even
Dionysos, but the dark, joyless gods of the north—gods
that were no longer the masters of their souls—the
Wotan of Wagner's mighty *Nibelung's Ring*.[2]

In this later nineteenth century the gods of Greece
were dead, vanished from the world, without seeming
hope of ever coming back. How dead they were we
see, if we turn to the nebulous, unplastic figures of

---

[1] This is the burden of Fritz Strich's suggestive work, *Deutsche
Klassik und Romantik, oder Vollendung und Unendlichkeit*, Munich,
1922.

[2] Yet perhaps, after all, behind the gods of Wagner's world lurk
the old gods of Greece. Cp. P. C. Wilson, *Wagner's Dramas and
Greek Tragedy*, New York, 1919.

Hamerling's *Venus im Exil* or *Amor und Psyche*, poems once popular, but now long relegated to the lumber-room of the effete and musty things of literature. The gods of Greece were surely never less alive than they are here.[1]

But again the whirligig of time brings its surprises. As the nineteenth century moved to its close, the cloud of depressing pessimism began to break. The finest minds of that age had, it is true, like Richard Wagner, turned, with deepening despair, to the East, to find a last word there with which to clench their faith in the Nirwana, to worship in Buddha a new saviour from the deluding optimism of a false world. But a new genera-tion was arising which demanded a truer actuality, a braver stand against the ills of life. The long reign of Schopenhauer—very much longer, as far as poetry was concerned, than Kant's or Hegel's—was visibly drawing to a close. In the apostasy of Friedrich Nietzsche from his old master, the gauntlet of the new time was thrown down. Nietzsche's breach with Wagner I have else-where singled out as the decisive moment from which the last epoch in German poetry took its beginning: the crossing of the swords. Nietzsche had begun life as a disciple of Schopenhauer, by proclaiming the doctrine, so comforting to the Romantic heart, that the ultimate basis of the Greek religion was Dionysiac and tragic, not Apollonic and serene; that the Greek dream of Olympos was, like Schiller's, merely a foil to a pessi-mistic outlook on the world. But, like Heine, this modern

---

[1] I am not forgetful of other isolated productions of this time, such as Paul Heyse's delightful *Der letzte Centaur*, or that most beautiful of all prose poems in the German tongue, Gottfried Keller's *Das Tanzlegendchen*; but in Keller's heaven there is no place even for the nine Muses.

Romantic philosopher became a renegade ; he disavowed his Romanticism, and proclaimed a new philosophy of optimism, a faith in ' man's unconquerable mind '.

Clearly the long night of Romantic pessimism was passing ; and in the fresher air that preceded the dawn, the old gods began once more to rub their eyes and think of a return to earth. As the century reached its close, they come once more to life in German poetry. In Switzerland was written a great poem, the greatest, I veritably believe, in this, the last epoch of German literature, the *Olympische Frühling* of Carl Spitteler. Here once again after a long span of time, we have in European literature an epic in the noble style, and moreover, an epic of the gods of Greece. Transformed, transfigured, rejuvenated, these old gods pass once more across the stage of Western Europe ; once more the marble museum gods of classic learning, the shadow gods who had faded before Heine's bleeding Nazarene, are forgotten; the old Olympians come back into our world in radiant, buoyant life.

I cannot here, at the close of an overlong lecture, speak to you as I should like of this wonderful epic.[1] Let me only say that Spitteler has followed the most dangerous of all courses for the poet who will succeed in this world ; he has scouted tradition ; he has defied alike the conventions of the epic and the century-old conception of the gods of Greece. These are things no contemporary criticism ever condones ; and Spitteler has paid the penalty of an incredible neglect. At the beginning of his epic he summons the old gods from the underworld, where they have slept their long sleep

---

[1] I have dealt with Spitteler in an article in the *Contemporary Review* of January 1921, on the occasion of the award to him of the Nobel Prize in literature.

while Chronos reigned in Olympos. And how different
is this underworld, this kingdom of Hades, from the
drab, colourless Styx landscape of the tradition! How
vivid the wondrous journey by which he leads his
gods to the upper world and the sun! And the gods
themselves! No pale shadows they of the classical
tradition, but real, living gods—yes, gods with a considerable dose of Swiss peasant blood in their veins;
and they face the riddle of destiny from sides undreamt
of by Schiller, or Goethe, or Heine. Spitteler lavishes
on his creations a wealth of genial humour that has
not had, I believe, its like in epic poetry since Ariosto.
He places his gods in the service of the burning ideas
of our time—he would be no real poet if he did not—he
accepts the challenge of the long age of Romantic
pessimism; and in his defiance of that pessimism he
voices the spirit of youth that has come into the world.
Ananke, the terrible machine, the ruler of gods and men,
has no longer the last word. Heine's phantoms had
faded before the Cross, and the great dynasty of the
North had gone down in Wagner's 'Götterdämmerung';
but Spitteler's gods do not relinquish their hold upon
the world of men. All that Jung-Siegfried was to be,
all that he failed to be, passes over into the Herakles of
Spitteler's imagination, this son of an immortal Zeus
and a mortal Hera, who descends to earth, with brave
defiance in his heart and the word 'dennoch' on his lips,
to proclaim to men new hopes in their high destiny.
Thus have the old gods of Greece returned, and returned
triumphantly into German poetry.

And here my survey may well close. But if you will
look around you in the literature of Germany and of
Europe, you will see, I think, how in other and unex-
pected quarters the old gods have been restored to

honour. Nay more, the classical scholarship of our
time has responded to the new demands of youth, and
denounced its allegiance to traditional shibboleths; the
eternally young tragedy of Greece has awakened to very
real life again.

In the course of this lecture I have not dealt with
new things; I have not asked you to accompany me
into untrodden paths of literature. I have rather tried
to show, by the light of poetry that is reasonably familiar,
what the beauty of Greece has meant for the Northern
mind. The gods of Greece have at no time been un-
welcome intruders in German poetry; on the contrary,
here, as elsewhere, they have always been the bearers
of the ideal. They take on the changing colours of
each new age; they are ever with us as the symbols of
harmony and conciliation in the imagination of our race.
'Die Götter sterben nicht,' sang old Opitz; 'der Todt
kan ihrem Samen mit keiner Sichel zu'; and Schiller:

> Rauch ist alles ird'sche Wesen;
> Wie des Dampfes Säule weht,
> Schwinden alle Erdengrössen,
> Nur die Götter bleiben stet.

G. G. DE BEAURIEU

ET SON

ÉLÈVE DE LA NATURE, 1763

By

ÉMILE LEGOUIS

The Taylorian Lecture 1925

Un disciple compromettant de *J.-J. Rousseau* : *Gaspard Guillard de Beaurieu et son* Élève de la Nature.

Quel état d'esprit a préparé et rendu possible la Révolution française ? Comment des millions d'hommes sont-ils arrivés à se mettre d'accord sur l'avantage qu'il y aurait à jeter bas la civilisation et à refaire une société toute neuve, sur la table rase, en repartant de rien ? Bien des livres ont répondu de manière diverse à ces questions. Il n'en est pas peut-être qui l'aient fait de façon plus satisfaisante pour l'esprit que ceux de M. Chinard sur *L'exotisme américain dans la littérature française.* C'est là que l'on voit le mieux se former, dans des récits véridiques aussi bien que dans des romans, les notions de plus en plus admises et répandues sur l'excellence de l'homme sauvage, sur la supériorité d'une vie toute conforme à la nature, sur ce devoir social qui consisterait à abolir la société. On va dans une première étape des narrations des explorateurs du Nouveau monde à Jean-Jacques Rousseau ; dans une seconde, de Jean-Jacques à Quatre-vingt-neuf.

Toute la partie subversive de l'œuvre de Rousseau apparaît comme préparée par les relations le plus souvent idylliques que les missionnaires, récollets ou jésuites, avaient faites des Indiens, particulièrement des Peaux-Rouges parmi lesquels ils avaient séjourné et en lesquels ils avaient cru reconnaître les vertus de l'homme naturel, non perverti par la civilisation. Le rôle des pères jésuites—ceux qu'on a pu appeler les jésuites philosophes—les Lafitau, les Buffier, les Charlevoix, est si proéminent qu'on pourrait presque sans paradoxe voir en eux les auteurs responsables de la Révolution. Mais il faut se garder de croire qu'ils aient été les seuls. Un homme tout pratique, comme ce M. Denys, qui s'intitule

Gouverneur Lieutenant Général pour le Roi, et qui consacre le premier de ses deux volumes en 1672 à la pêche à la morue, le second à l'histoire naturelle des côtes de l'Amérique septentrionale, termine sa description par un chapitre sur « la différence qu'il y a entre les coustumes anciennes des Sauvages et celles d'à présent », et il y place, probablement sans malice aucune, des remarques comme celles-ci dont la force explosive, pour peu qu'il y tombât une étincelle, ne saurait être exagérée :

> « La loy qu'ils (les Sauvages) observaient anciennement estoit celle de ne faire à autruy que ce qu'ils souhaitaient leur estre fait ; ils n'avoient aucun culte ; tous vivaient en bonne amitié et intelligence ; ils ne se refusaient rien les uns aux autres... Ils vivaient dans la pureté, les femmes estoient fidelles à leurs maris et les filles fort chastes... A présent ils se saoulent, se battent et s'assomment, sont devenus voleurs, se querellent pour des riens ; quant aux femmes, elles sont entièrement perdues,... elles sont larronesses et fourbes et n'ont plus la pureté du passé. Ils se vengent les uns des autres, dépouillent les étrangers quand ils peuvent, au lieu de les accueillir comme des frères, et ceux qui sont allés en France, et que les matelots ont promenés, pour s'amuser, dans des cabarets et des lieux infâmes, répondent, quand on leur fait des reproches, que nous en faisons bien d'autres. » [1]

Multipliez les passages de ce genre et vous arrivez sans surprise à la fameuse déclaration de Rousseau que « la nature a fait l'homme heureux et bon, mais que la société le déprave et le rend misérable, » — déclaration qui est la base de son *Contrat Social* comme de son *Émile*, et en somme de toute son œuvre.

Les romans ajoutent leur impulsion à la secousse donnée par les narrations authentiques : romans d'imagination, romans utopiques qui n'attendent pas

---

[1] G. Chinard, *L'Amérique et le rêve exotique dans la littérature française au XVIIe et au XVIIIe siècle*. Paris, 1913, pp. 156.

Rousseau pour se produire, car il en est de 1667 comme
L'Histoire des Sévérambes par Vairasse ; de 1699 comme le
Télémaque de Fénelon, avec sa fameuse utopie de la
Bétique ; de 1731 comme *Le Philosophe anglais ou
Histoire de M. Cleveland* par l'abbé Prévost ; de 1738,
comme *Les Aventures du Sieur Lebeau.* Mais c'est surtout après Rousseau que le roman se fonde essentielle-
ment sur le contraste entre l'homme naturel et le civilisé.
Voltaire lui-même, bien qu'il ait souvent fustigé Rousseau
de son ironie, cède à la tentation du genre quand il écrit
Le Huron ou l'Ingénu, la même année 1767 où Sébastien
Mercier publie son *Homme Sauvage.* Dans ce dernier
livre on voit le vieil Azeb, de la tribu des Chébutois,
horrifié par les crimes des Européens dévastateurs de
son pays, qui décide d'élever ses enfants dans une
ignorance complète du reste du monde. Il les aban-
donnera aux leçons de la bonne et sage nature,
persuadé « que tout ce qu'elle a fait est bien fait, et que
ce n'est qu'en la contredisant que nous nous sommes
ouvert la source de tant de maux. » [1]

C'est à cette littérature romanesque qui a suivi de près
les écrits retentissants de Rousseau qu'appartient le
livre sur lequel j'appelle votre attention. Il est de si
piètre valeur, mieux fait pour éveiller le sourire par son
absurdité que l'admiration par son éloquence, que j'ai
le devoir de m'en excuser. Mais, outre qu'on peut être
pardonné de présenter un ouvrage qui amuse, fût-ce
involontairement, les réflexions qui précèdent me servi-
ront de justification. Parmi les nombreuses utopies que
le xviiiᵉ siècle vit éclore, il n'en est pas de si naïve ou
même de si niaise qui soit tout à fait indigne d'arrêter
l'esprit. Chacune collabora en quelque sorte au drame
révolutionnaire, car elle fut à sa mesure force attractive et
cause d'action. Peut-être même ne sont-ce pas les plus

[1] Ibid., p. 414.

profonds et les plus glorieux de ces rêves de régénéra-
tion qui nous font le mieux connaître l'état d'illusion
spécial où se complaisait le public inférieur (partant le
plus considérable) de ceux qui savaient lire et croyaient
penser aux abords de 1789. Entre ce public et les
écrivains de premier rang, il y avait des intermédiaires
plus aisément compris, étant de niveau avec des intelli-
gences médiocres et des imaginations enfantines. Les
romans philosophiques d'un Rousseau, tout éloquents et
vivants qu'ils fussent, étaient encore trop abstraits et trop
sévères pour la plupart des esprits. Il a beau nous
paraître aujourd'hui d'une logique parfois bien croulante
et d'une invention bien chimérique, son *Émile* offrait en
somme une nourriture trop forte et substantielle pour le
grand nombre. Combien ne le connurent qu'à travers
quelque imitation ingénument caricaturale comme
L'Élève de la Nature de Gaspard Guillard de Beaurieu !

Sentimental et naïf Beaurieu ! Ce fils de l'Artois,
qui naquit à Saint-Pol en 1728, était animé d'un honnête
enthousiasme qui garde encore de nos jours je ne sais
quoi de touchant aux rêveries saugrenues dont il fit
part à ses contemporains. Il aima sincèrement le cam-
pagne avant de devenir une des plus insignes dupes
de la *Nature*. Et certes il eut quelque mérite à servir
d'un culte idolâtre celle qui l'avait crié « contrefait comme
Ésope, boiteux, d'une laideur repoussante ». Son incu-
rable optimisme n'était pas affaire de simple doctrine ;
il coulait dans son sang et colorait sa misérable vie. Il
se consolait de sa ressemblance avec Ésope en lançant
comme lui ses saillies contre les travers de la société, et
tirait avantage de sa laideur en la relevant par l'excentri-
cité du costume. Avec son chapeau de Crispin, son
manteau à l'espagnole, ses souliers carrés et son haut-de-
chausses du temps de François Ier, il goûtait la jouissance
d'être une vivante protestation contre l'artificiel de la

mode, et sans doute croyait en s'éloignant du coutumier
se rapprocher du naturel. Il vécut sans amertume dans
l'indigence, « ayant trop aimé l'honneur et le bonheur
pour avoir jamais pu aimer les richesses » . Il eut
vraiment l'amour des enfants, pour lesquels il essaya ou
rêva d'étranges éducations nouvelles. De la réforme
de l'enfance, il passa par une transition aisée à celle de la
société. A l'aube de la Révolution il espéra voir s'établir
sur le sol français quelque république agricole aux
fermes espacées, débarrassée des villes corruptrices, un
état patriarcal aux mœurs pures et simples, pareil à cette
région favorisée de l'Amérique du Nord que, trompé
par son journal préféré, *Les Ephémérides du Citoyen,* il
plaçait d'abord étourdiment dans l'État de New-York avant
d'être corrigé par le grand Benjamin Franklin en personne, et d'identifier définitivement ce paradis terrestre
avec « l'heureuse Virginie » . La Terreur ne réussit pas
à le désabuser. Quand la Convention ouvrit l'École
normale, on le vit, vieil écolier de soixante-six ans,
s'asseoir sur les bancs ; et il était à la veille de mourir
à l'hôpital de la Charité, en 1795. La mort seule put
arrêter les jeux de son utopique cervelle.

Or, quelque trente ans plus tôt, en 1763, Beaurieu,
— tout chaud de la lecture de l'*Émile* qui avait paru l'année précédente, hanté par le souvenir des aventures du
Robinson Crusoë, la cervelle farcie de force romans
utopiques, stimulé d'ailleurs par de vagues notions de
Locke sur la formation des idées et de Shaftesbury sur
le sens moral qui porte l'homme à désirer le bonheur des
autres êtres, — avait imaginé ce que pourrait devenir, de
cœur et de tête, un enfant confié à la seule discipline de
la nature, et il avait écrit le curieux roman dont nous
voudrions donner un aperçu.

C'est, comme il convient, sur le sol britannique que
Beaurieu fait germer l'idée hardie de cette éducation

nouvelle. Les intrépides extirpateurs de préjugés sociaux tendaient à être dans le roman d'alors aussi inévitablement anglais que l'ont été de nos jours les coureurs d'aventures merveilleuses célébrés par un Jules Verne. Mais le patriotisme français aurait tort de s'alarmer : le père du héros a du sang de huguenot dans les veines ; il revient à la France une part de lui, quoique ses ancêtres aient anglicisé leur caractère et, croient-ils, jusqu'à leur nom pour prendre celui de Willams (*sic*). Peut-être avons-nous le droit de revendiquer la moitié sensible de son être qui fait un heureux équilibre à son impassibilité d'expérimentateur. Il est capable de chérir son enfant comme Abraham chérissait Isaac, sans hésiter d'ailleurs à le sacrifier sur l'autel de la déesse Nature. Oyez-le raconter à son fils devenu homme l'origine de l'éducation très spéciale qu'il lui a donnée :

« Tu as quatre sœurs et deux frères, tu es leur cadet. J'avois obtenu de ma femme, au moment de notre mariage, que si jamais nous avions plus de six enfans, elle me permît de rendre à la nature, d'abandonner au seul instinct, tous ceux que nous aurions ensuite ; tu fus le septième et dernier ; j'ai tenu parole, et tout en toi m'annonce que j'aurois tort de m'en repentir . . . Tu dois trouver dans mes derniers mots l'éloge de ta mère et le mien. Si elle était une femme ordinaire, une femme à vapeurs, une femme à grands sentimens de parade, et rien de plus, elle n'auroit pu faire le sacrifice que j'exigeois d'elle. »

La France constatera avec fierté que cette mère antique, digne compagne de l'énergique Willams, est aussi sienne à moitié. Elle est issue du même heureux croisement de races anglaise et française que son mari. Tous les deux sont d'accord pour faire de leur fils une preuve vivante des vérités enseignées par Rousseau. Ce fils viendra « prouver aux hommes, par son exemple, qu'ils naissent bons, sensibles, vertueux ; que l'éducation la plus parfaite n'est point celle qui leur donne ce qu'on peut appeler *des talents et des vertus à grand bruit*, mais celle qui éloigne d'eux les vices de la société, qui les rapproche de la nature et qui les remet, pour ainsi dire, entre ses mains. »

Tel étant le but, admirables de fermeté et de décision sont les moyens. Ici Rousseau est laissé loin. Quelle transaction regrettable, quel timide pis-aller que l'éducation de son Émile mal préservé du funeste contact humain par les soins d'un précepteur, vigilant sans doute, mais qui a l'irrémédiable tare d'être lui-même un homme! Plus de ces demi-termes. Avant qu'il ait pu recevoir la moindre empreinte et garder le plus petit souvenir, l'innocent objet de la grande expérience est enfermé dans une cage de bois « exactement fermée de toutes parts ».

« J'y étois nud, nous dit-il, mais un poële allumé pendant tout l'hiver, échauffoit la chambre où étoit ma cage. La paille sur laquelle je couchois fut toujours la même pendant au moins douze ans que j'y restai ! On m'en donnoit seulement une nouvelle botte tous les six ou huit mois. Je la trouvais à mon réveil ; on la faisoit descendre sans bruit pendant que je dormois, en levant une trappe qui couvroit ma cage. Mais on n'auroit pas pu enlever la paille que j'avois déjà, sans m'éveiller, et il étoit ordonné que je ne visse, ni n'entendisse jamais personne, jusqu'au jour ou l'on devoit me rendre tout à fait à la société. »

Si cette paille permanente vous inquiète, de Beaurieu a une note qui vous rassurera :

« Pour ne rien laisser d'inconnu à ceux de mes lecteurs qui veulent être instruits de tout, et qui prouvent par là qu'ils lisent avec réflexion, je crois devoir les avertir que j'avois *des lieux à l'angloise,* mais sans siège, c'étoit une pierre taillée en évier, placée au fond de ma cage, et inclinée en dehors, de manière que rien n'y pouvoit rester. »

Grâce à un mécanisme semblable au tour des couvents, l'enfant reçoit sa nourriture sans voir qui la lui apporte.

Ou plutôt il y a deux tours superposés dont le plus bas lui sert jusqu'a neuf ans environ, le plus haut de neuf à quinze ans. Une petite « boëte » de carton, posée sur une tablette à la hauteur de quatre ou cinq pieds, et qu'il lui faudra grandir pour atteindre, lui permettra de se rendre compte de son accroissement.

C'est là tout le mobilier, pas très *naturel* peut-être, mais à coup sûr suffisamment réduit. La vie est, dans cette cage, simple et sans évènements. L'enfant s'y développe en liberté (?). Il tient du singe et du perroquet. Dans l'eau de sa cuvette il aperçoit un jour son visage et prend plaisir à lui faire répéter ses sourires et ses grimaces. Une autre fois, les domestiques invisibles chargés de le nourrir l'ayant taquiné en faisant mine de lui retirer sa portion quotidienne, il a entendu une voix lointaine (inconnue, mais instinctivement chère), la voix de son père, leur crier : *Qu'on l'laisse en repos !* Et ces mots dont il ignore le sens se sont gravés dans son oreille ; il se les répète pour son plaisir tout le long du jour et les met en musique. Ce sera le seul langage de sa jeunesse. Gardons-les en mémoire, car ils reviendront comme un *leit-motiv* à travers ses aventures.

Régime bien rigoureux, murmureront des parents sans héroïsme. Qu'ils se gardent toutefois d'imputer au père et à la mère du prisonnier la moindre dureté de cœur. Rappelez-vous qu'à leur fermeté britannique s'allie la sensibilité française. C'est l'âme débordante de tendresse qu'ils poursuivent la sévère expérience :

« Tu étois notre fils, expliquera plus tard Willams à son enfant, nous voulions que tu fusses encore celui de la nature, juge combien à ce double titre nous devions t'aimer ! Ah ! si tu avois vu avec quel empressement nous venions plusieurs fois chaque jour te regarder, t'observer, par des petites ouvertures que nous avions fait faire au haut de ta loge ! »

D'ailleurs le séjour de l'enfant dans la cage n'est dans leur idée que le préambule nécessaire de l'éducation naturelle qu'ils entendent lui donner. C'est comme le noviciat par lequel on le prépare à la consécration définitive. Quand il a quinze ans, la cage, avec son hôte effaré, est descendue dans la cale d'un vaisseau et, après avoir été ballottée trois semaines sur les vagues, est débarquée dans une île déserte. La voici maintenant qui s'ouvre et laisse échapper le captif enfin remis aux mains de la nature le 6 mai de l'année 1739,—grande date pour l'humanité ! C'est dans cette île perdue que pendant dix ans il doit, selon les desseins de son père, « continuer son cours de philosophie ».

Ici, pensons-nous, c'en est vraiment fait de l'intervention humaine, même indirecte et masquée. Plus rien qui doive gêner désormais la libre action de la nature sur celui qui lui est confié.

Il n'en est pas tout à fait ainsi. Par une faiblesse dont il a dû rougir s'il en a eu conscience, Willams a cru devoir préparer les lieux pour l'enfant dès sa naissance. L'île est légèrement truquée. On y a fait des chasses générales par lesquelles on a détruit tous les animaux nuisibles. On y a aussi abattu la plupart des vieux arbres pour y substituer de jeunes plants. On est même descendu à des précautions plus humbles et plus menues. Ce sont, autour de la cage d'où il va sortir, des fruits suspendus aux branches par des fils afin que l'émancipé apprenne par cette leçon de choses à chercher dorénavant sa nourriture parmi les arbres et les haies. C'est un chien laissé près de là, à l'attache, pour épargner à l'adolescent la surprise et la peur de voir cette bête inconnue s'élancer vers lui avec impétuosité : « On était sûr, nous dit-il, que je ne manquerois pas d'aller de ce côté-là quand j'aurois faim, et on se doutoit bien qu'un homme naturel étoit trop bon, trop sensible pour voir un animal r⋯

distance de sa cage cette fois, une grande serpe soigneuse-
ment cachée entre des pierres : « On l'y avoit sans doute
mise le jour de mon débarquement et l'on avoit eù
l'attention de la mettre ainsi un peu loin du lieu où l'on
devoit me descendre afin que je ne la trouvasse qu'après
quelque temps, et lorsque j'aurois acquis par l'expérience
assez de lumières pour deviner l'usage de cet instrument
et ne m'en pas blesser. » Willams lui-même n'aurait-il
qu'une confiance limitée dans les leçons directes de la
nature ? Quelquefois, vous le voyez, il rejoint Rousseau
par l'ingénieuse façon dont il ruse avec elle.

Mais ne chicanons pas. A ces exceptions près, l'île
est vierge d'empreintes humaines. C'est en pleine
solitude que l'adolescent apprend à connaître et à sentir?
Douterez-vous, hommes de peu de foi, que son intelligence n'y fonctionne bien et que ses sentiments n'y
soient purs et généreux ?

Il est bon logicien. et voit clair en lui-même. Un
romancier de nos jours représenterait un être pareil avec
la conscience obscure de la bête. Mais la nature était
pour le xviiie siècle à peu près exactement le contraire
de ce qu'elle est pour le nôtre. Conçue alors comme
l'antithèse de la civilisation, elle se ressentait étrange-
ment de la négation qui lui avait donné naissance. Vidée
de tout préjugé, de toute routine, voire même de toute
expérience et de tout passé, elle arrivait à n'être qu'une
forme sans substance où se reflétait à son gré l'intelligence courte et claire de l'individu. L'homme admirait
naïvement en elle sa propre petite raison projetée sur le
vide. Celle dont l'infinie et ténébreuse complexité nous
confond était donc alors synonyme de tout ce qui est
simple, manifeste, lumineux. Aussi ne s'étonnera-t-on
pas de voir son disciple raisonner avec justesse sur tous
les phénomènes qui tombent sous ses sens. Dans sa
cage, nous dit-il, il se contentait encore « d'accumuler

des faits ». Mais à peine libre, son esprit éprouve une
expansion analogue à celle de son corps. Il est maintenant curieux du pourquoi des choses. Ce n'est plus le
Robinson primitif dont les mains actives créèrent autour
de lui une sorte de civilisation matérielle en plein désert.
C'est un Robinson qui n'agit guère et qui pense beaucoup,
plus enclin à questionner les choses qu'à tirer parti
d'elles pour se faire une installation confortable. Si
dans ses conjectures il se porte vers quelques erreurs, il
ne cesse de s'élever avec une agilité merveilleuse sur
l'échelle des causes, découvrant les lois de la perspective,
la raison de l'ombre que fait son corps sur le sol, de la
disparition quotidienne de la lumière, de la décomposi-
tion des êtres vivants, remontant de la terre au soleil,
et du soleil au Dieu du Vicaire savoyard. Quelques
rêveries poétiques sur l'origine de la rosée, de la neige
et de l'écho sont à peu près tout ce qui le fait retarder
un peu sur les physiciens de son époque.

C'est ici la partie sérieuse entre toutes du roman,
celle où le brave Beaurieu a sûrement mis le plus
profond de sa philosophie. Il convient donc de montrer
par une citation les raisonnements intérieurs qu'il prête
à son silencieux héros. Voyez comment celui-ci, sans
autre aide que son bon sens, se rend compte des conditions et des raisons de la perspective. Il s'est d'abord
fâché contre ses yeux qui lui montraient le même objet
tantôt grand, tantôt petit. Mais il réfléchit et voici la
suite de ses réflexions : C'est une application du fameux
« Je pense, donc je suis » de Descartes :

> « Je suis un être parfait. Le jeu de tous mes organes est
> admirable ; il règne, et entr'eux et dans les fonctions de
> chacun d'eux, un accord, une harmonie qui fait mon
> bonheur. Seroit-il possible que le plus beau d'entr'eux,
> mon œil, fût vicié ? Non, il faut sans doute que pour mon
> propre avantage, plus les objets sont éloignés, plus ils me
> paraissent petits, et je crois qu'en voici la raison. Si, à la

plus grande distance, je les voyais tels qu'ils sont, je n'en pourrois voir que cinq ou six à la fois, ils rempliroient toute ma vue ; encore ne les verrois-je que confusément : il vaut bien mieux que ma vue s'étende librement et puisse parcourir en détail tout ce bel et grand cercle que le ciel couvre. L'expérience m'apprend que plus un objet est vu de loin, plus il me paraît petit : eh bien ! je multiplierai la grandeur apparente des corps par la distance d'où je les verrai, et j'aurai leur grandeur réelle et je ne me tromperai plus. »

Qu'il est donc simple d'arriver aux théorèmes et combien superflue l'usure des culottes sur les bancs de l'école ! Mais Beaurieu n'oublie pas, même en ces graves endroits, qu'il est aussi romancier, et il mêle agréablement à sa leçon philosophique une fantaisie d'où il tire d'ailleurs de nouvelles leçons de sagesse. Son Élève n'a pas plus tôt résolu le problème de la perspective qu'il ajoute :

« Je fus si ravi d'avoir fait ce raisonnement, quoique d'une manière encore plus faible que je ne viens de le rendre, que dans un transport d'admiration pour moi-même je m'écriai : *Qu'on l'laisse en repos !* Je commençais à ne plus répéter si souvent ni si volontiers ce mot qui m'avoit d'abord paru si agréable : tant il est vrai que les plaisirs, même les plus vifs, s'émoussent par l'habitude, et que la modération dans leur usage est le seul moyen d'en prévenir la satiété ! »

Ainsi va rapidement s'aiguisant l'intelligence du jeune homme. Si toutefois il pèse encore sur sa raison, comme il a été dit, quelques voiles qu'il n'a pas pu soulever tout seul, il est une chose par laquelle il dépasse sans effort et du premier coup les élèves des hommes : il est vertueux infailliblement, comme on a deux mains et dix doigts. La bonté avec toutes ses délicatesses lui est innée et il en a conscience (oh combien !). A dire vrai, quand il vivait en cage il était enciin à se croire l'être unique et à faire de lui le centre du monde. Un jour il s'est emporté jusqu'à la fureur en ne trouvant pas son tour garni d'aliments à l'heure accoutumée. Il a eu des velléités de vengeance contre les inconnus qui le négligeaient. Mais la nature qui veille (celle de Shaftesbury) eut vite refréné ces élans mauvais, triste legs, apparemment, de la vie artificielle menée par ses ascendants : « L'humanité et la reconnaissance l'emportèrent dans mon cœur. » Il a même des attentions aimables pour ceux qui le servent ; afin de faciliter leur tâche, il place à portée de leurs mains le vase d'eau qu'on lui remplit chaque nuit : « Je trouvois un plaisir délicat à épargner de la peine à ceux qui étoient chargés de me servir ; je m'applaudissois de ce sentiment. » Une autre fois, la négligence des domestiques s'étant répétée, ce fut de sa part même mouvement de colère suivi de même pardon :

« Nous autres hommes naturels ne sommes pas vindicatifs. Notre cœur est une tablette où sont écrits d'un côté les bienfaits que nous recevons ; sur le revers sont les injures, et nous ne tournons jamais cette tablette. »

Toutefois certains voyageurs font courir de vilains bruits sur les indigènes des régions bénies où la civilisation n'a pas pénétré. Beaurieu s'attend à l'objection, il a lu ses textes et il répond par cette note triomphante :

« On pourroit opposer au bien que je dis ici des hommes naturels des faits qui semblent être contre eux. On voit, par exemple, en Amérique, un sauvage rester huit jours derrière un arbre pour attendre un Espagnol ou un Portugais, qu'il veut tuer seulement en haine de sa nation. Mais les Américains sont-ils encore des hommes naturels, et n'est-ce point les Espagnols et les Portugais qui les ont tirés de cet heureux état ? »

Notre héros n'en a pas été tiré, lui ; aussi a-t-il une chaleureuse sympathie qui s'étend sur toutes les créatures. Avec une petite mouche qui s'était introduite étourdi-

ment dans sa cage il avait naguère fait « une espèce
d'amitié plus vraie que n'est souvent celle des hommes ».
Sa tendresse déborde maintenant jusque sur le monde
végétal. A-t-il malmené un pauvre arbre qui lui semble
s'obstiner à retenir ses fruits, il se le reproche aussitôt :

« Tu as bien tort, me dis-je, ayant si bonne idée de toi-
même, d'en avoir une si désavantageuse des autres êtres.
Cette réflexion me fut agréable, je m'applaudis de l'avoir
faite. Plus elle me portoit à former de doux nœuds avec
tout ce qui m'environnoit, plus elle étendoit la sphère de
mon bonheur. »

Rien d'étonnant si à la tendresse s'allie chez l'homme
naturel (surtout lorsqu'il fut élévé en cage) un indompt-
able amour de la liberté. Notre héros (est-il besoin de
le dire ?) possède cet amour. Mais on est plus surpris
de trouver chez lui ces vertus secondaires qui passent
pour l'apanage de l'homme civilisé et par lesquelles il se
console, dit-on, du manque des vertus capitales. La
propreté est du nombre. Non seulement le disciple
a d'instinct deviné l'emploi de l'évier mis dans sa
cage ; non seulement il a commencé à se laver dès
le jour où il se fut éclaboussé avec l'eau de son gobelet,
mais peu s'en faut que dans son île déserte il n'importe
la brosse à dents :

« Je rinçois tous les jours ma bouche ; je m'en étois fait
un amusement. C'est une des plus saines opérations de la
propreté, je remercie la nature de me l'avoir apprise. »

L'homme naturel ne s'en tient pas à la stricte propreté,
il va jusqu'à la coquetterie. Il aime à se mirer dans
l'eau, car, dit-il, « la tête d'un homme vue par une imagination aussi neuve et aussi peu troublée que l'étoit la
mienne, est vraiment une belle chose. » Quand il se
voit tout entier dans la mer son admiration augmente ;
en effet, nous dit une note : « L'homme naturel est
ordinairement content de lui-même et il a le droit de

l'être : L'amour-propre est pour lui un bienfait de la Providence. » Il ne manque pas d'une certaine recherche dans sa mise quand il consent à voiler son beau corps. Entre deux peaux d'ours, l'une noire et l'autre brune, qui lui ont été laissées pour se vêtir l'hiver, il choisira la noire, « parce que ma main, quand je la posois dessus, me paroissoit plus blanche. On a un peu de vanité même dans une île déserte, et ce n'est pas un mal. »

Mais ce qu'il nous tarde d'apprendre, c'est comment l'homme naturel ressent et pratique celui de tous les sentiments que la civilisation a le plus perverti, comment il éprouve l'amour. Il eût été invraisemblable qu'un roman du xviiie siècle ne s'étendît pas avec complaisance sur cette question et qu'il ne reflétât rien de cette sensiblerie mêlée de sensualité et de vertueuse déclamation qui était la marque de l'époque. L'excellent Beaurieu se donne ici carrière, avec tant d'optimisme attendri, avec tant d'impétueuse allégresse, avec un si amusant effort aussi pour conserver çà et là les traits du naturalisme dans sa fiction romanesque, qu'il désarme la critique.

Le héros est fort obsédé par l'amour même avant de le connaître. La nature l'insinue peu à peu en lui, soit par quelque songe troublant, d'une précision suggestive, soit en faisant se becqueter devant ses yeux de tendres tourterelles, s'ébattre curieusement une biche et un cerf, soit encore en lui révélant le mystère de la génération, l'œuf qui éclot, le flanc de la biche qui s'ouvre pour laisser sortir le faon. L'obsession va croissant à chaque découverte ; la solitude lui devient pesante ; la mélancolie parfois l'envahit. Le moment est venu de lui présenter Julie. Un coin de l'île naguère déserte est maintenant habité par deux naufragés, un vieillard et sa fille, des civilisés (hélas !), mais que la nécessité a rendus presque naturels. Au costume et au langage près, ils sont dignes

d'être mis en présence du héros. Un jour que celui-ci est
parti pour une expédition (il est tout nu, car c'est l'été,
et il a quitté sa peau d'ours noir), il tombe dans un filet
tendu par Julie pour une tout autre capture. Le filet en
s'abattant fait tinter une sonnette inquiétante :

« Non, non, je n'avois rien à craindre... De quel bonheur
au contraire j'allois jouir !... J'entends marcher, je regarde
... je vois une femme !

Sa beauté m'enchante, je perds l'usage de tous mes sens ;
je crois que j'aurois perdu la vue même, si le bizarre assem-
blage de ses habits n'eût modéré mon admiration et mes
transports. Je fais un élan pour me dégager, pour voler
dans ses bras : je lui tends les miens, sans avoir la force de
prononcer même les seuls mots que je savois, et qui me
revenoient toujours dans les grandes occasions. Julie
s'arrête, elle pleure aussi, puis se tournant du côté d'où elle
est venue, elle fait un signe empressé et se tourne encore
vers moi... Le feu de ses yeux embrasoit mon âme. Je
luttois de toute ma force contre le fatal obstacle qui me
séparoit d'elle ; je la voyois combattue, et par le désir de
venir à mon secours et par la crainte de ce qui en arriveroit.
Elle avance, elle recule.

Un vieillard (c'étoit son père) accourt, il vient à elle en
haletant. Il me regarde : il voit les efforts que je fais ; il
craint pour elle et pour lui-même ; il l'embrasse et lui parle
avec action, et l'envoie dans sa cabane. Je pleure, je me
prosterne devant le vieillard, je lui tends des mains sup-
pliantes, la douleur m'avoit ôté la parole, et la parole m'est
rendue par l'excès même de la douleur, je lui crie d'une voix
étouffée de soupirs : *qu'on l'laisse en r'pos*, et tout cela c'étoit
pour lui demander Julie. »

Mais le vieil Euphémon n'est pas amoureux, lui ; la
vue du jeune homme tout nu, ses gestes et ses cris
bizarres, l'effrayent. Il le frappe d'une épée que Julie lui
apporte de la cabane ; elle-même sur son ordre blesse à
contre-cœur avec une autre arme le beau sauvage. Le
voici garrotté, mais sans peur, car il lit dans les yeux de
ses geôliers l'intention de ne pas lui faire d'autre mal.

« Un homme naturel, nous explique-t-il, ne se trompe guère sur ce que disent les yeux. » On s'empresse maintenant de soigner ses blessures : .

   « Julie commença par celle de l'épaule, elle y porta ses mains pour étancher le sang... J'éprouve aussitôt après une autre sensation plus douce encore, un frémissement délicieux... Julie me l'a avoué depuis, c'étoit un baiser de sa bouche... Je regardois Julie, je pleurois, j'avois saisi une de ses mains que je couvrois de baisers ; je ne pouvois étant lié la tenir que faiblement, elle me l'eût arrachée sans peine : mais peut-on, dans une Isle déserte, résister à l'amour ? »

La flamme de la passion dévore le cœur vierge du héros. Il en oublie, lui si observateur de tout objet nouveau, de regarder avec attention certaine « jatte de faïence » dans laquelle Euphémon apporte de l'eau pour laver ses plaies : « C'est un malheur d'avoir passé toute sa jeunesse sans voir de femmes : il en coûte la liberté et la raison quand on en voit une. » Suit une cour rapide dans laquelle le jeune homme déclare sa passion par des *qu'on l'laisse en r'pos* tendrement modulés. Julie n'est pas insensible à d'aussi éloquents appels, auxquels se joint l'ineffable langage des yeux et des gestes. Elle se consume avec lui. Le bon Euphémon trouve utile d'accélérer le mariage ; il fait taire sans peine les pudiques objections de sa fille, et huit jours après la capture du solitaire, ayant joint lui-même leurs mains, il sort pour laisser seuls les deux époux : « Nœud sacré de la Nature, vous nous unîtes en ce moment ! La pudeur et la délicatesse, compagnes inséparables de la vraie volupté, rendirent nos plaisirs plus piquants et plus vifs. L'amour et la vertu scellèrent notre union. » L'île est assurée de ne pas demeurer déserte.

Ici Beaurieu est dans la tradition du roman utopique qui volontiers substitue au mariage formel une sorte d'union libre ou remplace les rites coutumiers par une

bénédiction patriarcale sous l'œil bienveillant de la
Nature. L'abbé Prévost en avait donné un avant-goût
dans son *Cleveland*. C'est ainsi que son Milord Axminster
avait joint les mains de Cleveland à celles de sa fille
Fanny. Beaurieu avait de plus nobles précurseurs
encore, voire même des esprits comme celui de Milton
tout pleins de la Bible et grondant contre les contraintes
de la loi humaine. N'y avait-il pas comme un rappel
d'Adam et Ève dans la consommation des amours du
héros et de sa Julie ?

A partir de ce moment commence l'éducation artificielle d'*Ariste* (le meilleur des hommes). C'est le nom
qu'Euphémon a donné à son vertueux gendre. Après
quelques façons (car à quoi bon les paroles quand les
gestes sont si expressifs et si doux ?), Ariste se laisse
enseigner le français par sa jeune femme. Le pédagogue
qui est en Beaurieu se manifeste ici par l'invention d'une
méthode nouvelle—et sûrement très savoureuse—pour
l'enseignement pratique des langues. Écoutez son
élève :

> ‹ Euphémon résolut de m'apprendre sa langue, c'est-à-
> dire le français ; mais il se fût donné pour y parvenir
> beaucoup de peine en pure perte, si le besoin, et peut-être
> plus encore l'amour, ne m'avoient enfin persuadé de profiter
> de ses leçons. Il appeloit quelquefois sa fille et, dès qu'il
> avoit prononcé le mot *Julie*, elle répondoit *me voici*. Ces
> nouveaux sons me parurent si doux qu'ils me firent presque
> oublier *qu'on l'laisse en r'pos*. A tous moments, je disois
> d'une voix mâle *Julie* et je répondois en l'élevant et en
> l'adoucissant *me voici*. Cela amusoit ma jeune épouse et
> son père. Je riais de les voir rire.
>
> Un jour, après que nous eûmes dîné, Julie se mit en tête
> de faire avec moi le petit dialogue que l'on va voir. Plût à
> Dieu que les amants n'en eussent jamais su d'autres ! Cela
> vaudroit mieux que toutes les fadeurs qu'ils se disent. Elle
> me prend les mains, me baise et me dit d'un ton qui imitoit
> celui de son père *Julie, je t'aime* ; je répète aussitôt *Julie*,

je t'aime, je t'aime ; elle met sa main sur ma bouche et me dit de sa voix ordinaire, *Ariste, je t'aime* ; elle ajoute en grossissant la voix et en m'interrogeant, *M'aimes-tu beaucoup ?* Elle ôte sa main de dessus mes lèvres ; je répète du même coup *m'aimes-tu beaucoup ?* Elle répond en m'empêchant encore de parler, *oui, mon ami, beaucoup, oui beaucoup, et toi ?* Puis, reprenant un ton mâle et me rendant la liberté, *Oh, beaucoup, beaucoup !* et je répète *Oh, beaucoup, beaucoup !*

En trois leçons, qui ne durèrent ensemble qu'un quart d'heure, j'appris ce dialogue avec les tendres inflexions qui doivent l'accompagner. Je payai ma maîtresse de langue de plus de baisers que je n'avois prononcé de lettres et en bonne justice ce n'étoit pas assez la payer. Cependant elle me les rendit tous comme s'ils ne lui avoient pas été dus. Que le commerce de l'amour est beau ! qu'il est généreux ! »

Pourtant ce savoir nouveau faillit lui causer une peine cruelle, le jour où un écho répétant après lui *Julie, je t'aime*, lui infligea sa première torture de jalousie. Mais il faut glisser sur cette scène ainsi que sur mainte autre également curieuse, et entre plusieurs chapitres mémorables faire un choix. Citons celui où Ariste, pour couronner son « cours de philosophie », s'abîme dans l'adoration de l'Être suprême :

« Euphémon et Julie me voyoient avec un plaisir bien délicat, bien digne d'aussi belles âmes, tantôt lever mes mains vers Dieu, tantôt me prosterner, l'adorer, et en lui montrant ces deux autres moi-même, le remercier de ce que je les avois trouvés. Une chose seulement les inquiétoit ; je cherchois toujours le soleil, ils craignoient que ce fût à lui seul que j'adressasse mes hommages ; ils affectoient de lui tourner le dos en priant, pour voir ce que j'en penserois ; je n'en étois pas content, et je ne les imitois pas. Enfin, le bon Euphémon qui jusques là n'avoit pas encore osé me parler de Dieu, et ne m'avoit fait nommer (en les nommant) que les êtres qui frappoient mes yeux, tels que le ciel, le soleil, la terre, la mer, etc., me conduisit sur un rocher fort élevé. Là, de ses tremblantes mains, il prend une des miennes, il la sert (*sic*) tant qu'il peut, il me jette un regard

tendre, il verse des larmes, il lève au ciel la main qui lui
restoit libre, et d'un ton qu'il n'est pas possible d'exprimer,
mais qui se fait si bien entendre au cœur, il me dit : DIEU.
... Je me sens pénétré de respect, je regarde Euphémon :
ses larmes font couler les miennes, je rêve un moment, je
demeure immobile... ce n'est point le ciel qu'il me nomme
et cependant je ne vois que le ciel ; il me nomme donc le
grand Être que j'adore... oui, c'est lui, je viens de lire
son nom dans l'âme de mon père, tandis que sa bouche le
prononçoit... Après ce monologue intérieur, je saisis avec
un saint transport Euphémon et Julie et je leur dis, en leur
montrant les êtres que je nomme : « Euphémon... Julie
... Ariste... mer... terre... arbres... rochers... ciel... soleil...
Dieu. » Cette profession de foi étoit claire : ils la com-
prirent sans peine. Nous nous prosternâmes ensemble du
côté opposé au soleil. »

Après avoir atteint une telle cîme l'histoire ne peut
plus que redescendre en des climats plus tempérés. Le
jour vient où le père d'Ariste se présente pour chercher
son fils et le ramener en Europe. Willams ne paraît
éprouver aucune déception en voyant compromise par
le hasard l'éducation toute solitaire qu'il avait voulu
donner à son enfant. Il le trouve marié, vivant en
société, parlant le français, et il se déclare ravi. Il
s'applaudit de tout ce qu'il a fait. Ariste voyage alors
en Europe pour juger en homme libre et sain les
merveilles et aussi les fléaux de la civilisation. Il est
plus attristé qu'ébloui par ce spectacle. Il lui tarde
de revenir dans son île. Il y ramène, avec sa propre
famille, plusieurs émigrants éprouvés qui ont résolu
de fonder enfin une société naturelle. Ariste est le
chef tout indiqué du nouvel État. Il rédige le code
qui doit faire le bonheur de ses compagnons, puis, après
avoir solennellement brûlé sa plume et proscrit les arts
d'imprimer et d'écrire, il consacre sa vie entière à
l'application des lois qu'il a promulguées.

Le troisième volume de l'édition d'Amsterdam de 1771

(celle dont je me suis servi pour mon analyse) est tout
entier empli par la description des institutions sociales
qu'Ariste a introduites dans son île, « l'Isle de la Paix » .
Merveilleuse conséquence de sa libre éducation naturelle!
Il tire de son expérience l'idée d'une république à la
Lycurgue où les travaux agricoles remplacent d'ailleurs
les soins guerriers. La nature, prise pour guide, lui
inspire de bâtir une ville carrée et régulière comme un
échiquier, faite de maisons toutes pareilles et symétrique-
ment posées, où les mêmes heures sont employées aux
mêmes usages par tous les habitants, où l'éducation des
enfants (bien qu'il déclare ne vouloir point gêner leur
liberté) est en fait l'objet de soins si minutieux et de
règlements si précis, de précautions si tracassières et
d'honnêtes supercheries si indiscrètes, qu'elle ferait
presque regretter « les geôles de jeunesse captive » dont
se plaignait Montaigne.

Si cette contradiction nous choque, n'imputons pas
pour cela à Beaurieu un illogisme qui lui serait
particulier. C'est le propre de tous les utopistes, dans
leur effort pour égaliser les hommes et assurer leur
bonheur, d'instituer une tyrannie. Platon est à cet
égard le grand modèle et le premier responsable. Thomas
Morus a suivi son exemple dans son livre fameux dont
Beaurieu se réclame, dont il déclare s'inspirer, quand
il nous dit que les lois d'Aristie (la cité fondée par
Ariste) seront à peu près les mêmes que celles de
l'Utopie, « cette belle et heureuse république imaginée
par Thomas Morus » . Une effrayante monotonie règne
dans tous ces États sortis de l'imagination d'un seul
homme, fût-ce un homme de génie. A ce qui fut la
création successive de forces innombrables et mysté-
rieuses, se substitue la conception d'une intelligence
unique, donc nécessairement rectiligne, pauvre, et limitée.
A l'incessant mouvement d'une chose vivante qui change

et se développe succède l'immobilité d'un plan parfait qui
ne doit plus être modifié et qui désole par ce qu'il a de
fixe et d'invariable non moins que par ce qu'il a d'uni-
forme.

Ce qui distingue l'Aristie des autres cités imaginaires,
c'est ce qu'elle doit aux goûts champêtres de l'auteur,
tout plein de réminiscences de Virgile, du jésuite
Vanière, ce poète latin moderne dont le *Praedium rusti-
cum* avait alors un éclatant succès, de Thomson, le
chantre des *Saisons*, et aussi des *Idylles* de Gessner.
Beaurieu n'était rien moins qu'un ignorant. Il avait une
certaine culture, et sa cervelle, si elle n'était pas très
solide, était meublée de lectures bucoliques comme celle
de Don Quichotte l'avait été de romans de chevalerie.

A coup sûr son roman est caractéristique. S'il est
surtout à conseiller aux lecteurs en quête d'un livre qui
les déride, il faut se garder d'imputer à l'auteur le
moindre dessein de caricature. Tour à tour sentimental
et solennel, sérieux et convaincu toujours, Beaurieu
a été lu sérieusement, soyons-en assurés, par beaucoup
de ses contemporains. Huit éditions de 1763 à 1794
(dont l'une fut mise sous le nom de Rousseau) attestent
la popularité de son livre. Celui-ci mérite de demeurer
comme le plus curieux monument peut-être de l'uni-
verselle duperie que le mot *nature* fit subir à un siècle.
Il ne nous déplaît pas de nous dire en le lisant que nos
pères étaient vraiment bien jeunes et bien naïfs, et que
nous sommes nous-mêmes plus avisés. Ce n'est pas
nous, n'est-ce pas ? qui autoriserions jamais nos désirs
et nos chimères en les mettant sous le patronage de
quelque grand vocable mystérieux. Aussi sourions-
nous avec complaisance en songeant aux illusions du
temps jadis.

CARDUCCI

BY

JOHN BAILEY

The Taylorian Lecture 1926

CARDUCCI

I WILL not occupy your time unnecessarily by expressing at any length my sense of the honour done me by the Curators of the Taylor Institution in asking me to deliver this lecture. I am very grateful to them. Indeed I have older reasons for my gratitude which dates back to forty years ago when under their auspices and the guidance of the teacher who was, I think, on their foundation—Signor Coscia—I first made acquaintance with the beautiful language of Italy.

But I confess that to-day my gratitude is mingled with not a little alarm. I think all the distinguished men who have held this Lecturership, except the first, Sir Edmund Gosse, have been University Professors, and all have been able to use it, and have used it, for the increase of learning in some branch of the study of modern languages. I have not felt able to follow their example. It seemed to me, when I came to consider what I could speak of, that I must try to find something in modern literature which I had myself enjoyed and to which I might venture to try to direct or recall your attention. My acquaintance with foreign literature is not very wide or intimate and most of what has given me pleasure was too generally known and enjoyed to leave me much to say about it. So that I did not find it easy to choose a subject, and even felt tempted to decline the alarming adventure. You remember the characteristic sentence in which Gibbon declined the adventure of marriage. ' The choice is difficult, the success doubtful, the engagement perpetual.' If I have after all not declined the adventure of this lecture, my courage is due to the fact that the engagement is only for a single hour.

I am going to speak of Carducci ; and part of my reason for taking him as my subject is that I know no poet whose reputation appears to me to be so far below his desert. Even Mr. Geoffrey Bickersteth, to whose admirable edition all

me to realize rather imperfectly the poetic greatness of the
subject of his study. For my part I should imagine that at
the time of his death Carducci was the greatest poet in
Europe with the doubtful exception of Swinburne. That is
less than twenty years ago and it may very well be that
posterity looking back will give the palm to some poet quite
unknown to me and even to people far better acquainted
with the literatures of Europe than I am ; perhaps to a poet
writing in some language which very few of us can read.
One can only speak of what one knows and so far as that goes
I should say that Carducci had no rival but Swinburne ; the
rival whom of all others I suppose he would have liked. For
though there was much in Swinburne, notably in *Poems and
Ballads*, utterly alien and repugnant to the sane and healthy
virility of Carducci ; yet he would have been ready, I expect,
to forget all that in gratitude to the devotion to Italy shown
throughout his life by the author of *Songs before Sunrise*.
And in any case Swinburne is himself an illustration of the
first point I wish to make about Carducci : I may say of the
first two points. Utterly and wholly unlike as men, and
a complete contrast to each other in some aspects both of
the manner and of the subjects of their poetry, they yet
shared two important poetic characteristics. They were
both political poets ; and they were both literary poets.
And they have both suffered for their literature and for their
politics. I believe a common notion about Carducci is that
he was partly a Professor making imitations of ancient poets,
and partly an Italian patriot putting ephemeral politics into
verse. And what sort of poetry could be less worth troubling
about than a mixture of political speeches with Prize-medal
echoes of the Classics ?

Now that notion has some truth in it and, so far as it is
true, it is fatal to Carducci. I should not recommend any one
who was not making a very special study of Carducci to
spend much time over the *Juvenilia* where the scholar has
hardly escaped from the schoolmaster, or even from the
schoolboy, stage of development. Nor should I think him
wise to trouble himself much with the *Giambi ed Epodi* for

the reason that they mainly deal with events of passing political interest which the poet has hardly known how to lift into that atmosphere of the universal and eternal which is the atmosphere of great poetry. But what of that? To confess so much is only to confess that Carducci, like most other poets, produced a good deal of mediocre work now best ignored by the judicious reader. The accusation only becomes damaging if it can be upheld against his poetry generally. But can it? It is true that in all his work, including his finest, there is almost invariably a felt presence both of literature and politics. And there are people in whose eyes that is enough to condemn him. One of the truest poets we have in England to-day, Mr. W. H. Davies, remarks in his Preface to one of the best selections of recent poetry that in it 'patriotic poetry has been purposely avoided as it is seldom enjoyed by lovers of real poetry'. It is this kind of feeling which acts against Carducci. Somehow or other it is common to-day: part of the price, I suppose, which we have to pay for those seekings after a better international feeling which are among the most hopeful political signs of our time. But we ought not to pay it. Few things would appear more certain than that if we cannot be internationally-minded without ceasing to be patriotic we shall never be internationally-minded at all. And to any one who knows even a little of the history of poetry can any statement be more ignorantly absurd than that statement of Mr. Davies? 'Patriotic poetry is seldom enjoyed by lovers of real poetry!' Were the Greeks, then, not lovers of real poetry? Is it suggested that they did not enjoy the outbursts of pride in Greece or in Athens which occur in all their great poets, in Pindar, Aeschylus, Aristophanes, Sophocles, Euripides? Did not the Romans at once enjoy the *Aeneid* and the political Odes of Horace, and has not the whole world gone on enjoying them ever since? Are we blockheads when our hearts swell at the two Agincourts of Shakespeare and Drayton, at the Sonnets of Milton or the Sonnets of Wordsworth? Is an Italian less a lover of poetry because he delights in the love and praise of Italy as

they come from Dante and Petrarch, and Filicaia and
Alfieri and Leopardi and Carducci ? The truth is that if the
readers of poetry must avoid patriotic poetry they will have
to avoid many of the very greatest poets of all times and
countries. I admit that two of the half-dozen greatest poets
of the most nationalist of all countries never, so far as I
remember, strike the patriotic note. But neither the
tragedies of Racine nor the Fables of La Fontaine offered
much scope for the praise of France. Perhaps the only poet
of the very first order who had such opportunities and
did not take them was Goethe. And he had the excuse
that in his greatest days Germany was hardly either a
memory of the past or a dream of the future. Italy never
ceased to be both ; and for my part I feel that Carducci
would have been not more but less a poet if he had forgotten either the memory or the dream.

The other attack I can hardly need to repel in this place.
Here in Oxford I hope we are not very likely to think learning fatal to a poet. We know that the history of European
poetry is an almost unbroken tradition, and that every poet
of importance inherits a past and creates a future. And we
know how much the scholarship of poetry, in hands that
know how to use it, can enrich and glorify its own verse with
memories and suggestions of the art and thought of older
masters. It would be knocking at an open door to ask here
how much of the charm of Virgil and Milton is due to the use
they make of their learning. Can there be any place in
which the doctrine that learning and poetry are incompatible
needs so little refutation as it needs in Oxford where Virgil
has had the highest place among our studies for centuries,
where Dante and Milton have lately been given an official
place among them, where you have had resident for many
years in your midst one whose work has been from first to
last a proof that the marriage of art and inspiration, of
learning and life, is no barren union of opposites but one
which may issue in poetry never to be forgotten ?

We are entitled, then, to reassure ourselves. Carducci
may have to plead guilty to both those accusations ; he may

be learned and he may be political ; and yet neither his learning nor his politics may be fatal to his poetry. I believe, even, that as he has used them in his happiest moments, they are both of its essence. If they are present in his failures they are also present in his triumphs. They were in fact an inseparable part of the man himself. As he called his son Dante and two of his daughters Beatrice and Lucia, and as he insisted that the wedding-day of his Beatrice should be the twentieth of September, so poetry and Italy, past and present, are felt in all his poems and certainly not least when he is most moved and most moving. What separates his successes from his failures is not a difference of subject but a difference of quality ; the presence or the absence, or the presence in a greater or a less degree, of the mood and power of poetry What is poetry ? There are a hundred definitions and I shall certainly not attempt a new one. But I suppose we shall all agree that, if the essence of the thing escapes exact or formal definition, it is certainly something in which we perceive a heightened and unusual energy of a combination of human faculties. Poetry gives us a picture of life and the world in which the imagination sees much more than is commonly seen, the heart feels much more than is commonly felt, the mind thinks more than is commonly thought, and the tongue or the pen, whatever name you give to the power of expression, expresses much more of these feelings, thoughts, imaginations, than can be expressed at ordinary times or by ordinary persons. Well, all poets have their ordinary times ; and unfortunately they sometimes write in them. And they are in part ordinary persons ; and sometimes the ordinary person confuses himself with the poet and puts on the poet's mantle. That happened in Carducci as in others ; and as in him the ordinary person, the person who was not a poet, was sometimes a pedant and sometimes a journalist, we have some poems published in his complete works which are exercises in pedantry and others which are outbursts of journalism. But they are not the poems with which we are concerned to-day ; for they do not affect, or ought not to affect, our estimate of the poet Carducci.

If you look through the whole of Carducci's work, what do you find ? You find, I think, that, to an unusual degree, Carducci is the same man and the same poet from first to last. Born in 1835, of a father who was at once a Revolutionary and a Manzonian, he developed, as most of us do, partly by acceptance and partly by revolt. He caught and kept all his life his father's passionate patriotism, as he retained all his life the love of the actual soil of Italy, her hills and streams and coasts, which grew up in him as he ran wild about the countryside near his home in that Tuscan Maremma to which he returned with such affection in several of his finest poems. But he reacted from the beginning, and very violently, against his father's worship of Manzoni and all that went with it. Europe was then under a wave of medievalism which came from the Germans, was carried all over Europe by the genius of Scott, conquered Italy under Manzoni, and was everywhere accompanied by a revolt against eighteenth-century rationalism and by a revival of ecclesiasticism in one form or another. That was the atmosphere of the school to which the young Carducci was sent and he hated it at once with an instinctive and undying hatred. These loves and hatreds are already to be found in the *Juvenilia* and in the *Levia Gravia* which are the two earliest sections of his poetry as finally arranged. The first words of the most famous volume of his maturity are ' Odio l' usata poesia ' : and what he hated in it then, its slack sensuousness, self-indulgence and sentimentality, is already the mark of his angry contempt in these early poems. Poem after poem pours scorn on the neo-clerical absurdities and worse than absurdities of the *secoletto vil che cristianeggia*; the generation which was busy at one moment in digging up the bones of pseudo-saints and at another in turning the Cross of Christ into a flag of slavery. And he has hardly less scorn for the Romantic poetasters of his time who have the names of Byron and Shakespeare always on their lips and have to be told that they may rant and rave as they like but it will not make them Byrons ; and that no quantity of fine phrases will bring Shakespeare back to earth. In these first poems, as all through, Carducci calls for life and nature, the full and healthy life of both mind and body. He is filled with an angry sadness of patriotism as he sees the plight and temper of his countrymen, crying to them in the spirit of Leopardi

Al gener vostro ozio é la vita, scherno
Ogni virtude : in questi avelli or vive,
Qui solo, e in van, la patria nostra antiqua.

But his physical and mental health was from the first too strongly built to allow him to sit by the wayside weeping splendid tears, like Leopardi: he longs for action and calls for 'Guerra a' tedeschi, immensa eterna guerra'; a feeling which was not merely political but partly intellectual, an expression of his lifelong faith in the Latin and classical civilization of which the northern barbarians were the eternal enemies.

I must not dwell on these early poems which as I have said are of comparatively little permanent importance. They are chiefly interesting as showing how free Carducci was from both of the two opposite (or are they opposite ?) vices of youth : its coarseness and its gushing sentimentality. In youth as in age he is muscular, sane, clean, virile in manner and thought : and, immature as these *Juvenilia* are, they already have style and are the work of a scholar and an artist. Only the three elements of scholar, artist, and patriot are not yet fused, as they presently will be, into the poet. Did I speak of three elements ? There is a fourth more important than any of them. In the scholar, the artist, the patriot there is always visibly present a man. It is sometimes said that Carducci lacks heart. Even Mr. Bickersteth says of him such things as that he cannot be called a poet of the 'human soul' and that 'to repress all merely personal emotion was the end at which he aimed'. Both these remarks, even partly qualified as they are by their context, are in my judgement serious misrepresentations of the truth. It is quite true that Carducci had little of the religious and nothing at all of the philosophic habit of mind : and therefore made no attempt at using his poetry to utter the deepest searchings of the human spirit, still less to offer a solution of the ultimate problems which confront the human mind. He

was no Job, no Lucretius, no Dante, no Goethe : he was
entirely without the speculative curiosity of his contemporary Browning ; and though some of the poems of his old
age, waiting outside the dark portal, are curiously like those
which the old age of Tennyson was producing a few years
earlier, yet he had in him little or nothing of that continual
sense of a Mystery, unknown indeed but certainly Divine,
which was never many hours absent from the mind of Tennyson. But to admit this is only to admit that he was not one
of the great seers of poetry. It is not at all to admit either
that he had no heart or that he did not allow it to make itself
felt in his poetry. It is true that he made it his business from
the first to turn utterly away from the facile and gushing
emotionalism of the Romantics. He defiantly promised his
critics that they should never be able to accuse him of having
written poems with the object of showing what a fine fellow
he was. He did not wear his heart on his sleeve and once
even called it ' vil muscolo nocivo Alla grande arte pura '
But have we yet to learn that a fluent verbosity of sentiment
is no proof of heart ? Which moves us most in the Anthology,
the few words of Simonides or the many of Meleager ?
Which are the great moments in Shakespeare, the bursts of
exuberant rhetoric, or the brief sentences which utter a world
of emotion in three or four monosyllables ? So with Carducci. I do not envy the man who has read him without per-
ceiving that he has in him more heart than a whole tribe of
Rousseaus and Chateaubriands and Mussets. I say without
any doubt or hesitation that few poets have gone so deep
down into those secret places of the human heart where alone
we realize all the meaning that there may be in such words
as son and brother and father, home and country. The proof
is there for all of us to see. The grave and poignant beauty
of the poems about his little son Dante, whom he lost so
young, is a thing unforgettable : and except the brother of
Catullus I do not remember any brother whose memory lives
in such verse as Carducci gave, and more than once, to his.

Let me, then, insist that beside the scholar and artist and
patriot whom all can see in Carducci there is also, what has

not always been seen, a man of large and tender heart, who has again and again written verse which some of us find among the most moving we know. And let me try now to show how much poetry he has left us in which those various elements escape from their isolation.

To see that we must come to his mature work. I spoke briefly of the *Juvenilia* and *Levia Gravia*. I need say even less of the *Giambi ed Epodi* which follow. They are the product of Carducci's disillusion with the kingdom of Italy and what seemed to him its compromises and cowardices. In his earlier years he had addressed poems to Victor Emmanuel, calling him the champion for whom Italy was waiting and the son of a noble father ; and he was later on to return to loyal acceptance of the House of Savoy, addressing odes to Queen Margaret and making of Charles Albert the most human and moving of all his historical portraits. But poets have hardly ever understood that politics are, in the main, an art of awaiting opportunities and of accepting compromises ; and Cavour, who understood that so well, was hardly dead before Carducci was clamouring for action which might easily have strangled the infant Italy in its cradle. No doubt there was plenty of field for righteous scorn and hatred in the Italian politics of those days. But Carducci's angry impatience made journalism rather than poetry : the patriot feels only the happenings of the moment which are sufficient food for the journalist but never for the poet : and after the fine prologue with its note of

> Be through my lips to unawakened earth
> The trumpet of a prophecy

we do not get much from the *Giambi* but rhetoric, invective, and epigram. Two of these last give in a single phrase the political and literary impatience which is the essence of the book. There is the

> Impronta Italia domandava Roma,
> Bizanzio essi le han dato ;

and there are the two words, ' sublimi ammalati ', in which the *Intermezzo* sums up his old scorn of the Romantic poets. It is at the bottom the same faith in a sound mind and healthy body, the same scorn of weaklings and palterers, which is the inspiration of the famous, or notorious, *Hymn to Satan*. I cannot, of course, discuss it here from the point of view of religion. It gave, and no doubt was meant to give, great offence to Catholics : and indeed to all Christians : and still does : offence which in his later years Carducci regretted. We must admit that he was always definitely a pagan : and often, especially in the first half of his life, not merely a pagan but an anti-Christian. This attitude is seen at its height in the *Satan* though the title is, as we shall see, a misnomer. But to judge him or it fairly we must remember the time and place in which he wrote : an Italy which had long been ruled by priests who allied themselves with foreigners and tyrants, in which the Pope who had deserted the national cause still held Rome : in which one Pope had declared the steam-engine to be an invention of the devil and another was now replying to the spirit of the nineteenth century by getting himself declared Infallible. The Ode was written in one day in 1863, published in 1865, and again on the day of the opening of the Vatican Council. It is enough if it stood alone to disprove the notion of Carducci as a mere academic pedant. It splutters with fiery life from the first word to the last. But the Satan whom it proclaims and glorifies is not the spirit of evil ; there is no less immoral poet than Carducci. His Satan is reason and nature, the body and the mind, all that revolts against the asceticism, sacerdotalism and obscurantism which have so often claimed to represent the Christian religion. The *Hymn* is as full of imagination as it is of spontaneity, sincerity and strength. What it is not full of, either in thought or in language, is that grave music of the mind and of the word without which poetry cannot be entirely itself. When Shelley asks

> Why fear and dream and death and birth
> Cast on the daylight of this earth
> Such gloom

he asks, in part at least, what Carducci asks in *Satan* : but, by the side of Shelley's *Hymn*, Carducci's reads as little more than a piece of polemical journalism.

With the next section of the poems, *Rime Nuove*, of which the earliest are much earlier and the latest are much later than the *Giambi ed Epodi*, we reach the Carducci who is one of the poets of the whole world. There are still here many more or less commonplace exercises in verse, imitations and avowed translations : and there is still a little political invective of the journalistic order. I cannot but think that in the line he puts into Luther's mouth ' Pregar non posso senza maledire ' he is not thinking only of Luther ; the confession, and perhaps the repentance, are a little also his own. But in the finest of the *Rime Nuove*, all that was in Carducci, scholar, artist, historian, patriot, human being, are fused into a union in which memory and mind, heart and imagination, the sense of literature and the sense of life, all unite in something rarer than themselves, something which is great poetry. Take, first of all, the pieces in which the scholar and artist predominate. They are not all successes. I confess to finding the *Primavere elleniche* rather frigid : and of the three sonnets to Homer only the first seems to me quite worthy of so great a poet as Carducci. That one certainly has a magnificent close. There are no gods left on Olympus, it says ; and the sacred Scamander no longer flows in its old bed and Turkish towers insult its sea. But the world still bows in awe before the nod of Homer's Zeus and trembles before the wrath of Achilles :

> E trema, o vate, allor che d'omicide
> Furie raggiante lungo il nero Egeo
> Salta su'l carro il tuo divin Pelide.

But though Carducci was always returning to the Greeks and more than once declared that Greek poetry was the supreme poetry which had no equal, yet he was a Latin in heart and mind as well as in blood, and, as it is Horace who was the chief model of his verse, so it is Virgil who moved him to the noblest oi his poetic tributes. What a poet he must be who after two thousand years can still move two such poets as Tennyson and Carducci to two such poems as the lines to Virgil and this incomparable Sonnet ! I venture to give myself the pleasure of reading it !

Come, quando su' campi arsi la pia
Luna imminente il gelo estivo infonde,
Mormora al bianco lume il rio tra via
Riscintillando tra le brevi sponde ;

E il secreto usignuolo entro le fronde
Empie il vasto seren di melodia,
Ascolta il vïatore ed a le bionde
Chiome che amò ripensa, e il tempo oblia ;

Ed orba madre, che doleasi in vano,
Da un avel gli occhi al ciel lucente gira
E in quel diffuso albor l' animo queta ;

Ridono in tanto i monti e il mar lontano,
Tra i grandi arbor la fresca aura sospira ;
Tale il tuo verso a me, divin poeta.

What a world away from imitation and pedantry we are in these lovely lines in which art and nature and the heart of man all confess by the mouth of the modern Italian that they still find their perfect expression in the words of the Latin poet !

A very different poem, in which the scholar, this time the Italian and post-classical scholar, is seen, is the Ode to Rhyme which stands at the head of *Rime Nuove*. Like Milton, Carducci is chiefly known by poems in which he broke away ' from the troublesome and modern bondage of rhyming '. But, again like the denouncer of that bondage, he used rhyme in some of his loveliest poems ; and here, confessing himself a heretic, he yet brings a splendid offering to the temple of rhyme. *Alla Rima* is a thing of rushing verve and go, full at once of the learning and of the vigorous personality of Carducci. He shows how the troubadours by whom rhyme was carried all over Europe made it serve all the purposes for which they used poetry, and then how Dante called it to other tasks and made with it the first great poem of the post-classical world. And there he leaves it, queen, as he admits, of Latin metre :

Ave, o bella imperatrice,
O felice
Del latin metro reina !
Un ribelle ti saluta
Combattuta,
E a te libero s'inchina.

Poetry is the union of opposites, the solution of contradictions. As the poet of *Odi Barbare* pays his homage to rhyme, as the pedant is absorbed in the man, so it is curious to see that even the hater of the Romantics, the lifelong classic both by temper and education, could transcend these antitheses and write poems which are purely Romantic in temper. The four stanzas called *Pantheism* might well have come from Heine by whom he was much influenced at this time, though a hundred things, and chiefly health and daylight, kept him from ever becoming either the cynic or the sentimentalist, each of whom was a large part of Heine. ' I never uttered her name ; it echoed only in my silent heart : but the stars told my secret to each other and the setting sun whispered it to the moon, and birds and trees and flowers, nay, earth and heaven themselves, murmur all round me " She loves you, she loves you " '. And, if in the poem ' Classicism and Romanticism ' he puts all his weight into the scale of the sun which is his symbol of the Classical—the sun, the giver of corn and wine and spring and light and joy—and none into that of the Romantic moon whose milky languors bring neither flowers nor fruit and only flatter idle poets and empty loves, yet in the purely Romantic ' Moon's Revenge ' which follows, he actually makes of this same ' lewd and barren nun with the stupid face ' the giver to his mistress of all the beauty in which he desires to drown his soul. Who, again, has written a ballad fuller of medieval romance than the rhymed stanzas of *Jaufré Rudel*, which are to be found in his last volume ? So varied, so contradictory, so double-faced, such reconcilers of opposites, are even the most definitely doctrinal of poets ; as we may see in the fact that some of the most purely Romantic lines of English verse are to be found in Milton and some of the most entirely classical in Keats. Indeed in their happiest moments, all poets, the Classical as well as the Romantic, the Romantic as well as the Classical, transcend these distinctions, or exhibit the two moods at once. Carducci believed deliberately in severity of poetic form and all his best poems are marked by it. But how much of the temper which would generally be called Romantic there was in that lovely sonnet to Virgil which I read just now ! And if we look at the famous Sonnet, *Il Bove*, which precedes it, one of such extraordinary quality that it could hardly be excluded from any selection of the finest sonnets in the world, do we not find in it an almost miraculous combination of classical directness, simplicity and truth with a sentiment, a ' dolcezza ', to use its own word, which moves us as we are moved by the masters of Romance ? So, also, the two poems about his brother and his child are as simple as a Greek epitaph or a marble stele of Athens : yet Carducci's marble, like that of Greece, can take us very close to tears, perhaps beyond them. The Sonnet *Funere mersit acerbo* and the brief stanzas *Pianto Antico* are very well known to every one who has ever looked into Carducci. But I lay stress on them because, even if they stood alone, they would be a complete refutation of the notion which keeps many people from making trial of him ; the notion that he was never really stirred by anything more human than old books and contemporary politics. It is impossible to make a greater mistake. Carducci was a man of passionate nature and, if he put passion into his love of literature and his love of Italy, as he assuredly did, he had abundance left in him for the love of men and women and children. I said that in his best things various elements in him, the artist and the scholar and the patriot, were found united in the human being and expressed by the poet. And so they are here. The artist is in their beautiful form : the scholar, and perhaps the patriot too, in the thought of the supreme Italian poet whose name was borne both by his brother and his son ; and the human-hearted brother and father speaks to us from every word. I will read the *Funere Mersit Acerbo* :

> O tu che dormi là su la fiorita
> Collina tosca, e ti sta il padre a canto :
> Non hai tra l'erbe del sepolcro udita
> Pur ora una gentil voce di pianti ?
>
> È il fanciulletto mio, che a la romita
> Tua porta batte : ei che nel grande e santo
> Nome te rinnovava, anch' ei la vita
> Fugge, o fratel, che a te fu amara tanto.

Ahi no ! giocava per le pinte aiole,
E arriso pur di visïon leggiadre —
L'ombra l'avvolse, ed a le fredde e sole

Vostre rive lo spinse. Oh, giú ne l'adre
Sedi accoglilo tu, ché al dolce sole
Ei volge il capo ed a chiamar la madre.

And while I am insisting on the heart of Carducci let me
add that it is not only death that shows it to us. How many
poets have so often written about the marriages of those
whom they loved and with such evident personal feeling ?
Many have written *Epithalamia* for the marriages of great
personages to whose hopes and fears they were entirely indifferent, and sometimes the result has been a great poem.
But that was not Carducci's way. On these subjects at any
rate he wrote no verses into which he did not put his heart.
And what a collection of them, those poems of death and
marriage and home and friendship, he has left us ! If we
included only the very finest the list would not be a short
one : for, beside these two poems on his dead child and
brother which are only the finest of several, it must at the
least include the *Ave* of *Odi Barbare* and the Funeral of the
Alpine Guide in *Rime e Ritmi* : while to marriage he returned
again and again, always with the same grave tenderness, his
heart speaking in every word, from the two fine sonnets in
Levia Gravia, For a Marriage in Spring and *The Marriage
of a Geologist,* to the two beautiful *Odi Barbare* about his
daughter's marriage, *Colli Toscani* and *Per le Nozze di mia
figlia,* and the touching stanzas in *Rime e Ritmi* addressed to
the daughter of Crispi on her marriage. And the list would
have in it more than one showing his love of children, such
as the pretty little lines put at the head of *Rime e Ritmi* and
the poem called *Sabato Santo* written for the birthday of the
daughter of an old friend. And then there would be some
at least of the many poems in which he returned to his home
and his childhood and his first love : *Davanti San Guido* and
Idillio Maremmano, if nothing else ; and one or two at any
rate of the poems he gave to friendship which in him had a
Roman constancy and strength. Whatever else was omitted

the four stanzas of *Alla Mensa dell' Amico* would have to be included ; for, though others address particular friends with more open and personal affection, none has more of Carducci than this. All his worships are in it, not only friendship but the Sun God and the God of Wine : all his strong, and again partly Roman, feeling for the family, for him the greatest of all human institutions : and finally the grave and quiet tenderness, without fear, without revolt, without impatience, with which he always met the thought of death. I am well aware that translating poetry is a vain thing, of little advantage except to the translator : and indeed that the old Italian *traduttore traditore* has too much truth in it : yet reading foreign poetry which one pronounces imperfectly is so difficult a business even to a University audience that I will venture to offer you an attempt at rendering *Alla Mensa dell' Amico* which I made a good many years ago.

> O godlike sun, never all so bright
>   In the place where I was born
> Didst thou smile on me in my childhood's days
> As now when thou floodst with thy light the ways
>   Where I walk in wide Leghorn.
> O Bacchus, kindly friend and sage,
>   Never yet didst thou fill thy wine
> With such fire of spirit for me as here,
> Where I sit at the board of a friend long dear,
>   With my heart in the Apennine.
> Grant, Lord of Light, and Lord of Wine,
>   That we with hearts entire
> Down to the quiet shades below,
> Where Horace waits, with love may go,
>   With love and with the lyre.
> Yes, grant us rest, my friend and me ;
>   But to our lives' new flowers
> Grant hopes that shall grow bright with truth ;
> Peace to their mothers ; to our youth
>   Brave lives and crowded hours.

The genius of many poets, as we know, pales in middle life. The exact reverse of this is seen in Carducci. He published little of importance before he was thirty : of the *Odi Barbare*, by which he will always be chiefly remembered, the first did not appear till he was forty and the final series not till he was past fifty : and his last volume, which is as fine as *Odi Barbare* and much finer than any of its predecessors, appeared in 1899 when he was sixty-two. That long scholarly life spent in a Professor's Chair at Bologna had in no way dulled his fire or dried his heart. It had made him wiser and gentler and less of a partisan : but he never loved Italy more, or showed his love more passionately, than in those later years ; and his love of the great dead, who were to him so alive, his love of Nature, of Man, of all the wonder, mystery and tenderness of life, is seen at its height in his last two volumes. For any one who wishes to read a little of Carducci and has no time to attempt the whole there is no question that these two small volumes are the things to be recommended. No doubt such a reader will miss a few wonderful things, especially the Sonnets of which I have spoken. But they are not much more than a few : and whoever has read *Odi Barbare* and *Rime e Ritmi* knows Carducci and knowing him will probably not be content with two only of his books. There is a special reason too why these two volumes are the best to be read. The scholarship of literature is nothing if it does not teach the man who gives himself to it the gulf which separates the only perfect word from the many imperfect. Carducci was learning that all his life. In his later poems, very much more than in his earlier, one continually feels that he has not been content to let his pen touch his paper until he has found the one word which will give all he wants to give of meaning and association and music. So with the artist. Carducci loved form and he loved it more and more as he grew older. Only a few times in these last volumes—perhaps in *Bicocca di San Giacomo*, perhaps in the Ode to Ferrara—does he allow the garrulity of age to ignore the first rule of art, that the half is greater than the whole. He had shown in his early volumes more than enough of the exuberant rhetoric of youth. Now he almost always compresses his thought and emotion into a mould of sculpturesque severity. It was no mere whim of classical scholarship that made him rewrite the Alcaics and Sapphics and Asclepiads of Horace on a system of his own.

He chose very definite forms for his verse because he thought poetry gained by strictness and was weakened by looseness of structure. He put at the head of his *Odi Barbare* some elegiacs of Platen's which declare that for a muddle of bungled verses any subject will serve : but for fine form only a great theme will do. Many poets have professed the faith that

> l'œuvre sort plus belle
> D'une forme au travail
> Rebelle.

But Carducci really believed it and exhibited its truth in himself. There can be no question that his later work, almost all in one or another form which resists the poet and make his task a difficult one, is not merely finer art but richer stuff than his earlier. All his subjects have grown larger. His politics are not less Italian, less actual and contemporary : but now they are put into the presence of history without which politics cannot make literature. He is still himself in every poem. But the self that is felt in them is now, what it was not always, at once himself and all the world. He has in fact risen to the full stature of a poet ; who is at once more of an individual than other men, more arresting, singular, and solitary, and also more representative of the whole of humanity, abler to think and feel for all men, abler to say what, when it has been said, they all recognize as their own.

One might roughly divide the contents of these last volumes into poems of nature, poems of politics and history, and poems of the human affections. I will say a word of each. Carducci's attitude to nature is like his attitude to life, simple and direct. He has no philosophy here or elsewhere. Like our own Landor with whom he had many points of resemblance, he disliked all speculative inquiries : and though he really believed as strongly as Wordsworth that men are made what they are by their natural surroundings, yet he would never have written a *Prelude* or an *Excursion* on the philosophy of the unity between Nature and Man. His faith in Italy and her people was built partly on the memory of the great Italians of the past and partly on the two seas of Italy and the lakes, rivers and mountains among which Italians live. Such a people, he thought, with such a past and so lovely a land to inspire them, must have a future too. Wordsworth would have agreed with every word of that. But that was only a part of Wordsworth's faith : and when he said such things as

> Winds blow and waters roll
> Strength to the brave and Power and Deity

part of his meaning was a mysticism which was outside Carducci's ken. Carducci did not ask what was behind Nature. He was content with her as a visible presence of beauty and delight, and as the giver of good things to men, especially of bread, the strength of man's labour, and wine, the joy of his rest. As woman was for him, not, as for the Romantics, a dream of sensuous or sentimental beauty, but always a power of life as daughter, wife, or mother, often too as worker in the fields, so his Nature was not a vision but an energy of life, perpetually inheriting, and perpetually using its inheritance for new creation. To this conception of a working and beneficent Nature, which has its parallel in our own Meredith, he continually returns. The *Georgics* were never far away from his mind, and when he makes his salutation to Italy at the end of that Ode to the Springs of Clitumnus which some have thought his finest poem it is as mother of oxen and horses, corn and vines, as well as of arts and laws, that he hails her :

> E tu, pia madre di giovenchi invitti
> a franger glebe e rintegrar maggesi
> e d'annitrenti in guerra aspri polledri,
> Italia madre,
>
> madre di biade e viti e leggi eterne
> ed inclite arti a raddolcir la vita,
> salve ! a te i canti de l'antica lode
> io rinnovello.

This realism of Carducci's was at once an instinct and a doctrine. 'Away with metaphysics' he said : 'let us poets get back to nature and reason and reality : let us return to the ancients who are at once realistic and free.'

But his realism was no mere utilitarianism. He saw the things of nature as they are, as few men see them : and loved the sight and could render it in verse with extraordinary exactness and vividness. There is more than one wonderful picture of snow in poetry : but is there any, even that of Mr. Bridges, which more makes us feel as if we were ourselves in it than the *Nevicata* of Carducci, his only and not too successful experiment in the accentual hexameter ? It is done in quite a different way from *London Snow*, with far less detail and with a greater insistence, natural to an Italian, on the silence and gloom of snowfall. But I find myself almost equally conscious of the snow in both poems. And everywhere Carducci's poems are sown with little pictures of particular scenes, or seasons of the year, of a wonderful clearness of beauty. One feels oneself on the Italian Alps as one reads *Piemonte* ; when one reads *Mezzo Giorno* one is as conscious of a southern noon as one is when reading the *Midi* Stanzas of Leconte de Lisle. And though Carducci will never put a philosophy into his landscapes he will often put himself. How many poems of Spring are either lovelier or tenderer than his *Primavera* ? It is more fanciful than he commonly is. But how well the fancy is fitted into the facts, how exactly the epithets chosen at once help out the fancy and express the facts ! And, simple as all the words are, how hard it would be to change one without injuring the poem ! Like all Carducci's later work these four short stanzas are a lesson in the art of expression.

> Ecco : di braccio al pigro verno sciogliesi
> ed ancor trema nuda al rigid' aere
> la primavera : il sol tra le sue lacrime
> limpido brilla, o Lalage.
>
> Da lor culle di neve i fior si svegliano
> e curïosi al ciel gli occhietti levano :
> in quelli sguardi vagola una tremula
> ombra di sogno, o Lalage.
>
> Nel sonno de l'inverno sotto il candido
> lenzuolo de la neve i fior sognarono ;
> sognaron l'albe roride ed i tepidi
> soli e il tuo viso, o Lalage.

Ne l'addormito spirito che sognano
i miei pensieri ? A tua bellezza candida
perchè mesta sorride tra le lacrime
la primavera, o Lalage !

There may be some here who do not follow the Italian. I
ask the pardon of those who do for adding a translation of
my own :

Behold from sluggish winter's arm
  Spring lifts herself again :
Naked before the steel-cold air
  She shivers as in pain ;
Look, Lalage, is that a tear
  In the sun's eye which yet shines clear ?

From beds of snow the flowers awake
  Lifting in deep amaze
To heaven their eager eyes : but yet
  More in that wistful gaze
Than wonder lies : sure trembles there
  O Lalage, some memory fair,

Some dream which 'neath the coverlet white
  Of winter snow they dreamed,
Some sleeping sight of dewy dawns
  And summer suns that gleamed,
And thy bright eyes, O Lalage ;
  Was not the dream a prophecy ?

To-day my spirit sleeps and dreams ;
  Where do my far thoughts fly ?
Close to thy beauty's face we stand
  And smile, the spring and I ;
Yet, Lalage, whence come those tears ?
  Has spring, too, felt the doom of years ?

These Lalages and Lydias whom Carducci occasionally intro-
duces are of course only Horatian shadows. But he will often
connect his landscapes with historical figures, Dante or
Titian, the Emperor Maximilian or Charles Albert, Garibaldi
or Cairoli or Calvi. And sometimes with figures belonging to
his own private affections like the Maria of the *Idillio Maremmano*, his first love whom he half enviously pictures on some
farm with stalwart sons around her ; like his summer
hostess of the Inn at Gaby : or again like his daughter for

whom in *Colli Toscani* he prays to the beautiful hills which he once knew and loved so well to give her the happiness they had denied to him and to whisper to her no word of her near ones whom she never knew, who lived there in sorrow and died in despair, and may be greeting her, perhaps even awaiting her, in their graves.

> Colli, tacete, e voi non susurratele, olivi,
> non dirle, o sol, per anche, tu onniveggente, pio,
> ch' oltre quel monte giaccion, lei forse aspettando, que' miei,
> che visser tristi, che in dolor morirono.

I have left to the last those historical and political odes which are unquestionably the most original work of Carducci. There is nothing quite like them anywhere so far as I know. The passion for history had been a feature of the Romantic movement. Carducci took history out of the hands of the Romantics and made it the chief subject of poems of classical form and classical temper. What the Romantics had often made an amusement or an embroidery or a languishing sigh over a shadowy and often imaginary past became in Carducci's hands a fountain of moral energy and political life. Hating the dilettantism which was so common among Romantics, he took care to know every inch of the ground over which he travelled ; and the great figures of his historical odes have the substance and solidity of truth. But of course truth of history will not alone make poetry, and too much truth in the shape of too many facts may easily, as sometimes in Carducci himself, stifle poetry in information. But there is no mere history in the best of Carducci's Odes. The facts and personages are selected : Carducci was never one of those poets who think that all subjects are equally suitable for poetry. He knew the immense advantage with which a poet starts who has chosen for his theme, as he chose, such figures as Maximilian or Charles Albert or the mother of Napoleon. And more than that ; even in these selected subjects he never confined himself to history. In his most historical poems there are always present two things which are not history, or were not then, himself and the Italy in which he lived. History was for him, in no meagre or pedan-

tic sense, a living lesson : and as Horace when he wrote of
Regulus thought of the Rome of Augustus, so when Carducci
wrote of the Rock of Quarto he thought not only of Garibaldi's Thousand but of those who had so soon forgotten
them and the cause for which they had set out into the unknown that wonderful night. His Odes are no page of dead
history ; they are chapters in the life of a poet and a nation,
and both speak through every burning word of them, the
poet in his own voice and as he really was, Italy, as she was
not always, in the voice the poet gave her.

As I said before, I know nothing quite like them. People
of wider reading could probably suggest nearer parallels ;
but the two poets who seem to me to exhibit some striking
points of likeness, as no doubt also of unlikeness, with this
side of Carducci are Pindar and our own Walter Scott. Scott
loved the Christian Middle Ages which, except for Dante,
Carducci detested and despised. Scott carried the Romanticism which Carducci hated in triumphant progress over
Europe. But though in one sense the greatest of the Romantics, Scott had nothing in him of the things which Carducci
most disliked in Romanticism. He was the very sanest and
healthiest of men. His was not that ' Romance with the
death-rattle in her throat ' of which Landor made Hume
speak before its time. And in Carducci's bitter sentence, ' il
Manzoni trae la gente in sacrestia, il Byron in galera, il
Leopardi al ospedale ', it would not have been easy to make
room for Scott. He never idealized either the criminal or the
sickly : and as to sending people to the sacristy, if his
medievalism had its share in the Oxford Movement, he himself was always a common-sense Protestant equally free from
pietism and sacerdotalism. Still Scott was as definitely a
Christian as Carducci was definitely a Pagan ; and the one
was as little, as the other was much, of a scholar. But these
differences are not my point, which can be put in this question : are there any other imaginative writers who have been
so continuously inspired by the history of their own country
as Scott and Carducci ? Everything Scott wrote is inspired
by the history of Scotland except what is inspired by that of

England, which he regarded as almost equally his own. So, if a book were made containing all the best poems of Carducci and no others, there would hardly be one in which you were not conscious of the presence of Italy. That is the parallel in which perhaps no third poet has anything like an equal share. Scott is as full or fuller of legend than of history : his verse is half ballad, half epic, instead of ode : the history of Scotland compared with that of Italy is brief, petty, and obscure. Scott's writing is fluent and careless, as unlike as writing can be to the scholarly if sometimes laboured art of Carducci. I think Carducci clearly a greater poet, though a so much smaller man of letters. But there remains the significant likeness. In no one else as in these two, in no other poets, masters of the imagination, call them what you will, has the love of a country, its past, its people, its natural features, played so decisive and continuous a part as it played in Scott and in Carducci.

I ventured just now on a bolder comparison, one very dangerous to risk in this place of learning. I spoke of Pindar. Here again the differences impose themselves on us at once. If Scott as a poet is less than Carducci, it is plain that Pindar is immeasurably greater. If Carducci excels Scott both in seriousness of mind and in the conscience and achievement of his art, it is plain that he cannot approach Pindar in either. And it would be easy to enumerate other differences. But here again there is, I suggest, a real parallel. In Pindar's day the distinction between history and legend, between the actions of warriors or patriots and those of gods, was not very clearly defined. Pindar took the legends which for the Greece of his time stood in the place of history, and out of them, with what little actual history was then coming into being, made the most splendid odes the world possesses. The Greece of his day, its present and still more its past, went into his odes as the Italy of the nineteenth and all previous centuries went into Carducci's. Pindar used the victory of some boxer or charioteer as a path to greater victories of another order, to Himera, or Cumae, or Salamis ; or as an excuse to travel back to the wonders or glories of the past. Carducci was not forced to occupy himself with boxers. But he used the same method. Both poets ennobled and glorified the present by setting it in the light of the past. Pindar, of course, does this on a far more magnificent scale than Carducci and in a language and manner which have been the wonder and despair of poets ever since. But it is essentially the same thing which he does ; indeed in some respects the difference is all in Carducci's favour. The death of Maximilian, the death of the young Napoleon, are far happier starting-points for a poem than the unimportant achievements of some youthful athlete. Carducci can dwell at length on his primary subject and put his heart and mind into it : whereas we can often almost hear the relief with which Pindar makes his escape to his ancestral legend or divine myth. And another and kindred advantage of the modern poet is that the transition from Maximilian to Montezuma and Huitzilopotli, or from the Prince Imperial to the ' Niobe of Corsica ', is obvious and natural while the connexion between, say, the victory of Arkesilaos and the tale of the Argonauts may invite pages of not always convincing commentary. The fact remains that what Pindar did for Greece Carducci, on a much smaller scale and with much smaller powers, did in a not very dissimilar way for Italy.

There are a good many of these historical odes, as everybody who has looked at Carducci knows. It would be difficult to say which are the finest. But at least six, those to Rome, to the Springs of Clitumnus, on the death of the Prince Imperial, *Miramar, Piemonte*, and *La Chiesa di Polenta*, must certainly, I think, rank among the very finest examples in all the world of what poetry can do with history. Many would add to this list the ode to the statue of Victory at Brescia, that on the River Adda, the two Garibaldi Odes, that called the Rock of Quarto and that written after Garibaldi's death, or those to Cadore and Ferrara and that called *Bicocca di San Giacomo*. But the Garibaldi poems, marvellous as is the vividness of their pictures of the hero himself and of the scenes of his embarking at Quarto and of his retreat after Mentana, are not entirely characteristic of Carducci's manner

in these odes ; for the present in them hardly takes us back
to the past at all.   They are rather contemporary than
historical.   There are some again, like the Victory Ode, in which
the range is much narrower than in the great odes, while in
others, notably in the *Bicocca*, poetry tends to be drowned
in a sea of obscure details of history and geography.   A Carduccian will find in all of them, and in others which I have
not mentioned, things to delight in, things to stop and read
aloud again and again till all the pleasure of art and thought
and imagination has been got out of them.   But I would not
advise any one to expect that reading the *Bicocca* and *Ferrara*
odes will make him a Carduccian if he is not one already : for
there is no doubt at all that they are long, and not much that
they are in parts both obscure and tedious.

I will give my last minutes to saying a few words about the
great six, with a final word about what seems to me the
essence of the poetic genius of Carducci.

The first of my six is the ode written in 1877 to celebrate
the 2630th year of Rome.   Other odes of Carducci's may
have more imagination ; none equals this in passionate concentration.   It begins with the contrast between the Rome
of Romulus looking out on wood and wilderness, and the
Rome of to-day, the capital of the Italian race.   It is a small
point, but I always wish I could find in the first line a various
reading of ' redimita ', in the feminine, agreeing with Rome,
instead of the ' redimito ' of the text, agreeing with April.
It seems to me that ' redimita ' would make a much better
point with its contrast between the hills once crowned with
flowers and now, ' dopo tanta forza di secoli,' crowned with
monuments and memories which are the greatest in all the
world.   However, all the editions I have seen read ' redimito ' ; so evidently Carducci judged otherwise.   The ode
goes on to the opposite contrast, that between the Forum of
consuls and triumphs and the silent and solitary Forum of
to-day.   And the poet takes the opportunity, after his
wont, to work in some famous ancient words and make
them no longer Latin but Italian, no more Virgil's but
his own.

Se al Campidoglio non piú la vergine
tacita sale dietro al pontefice
né piú per Via Sacra il trionfo
piega i quattro candidi cavalli,

questa del Foro tuo solitudine
ogni rumore vince, ogni gloria :
e tutto che al mondo è civile,
grande, augusto, egli è romano ancora.

The proud boast, that all that is humane and all that is
great in the world is Roman still, leads to a rebuke of certain
Germans, notably Mommsen, who had spoken disparagingly
of Latin civilization :

Salve, dea Roma ! chi disconosceti
cerchiato ha il senno di fredda tenebra,
e a lui nel cuore germoglia
torpida la selva di barbarie.

And so, after several more stanzas of passionate pride and
devotion, he ends with a final contrast between old and new
as he looks at the

Columns and arches now to see
   Triumphs, no more of kings, go by ;
No more Caesars in ivory cars,
   Chains and slaves and cruelty.
Now a people's triumphs shall lead
   Captive all dark things and base ;
Now from ancient powers of ill
   Justice frees the human race.
O Italy ! O Rome ! that day
   Thunders of heaven shall sound on high
O'er thy hills : and glory's voice
   Fill the blue Infinity.

At Rome, at any rate, the fame of Carducci and of this
ode should be as eternal as that of the very City herself.

The ode to the Springs of Clitumnus, equally Roman in
spirit, is very much longer, is in Sapphics instead of Alcaics,
and is besides in rather a different poetic manner. It was
conceived on the spot in 1876, a year earlier than the Roman
Ode. It contains far more historical detail and begins with
one of those landscape scenes, with nature and man and the
animals all playing their parts, in which Carducci has few

poetic rivals. Very likely it is founded on something he saw
when he went there. The flocks still come to the ancient
springs : and the Umbrian boy still plunges the shrinking
sheep into the stream while his sunburnt and barefoot
mother sits singing by her cottage door and the chubby baby
at her breast throws his big brother a smile ; while close by
is the father, clothed in goatskin like a faun, driving his
painted plough and his team of the famous oxen, strong and
beautiful in all the beauty of their massive breasts, of the
horned crescents above their foreheads, of their snow-white
skins and those wistful eyes which the gentle Virgil loved !
From this incomparable picture of the present which is also
the past, he goes back to the beginning, to the past which is
lost in obscurity : the original Umbria and its native gods,
its woods of ilex and ivy and cypress. And so we see the
Umbrian surrendering to the Etruscan and the Etruscan to
the Roman, and conquerors and conquered uniting to resist
the Carthaginian : the disaster of Trasimene, the victory of
Spoleto, and all the crowd and noise of both, where now all is
once more so silent, as the poet sits alone among the mountains, valleys and streams which he declares to be the source
and life of Italian poetry. And so remembering that the
oxen of Clitumnus were once the chosen victims for Roman
triumphs, he laments that Rome triumphs no more since the
native nymphs fled before Christian monks, who took men
from their fathers and their wives and their ploughs, and
made them renounce all the works of life and love. But, the
ode ends, the dark days are gone : Italy is again the mother
of corn and wine and human laws : and the dirges of monks
are replaced by the whistle of the engine with its promise of
new conquests of the earth.

An abstract of this sort can of course give little idea of the
poem. It only serves to indicate something of the ground the
ode covers, and of its varying moods, at once more realistic,
more sentimental (if that were a word one dare ever use of
Carducci), more historical and more controversial than the
Ode to Rome. Many think this Carducci's finest poem : no
wonder that an inscription has been placed near the fountain
with his name upon it.

The third of my six is the ode on the death of the Prince Imperial, killed by Zulus in Africa in 1879. Here we get a feature of the Carduccian ode which neither of the two of which I have been speaking exhibit ; and that is the contemporary or historical portrait. The ode begins with the sons of the two Napoleons, both dying so young, so far from the thrones they had been destined to fill, so far from the mothers who bore them. And then we go on to the mother of the race, Letizia Buonaparte, the ' Corsican Niobe ', who is the most imaginative creation, though not the most moving, in the work of Carducci. Her spirit haunts the empty home : she had never cared to wear a crown : she dwells among the old tombs and altars, and there she waits. Her children all lie far away from her : the son of fate with the eagle eyes, the daughters radiant like the dawn, the sons breathing dreams of hope ; and now she stretches out her arms across the wild seas, demanding whether from America, from England, from Africa, death will yet send home to her breast any of her tragic race. Poetry, outside the greatest dramas, has not many figures of more tragic power than this of the Letizia whose name of joy has, as Carducci says, through her become for ever a name of sorrow.

The fourth ode is *Miramar*, and takes its name from the castle at the top of the Adriatic from which Maximilian and his wife sailed to the fatal throne of Mexico. Carducci is a moralist who never preaches and has only one doctrine, that ancient one of the connexion between sin and suffering of which the Hebrew prophets are so full, which Aeschylus, I suppose, first gave to our Graeco-Roman world. As the burden of the Napoleon ode, more felt than uttered, is that the crimes of the two Emperors find their inevitable fate in the deaths of their innocent heirs and the ruin of their house : so here, in *Miramar*, the old sins of the Hapsburgs, especially the crimes they and their agents committed in Mexico, are seen paying their long delayed penalty in the miserable adventure which cost Maximilian his life and his Empress her reason. The Ode begins with a sinister landscape of Miramare and the gulf of Trieste. And yet how fair it all looked that April morning.

Deh come tutto sorridea quel dolce
mattin d'aprile, quando usciva il biondo
imperatore, con la bella donna,
          a navigare.

Dante and Goethe, whose portraits hung in Maximilian's study, warn him in vain : he leaves the book of old stories open on his table : an evil destiny, the Sphinx of Empire, entices him across the seas to a fate out of which no tales of love or knighthood will ever be made. Dirges sound around the ship as it sails away : and the beckoning sphinx takes in turn all shapes of horror ; the white face of mad Joanna, the murdered head of Marie Antoinette, the yellow cheeks and hollow eyes of Montezuma. And as they draw near the coast of Mexico the Mexican war-god is there on his pyramid, breathing flame through the dark woods of aloe, and scenting the young blood for which he has thirsted so long. ' Come, heir of Charles the Fifth,' he says ; ' thy ancestors, vile in heart, diseased in body, were not the victims for me : thee I desired, for thee I waited, thee I take, my offering to the mighty soul of Guatimozino, O flower of the race of Hapsburg, Maximilian, beautiful, and brave, and pure.'

I spoke just now of the gulf which separates an analysis from a poem. But analysis of this sort has a better excuse for itself when applied to Carducci than to most poets. For he had the ancient belief in action, not any action but a chosen, designed and formed action, as the proper subject of poetry. So that the historical or biographical facts which, reshaped by imagination, form the scheme of a Carduccian ode, are of primary importance for the understanding of his mind and art. And as they lend themselves to analysis, as the components of a purely psychological or emotional poem do not, it can give us, however imperfectly done, more of Carducci than of many poets. I hope that what I have given of *Miramar* may have been enough to suggest at least some faint idea of its intensity of daring imagination : more than enough to show how absurd it is to think of this passionate poet, breathing fire into the dark places of human story, as a cold pedant making imitative exercises in his study.

My two last odes are to be found in *Rime e Ritmi*. The

first is *Piemonte* which begins rather heavily, or at least rather geographically, with nine stanzas of the praises of the various cities of Piedmont. It is not till we get to the tenth that Asti gives us Alfieri whose name always set Carducci on fire, being, as he once said, that of the most Italian of all Italians except Dante and Machiavelli. With him the real poem begins ; Alfieri calling to Italy, Dante and Petrarch echoing his call, and the great dead arising to demand war for the deliverance of Italy. The rest of the ode is Charles Albert, the

> re a la morte nel pallor del viso
> sacro e nel cuore,

the Italian Hamlet, with the sword in his hand and the Christian's hair shirt on his breast. It was once said of him that he fought as a hero, lived as a monk, and died as a martyr ; and he is, I think, certainly the most moving, though perhaps not the grandest, figure in Carducci's gallery of historical portraits. The poet's own memory looks back to the first victory of Italy, the fall of Peschiera, and the first cries of ' Viva il re d' Italia ! ' The Lombard plain, that evening, was blazing in the sunset and Virgil's lake lay quivering like a bride's veil opening to the kiss of plighted love. But the pale king sat motionless on his saddle : his eyes saw the distant shadow of the Trocadero, where he had fought against freedom. And, indeed, Novara was close upon him, and abdication, and then the soon-following end at the villa far away on the Douro. Carducci never conceived anything more beautiful than the last part of this ode with its wonderful vision of the martyred heroes of Italy descending to the bedside of the dying king who had persecuted so many of them, who had sinned so against Italy, and yet had tried to serve her ; who now gave a smile of pride and joy to the news of Garibaldi's defence of Rome. The spirits conduct his soul to heaven :

> E tutti insieme a Dio scortaron l' alma
> di Carlo Alberto.—Eccoti il re, Signore,
> che ne disperse, il re che ne percosse.
>   Ora, o Signore,

Anch' egli è morto, come noi morimmo,
Dio, per l' Italia. Rendine la patria.
A i morti, a i vivi, pe'l fumante sangue
           da tutti i campi,

per il dolore che le regge agguaglia
a le capanne, per la gloria, Dio,
che fu ne gli anni, pe'l martirio, Dio,
           che è ne l' ora,

a quella polve eroica fremente,
a questa luce angelica esultante
rendi la patria, Dio ; rendi l' Italia
           a gl' Italiani.

Carducci had praised Charles Albert in his early days and called Victor Emmanuel the Caesar who was to save Italy ; but in disappointment at the first results of half-achieved unity, he had turned in bitterness against the Monarchy and the House of Savoy.   Then he changed once more : the grace and kindness of Queen Margaret helped the ' mitis sapientia ' which crowns all healthy old age to judge the royal House more fairly : and he wrote two odes to the Queen and this noble tribute to Charles Albert, the king, as he says, of his young years, whom he once could not name without blasphemies and groans.   The truth is, he was no ungenerous foe.   No one, for instance, ever hated Austria more than he : but the House of Hapsburg cannot have received many tributes of sympathy more moving than his *Miramar* and his poem on the murder of the Empress Elizabeth.

The last of my six is *La Chiesa di Polenta* which Carducci himself is said to have thought his finest.   It was written in 1897 as his contribution to the effort made at the end of the last century to restore the little church of Polenta, not far from Ravenna, whose walls may have held Dante worshipping within them, and may have looked down on his Francesca in her childhood playing outside.   It begins with them and with Carducci's anti-feudal joy that what remains of the old castle of Francesca's fathers is now the home of industrious peasants.   It goes on to a picture of the darker, earlier ages when the barbarians overran Italy, when Rome was forgotten and Gothic saints and devils replaced the fair forms of classical sculpture.   Ruin and misery were everywhere : nothing was left to the people but the church, at once their country and their home and their tomb. And then the conquerors are converted and come there too, and the great Gregory remakes the beginning of a new Italy and a new freedom. And so the poet turns from history to salute the little church :

> Salve, chiesetta del mio canto :

and bids Italy, born once more, to give back to it the voice of prayer and to let its bell once more sound *Ave Maria* from hill to hill. And as the humble folk uncover at the sound they will not be alone : Dante and Byron and a host of spirits will be with them.

> Una di flauti lenta melodia
> passa invisibil fra la terra e il cielo,
> spiriti forse che furon, che sono
> e che saranno ?
> un oblio lene de la faticosa
> vita, un pensoso sospirar quïete,
> una soave volontà di pianto
> l'anime invade.
> Taccion le fiere, e gli uomini e le cose,
> roseo 'l tramonto ne l' azzurro sfuma,
> mormoran gli alti vertici ondeggianti
> Ave Maria.

A call to prayer and to the *Ave Maria* issued by the writer of the *Hymn to Satan* could not but arouse surprise. There were rumours that Carducci was about to make his peace with the Church. But some stanzas of the ode itself were enough to refute that hope or fear. There had been a change. Carducci could not have written his *Satan* in his old age : he could now understand, and more than understand, he could respect and sympathize with, beliefs which he did not hold. In 1905 he wrote, for publication, a letter admitting that, even so late as in the Clitumnus Ode, he had allowed himself to be carried away by the ' Roman Spirit ' which was so strong in him, and had been led by it to say things about Christianity which he now regretted. The Polenta Ode may be said to complete him. It shows how entirely he had outgrown the poet of faction, negation, and con-troversy who was so large a part of him in his youth.

My object to-day has been to speak, as when speaking of poets one always ought, of what is great and permanent in the work of Carducci. I have said little or nothing of his metrical system of which so much has been written. The question of importance seems to me to be, not what its relations were to other systems, ancient or modern, but whether Carducci has been able to use it with power and make with it a living poetry, a poetry which affects our minds and imaginations as only living poetry can. I have made it clear that I think he has. No doubt much of his work, and the finest, demands a capacity for being stirred by history, and even by politics, which not everybody possesses. Nor, perhaps, will any one fully appreciate Carducci who does not take exceptional pleasure in the form of verse and in the fitness and felicity of language. But, for my part, I cannot think it a small thing that it can be said of him, as Mr. Bickersteth has said, I think with truth : ' probably no poet that ever lived has composed so few slipshod lines or written his own language with greater purity of diction '. And it seems to me a still greater thing that, in the words of another critic, ' Carducci has solved the problem which baffled the Renaissance, of linking strength of thought to artifice of form.' But it has been my object to insist that strength of thought and perfection of form are far from being the whole of what he brought to his verse. He himself in the fine *Congedo* of *Rime Nuove* compares the poet to a smith, shaping on his burning forge love as well as thought, memories and glories, past and present, and all the emotions they arouse, till he has made he knows not what ; only when it is done he looks upon it and is glad and asks no more.

The smith does not always succeed nor does the poet : each is clumsy sometimes and each sometimes finds his metal too hard to shape. What I have wished to say to-day is that Carducci succeeded often, and that when he succeeded it was with such materials, so finely worked, that his place among the poets is assured and immortal.

PAUL VALÉRY

BY

The Right Hon. H. A. L. FISHER

The Taylorian Lecture, 1927

Mais Degas, ce n'est pas avec des idées qu'on fait des vers, c'est avec des mots.

MALLARMÉ.

Mes vers ont été surtout pour moi des exercices.

VALÉRY.

PAUL VALÉRY

IN that year of the Great War which was marked by the success of the Russian Revolution and by formidable mutinies in the French Army, Paris exhibited two manifestations of literary interest which were in singular contrast to the poignant anxieties of the time. The first was the issue of a complete collection of the works of Baudelaire to celebrate the fiftieth anniversary of that poet's death. The second was the appearance of two short lyrical pieces from the pen of an almost unknown writer which seemed to announce an unusual talent with new and challenging melodies at its command. Save for their titles there was nothing familiar either about the manner or the matter of the two poems which appeared in 1917 over the signature of Paul Valéry. They seemed to be brought out of the hidden places of some remote and brooding nature, not only untouched by the patriotic preoccupations of that terrible year, but so austerely intellectual as to refuse enjoyment from the visible glories of nature herself. Both poems were intricate and difficult of comprehension. To earnest inquiries the author with a smile vouchsafed the information that *La Jeune Parque* was a *cours de physiologie*, seeing that it portrays a series of psychological changes which affect a human consciousness in the course of a night. The other poem, *L'Aurore*, is less ambiguous in its message and may with reasonable probability be described as a picture, true as the exigencies of a delicate lyrical metre may allow, of the psycho-physical processes of sleep and awakening. It will be admitted that as themes for the poet neither physiology nor psycho-physics is *prima facie* alluring. Lucretius, however, and later Dante, had succeeded with matter hardly less tractable, but then neither Lucretius nor Dante was French. The French genius, so essentially rhetorical, had shrunk from the marriage of science and verse. 'Our poetry', writes M. Valéry, 'ignores or even fears all the epic and pathetic of the intellect. . . . We have not among us the poets of knowledge.' The time had come to fill that gap.

Valéry was born in 1871, and was therefore in his forty-seventh year when he thus succeeded in attracting notice as a poet. His literary work had been hitherto so slight and casual that it would seem as if he hardly cared to win a name as a man of letters. In early youth he had been a fervent disciple of Mallarmé, and had published a few stray lyrics in the musical and apocalyptic vein of the master, choosing generally with a shy and wayward arrogance as his medium of publicity some ephemeral sheet struck off for a small coterie of exquisites, so that to have read a line of Valéry was in itself an achievement and the mark of an initiate in the school of symbolism. Thus for seven years he proceeded, decanting a slender and intermittent trickle of imitative music into vessels of the frailest porcelain.

Then in 1897, to quote from the poet's own words, 'a profound modification came over me. What modification? I cannot define it. It was perhaps due to a kind of substitution in the predominant hereditary functions.' Whatever may have been the cause, the trickle of poetry was arrested and at the age of twenty-six, when it might have been expected that his genius would begin to burst into flower, M. Valéry lapsed into a silence which was unbroken for twenty years. The friend of Henley and Meredith, of Huysmans and Heredia, had changed his allegiance from poetry to mathematics.

It is then as a symbolic poet turned mathematician, and with a mind equally alive to the delicacies of prosody and to the procedure of the most abstract branch of exact knowledge, that Valéry made his reappearance as an author. But while the passage of years had given him a new angle of vision and a more serious concentration of purpose, they had refused him any share of Ovidian fluency. It is not in M. Valéry's nature to be fluent. Verses do not come easily to him. He could never say:

> Sponte sua numeros carmen veniebat ad aptos;
> Et quod temptabam dicere versus erat.

He writes with difficulty, and it is part of his creed as a man of letters that the only writing worth having is the product of arduous and tortured labour applied to the deep-

est themes. It is not therefore surprising that his output
is slight.

The harvest of ten years could be easily garnered into two
volumes. There is a volume of his earlier verses (*Album de
Vers anciens*), a smaller collection of later poetry entitled
Les Charmes, published in 1922, there are two Platonic dialogues, some aphorisms and prose sketches and reported con-
versations. Save for one prose fragment suggested by the
war and characteristically unfinished, there is no sign that
any part of his activity is determined by the practical aims
of contemporary politics. The things that interest him are
the theory of the arts and the processes of his own thinking.
What is dancing, what is architecture, whence and how spring
the sudden, unexplained revelations which come to the poetic
mind, giving to it the phrase, the melody, the thought, the
image, which had lurked unsuspected in the hidden regions
and then swiftly, and as it were in a movement of caprice,
emerge above the threshold of consciousness, and flood the
soul with their convincing aptness and beauty? As he conceives the business of the poet, it is not to paint the outward
face of nature or the visible spectacle of human events, but
to dive into the recesses of the personal consciousness and to
extract whatever pearls the deep may yield. What if the
pearls be sometimes cloudy, and the treasures of the sea seem
dark and abstruse? It is only by the drag-nets of the mind
sunk to the uttermost depths of human nature that the most
precious secrets of the spirit are revealed. The French have
a word *Narcissisme*. Valéry is a Narcissist, contemplating
his own intellectual image in the mirror of consciousness.

Valéry then conceives himself as the poet of thought.
' J'aime la pensée comme d'autres aiment le nu qu'ils dessine-
raient toute leur vie.' It is, in his view, the thought which
makes the man. The ordinary biography affords no indication of what a man is like. It recounts his ancestry, the outer
facts of his education and activities, but the deeper part of
him, the inner functioning of the intellect, the mode in which,
and the passages by which, ideas flowed into his mind and
stirred his will, this, which is the true index of the human

character, is omitted. Valéry, on the other hand, only cares for this essential and inner kernel of history, 'the functioning of beings and the generation of works'.

Now Valéry is not the first poet who has been passionately interested in his own intellectual development. Wordsworth here finds an habitual and fruitful theme. He too endeavoured to penetrate into 'the hiding-places of man's power'. He too was concerned to note the wayward visitations of ancient surmises and thoughts:

> A shy spirit in my heart
> That comes and goes, will sometimes leap
> From hiding-places ten years deep
> Or haunt me with familiar face,
> Returning like a ghost unlaid
> Until the debt I owe is paid.

Apart from *The Prelu'* which traces the history in time of the poet's mind, there the *Ode on Immortality*, which, as Coleridge observes, 'was intended for such readers only as had been accustomed to watch the flux and reflux of their inmost nature, to venture at times into the twilight realms of consciousness and to feel a deep interest in modes of inmost being'. But whereas Wordsworth drew his poetry from

> The harvest of a quiet eye
> That broods and sleeps on his own heart,

Valéry works in singular independence of nature and no one would go to him, as we may go to Wordsworth, to enjoy 'the pliant harebell' or 'the sweetness of the common dawn' or the glories of sun and cloud upon the mountain side. Nor does he introduce into his poetry any delineation of human character. The reader must not expect to meet a leech gatherer or a rough dalesman or any French analogue of these Wordsworthian types in the rarefied atmosphere of Valerian poetry. He will not even see a woman face to face. For Valéry is a practising doctrinaire. Whatever he may be as a metaphysician, as a poet he is 'a solipsist' absorbed in the contemplation of his intellectual and emotional states. Moreover, he believes in the doctrine of *La Poésie pure*, by which he means that poetry is so fundamentally distinct from

prose, that nothing which is capable of being adequately de-
lineated in prose has its place in poetry. A sunset can be
described in a guide-book, a miser can be portrayed in a novel,
a statesman or a political transaction form the proper substance of a history. For this very reason no one of these
phenomena has a place in pure poetry. It is only after such
prosaic impurities have been drained away that we have the
quintessential spirit of verbal melody. Poetry is music:
where there is no music there is no poetry. A fact or a date
intruded into a poem is like the noise of a falling chair at
a concert.

This doctrine which he holds in common with the symbolists is never pushed to the length of saying that the content
of poetry is immaterial. The meaning in Valéry's poetry may
be difficult to define with certainty and precision, but there
is always some meaning, and even if there is nothing in the
least resembling moral direction, there are ideas and there are
symbols of ideas, shaping themselves and re-shaping themselves like a procession of clouds in the sky. The great
mathematician, Henri Poincaré, once compared the thoughts
in his mind to clusters of flies on a ceiling now assuming one
pattern, now another; and the image may serve for the
mental processes exhibited in the Valerian lyrics.

On all this business of what does and does not lie within
the scope of his intellectual interests Valéry writes with singular candour. 'There is an abyss between an impression and
an expression. I am quite capable of appreciating things
which I am altogether unable to describe. I prize and revere
the great art of the novelist, but I do not pretend to be at
home in it. It is a mode of literature based upon a view of
men which is not natural to me. I do not know how one
should go about creating characters. Novelists give life and
my only object is in a certain sense to eliminate life. This
singular angle of vision prevents me from forming a reasonable judgement on any matter concerned with novels, theatres,
politics, or even history. In brief on any kind of work which
takes man as he appears to us, as a unit or element in its
combinations.'

It must be admitted that the exclusions are comprehensive. A poetry which seeks in a certain sense 'to eliminate life' is a very different kind of poetry from that which the world has valued since the days of Homer. Psycho-analysis however subtle, set to music however delicate and scholarly, is not literature for the profane. It is no surprise to learn that it is very difficult literature to create; so difficult that we can well understand the author when he dismisses the idea of inspiration as part of the ordinary mythology of the mind, well understand him again when he preaches the gospel of hard work and assures us that there is no certainty about the art of versifying, that it presents at every instant insoluble problems and that a mere nothing may break a fine poem, spoil its accomplishment and destroy its charm. Nor is it surprising that the poet-mathematician who has set himself the task of trying to get as deep down into himself as possible should seek every possible assistance from nature in this arduous enterprise, and should make careful note of those natural circumstances which seem to hinder and those which on the contrary assist his arduous purpose. M. Valéry, who takes himself and his intellect with profound seriousness, does all these things.

'How many observations have I not made myself while working at my verses. I tried to write *Pythia* and some other pieces in a park planted with the finest trees I have seen, near Avranches. There was a small tidal river meandering through the rich white soil. I would go down into the park before dawn bare-footed in the cold grass. The first moment of dawn exercises a singular power over my nerves. There is sadness in that moment and enchantment and emotion and a kind of lucidity which is almost painful. Hardly was the sky stained with colour when I would return to the house drunk with freshness and with will.'

The admirers of Valéry have found in his work an original and inventive quality which, apart from an unusual sense for the niceties of French prosody, gives him a special place among the poets of this age. His critics admit the excellence of his technique but complain that his verse is cold, strained,

and difficult, and to them M. Valéry would at once concede
that neither in his choice of themes nor in his treatment of
them is he concerned to stir the common heart of man. If he
ever thinks of his readers, which may be gravely doubted, it
is certain that he does not view them as lost souls to be saved
by his verse. His gift to them is not ethical improvement
but the kind of subtle and intellectual enjoyment which is
excited by delicate chamber-music. Some of the audience
will discover deep meanings in the music, others will simply
enjoy the sounds, to others the whole performance will be
unintelligible. To all critics the author's reply would be that
he is giving them the deepest part of himself in the form most
satisfactory to his artistic conscience, and that if they do not
like it, they are under no obligation to listen.

But even the reader who finds little pleasure and profit
in introspective verse will be compelled to concede that
M. Valéry is a master of musical French.

There are single lines like:

> Sage Sémiramis, enchanteresse et roi,

or

> Te voici, mon doux corps de lune et de rosée.

Quatrains like this from the *Cantique des Colonnes*:

> Pour affronter la lune,
> La lune et le soleil,
> On nous polit chacune
> Comme ongle de l'orteil,

and Odes like *L'Aurore*, which begins thus:

> La confusion morose,
> Qui me servait de sommeil,
> Se dissipe dès la rose
> Apparence du soleil.
> Dans mon âme je m.'avance,
> Tout ailé de confiance:
> C'est la première oraison!
> A peine sorti des sables,
> Je fais des pas admirables
> Dans les pas de ma raison.

No reader can fail to note that there is here a happy and

dexterous audacity in the use of words. Let us recur to the
first example:

> Sage Sémiramis, enchanteresse et roi.

Semiramis, of course, was a woman, and *enchanteresse*, a
feminine adjective, reminds us of the fact. Why then *roi*
and not *reine*? There are three reasons: In the first place *roi*
is needed for the rhyme.

> Battez, cymbales d'or, mamelles cadencées,
> Et roses palpitant sur ma pure paroi!
> Que je m'évanouisse en mes vastes pensées,
> Sage Sémiramis, enchanteresse et roi.

This, however, is not decisive, for had *reine* been an equally
effective close of the last and most important line of the
quatrain, the second line could have been made to conform.
Roi, however, is better than *reine* for two reasons: first, because it makes a stronger and more euphonious ending, the
letter *o* being wanted as a contrast to the preceding *e*'s, *a*'s,
and *i*'s; secondly, because it enables the poet to express his
purpose more exactly. Semiramis has wisdom, seduction,
power. The poet wishes to point out that her power is not
based upon feminine seduction. It is masculine, kingly
power. In three letters he achieves his end. As Shakespeare's Cleopatra is Egypt, so Valéry's Semiramis is King.
The three epithets represent sexless wisdom, feminine enchantment, masculine power. Here is a happy and dexterous
grace in the management of words, and an avoidance of
anything resembling a cliché.

In Paris, as in Ancient Rome, a poet as soon as he has
attained to any small measure of renown, especially if it be
based upon a departure from established tradition, is apt to receive divine honours from a small circle of youthful admirers.
M. Valéry has not been exempt from this flattering destiny.
A good deal of incense has been, and is still being burned
upon his altar. Commentaries are written upon his works.
The distinguishing notes of Valerian poetry are singled
out for elaborate commendation—his surprising and re-
condite imagery, his attention to the subtler conditions of
metrical harmony, such as the sequence of vowels and con-

sonants, his employment of symbols, his austere concentration upon the inner processes of mind. The Delphic oracle of old did not win more renown for the obscurity of its deliverances than does M. Valéry from the worshippers who crowd to his shrine. We are even told that poetry should be oracular, and is the less effective the better it is understood.

These views are not unpalatable to the poet. He does not propose to himself to describe men and things but only the emotions which correspond with certain states of mind. The objective world is not, in itself, a fit object for contemplation. As Socrates is made to say in the prose dialogue entitled *L'Âme et la Danse*, 'Nothing is so fatal to nature as to see things as they are. A cold and perfect clearness is a poison which it is impossible to combat. Reality in a pure state instantly stops the heart.' Reality then must be masked. We must cultivate the state most opposed to 'mundane lucidity and inexorable clearness'. And certainly in many of M. Valéry's poems this state is cultivated to a high pitch of perfection.

It is not, however, in virtue of these affectations and obscurities but in spite of them that the lyrical poetry of this subtle and cultivated mathematical scholar will continue to attract attention. *Le Cimetière marin*, so much admired by good judges, is not improved by the comparison of the sea flecked with white sails to a quiet roof over which doves are walking, nor yet by the passage in which the sea is compared to a watchdog and the tombs in the cemetery to white sheep. These similes do not advance the main theme of the poem which we understand to be a meditation on the old maxim of Heraclitus that all things are in flux.

> Comme le fruit se fond en jouissance,
> Comme en délice il change son absence
> Dans une bouche où sa forme se meurt,
> Je hume ici ma future fumée,
> Et le ciel chante à l'âme consumée
> Le changement des rives en rumeur.

This is intelligible, and indeed the effective parts of the poem are those which are easily comprehensible, such as the fine stanza on the transitoriness of human love and the superb

concluding image of the freshening wind whipping the calm
southern sea into a thousand glittering splendours.

> Buvez, mon sein, la naissance du vent!
> Une fraîcheur, de la mer exhalée,
> Me rend mon âme. . . . O puissance salée!
> Courons à l'onde en rejaillir vivant!
>
> Oui! Grande mer de délires douée,
> Peau de panthère et chlamyde trouée
> De mille et mille idoles du soleil,
> Hydre absolue, ivre de ta chair bleue,
> Qui te remords l'étincelante queue
> Dans un tumulte au silence pareil,
> Le vent se lève!

The difficulty which confronts the poet in this, as in every
other part of his work, is that he is striving for two incompatible and incommensurable things, depth of thought and
pure music, and that he is disposed, whenever obstacles arise,
to sacrifice meaning to music. Nobody can read *Les Charmes*
without being impressed with the care which has been taken
to secure the right sequence of vowels and consonants, how
every musical effect has been studied, what use is made of
alliteration, and how often it would appear that the poet is
started off upon a new line of thought not by any inner logical
coherence but by the accident that a certain collocation of
beautiful sounds has captivated his ear. Now beautiful
sounds may sometimes suggest commonplace images, and
where this happens, the ordinary reader, who cannot altogether succeed in diverting music from meaning, experiences
all the effects of bathos. An example occurs in *Le Sylphe*,
a pretty lyric describing the sudden and gracious flash of
intuition, elusive and unaccountable, which from time to
time pierces the drab envelope of work-a-day thoughts.
Tennyson, in a fuller context and with a reference, absent in
Le Sylphe, to the problem of immortality, has touched lightly
in the *Two Voices* upon these mysterious visitations of thought
and feeling:

> Moreover, something is or seems,
> Which touches me with mystic gleams,
> Like glimpses of forgotten dreams.

Valéry is not thinking of intimations of immortality. *Le Sylphe* would seem to be the divine moment in the process of artistic and intellectual creation:

> Ni vu ni connu
> Je suis le parfum
> Vivant et défunt
> Dans le vent venu.
>
> Ni vu ni connu,
> Hasard ou génie?
> A peine venu,
> La tâche est finie!
>
> Ni lu ni compris?
> Aux meilleurs esprits
> Que d'erreurs promises!

Then comes the bathos. A rhyme must be found for *promises*. M. Valéry lights upon *chemises*, and so we have

> Ni vu ni connu,
> Le temps d'un sein nu
> Entre deux chemises!

Clearly the sylph has made a precipitate retreat. The *deux chemises* may be euphonious, but they are not inspired, and it is difficult to believe that a poet, guided by considerations other than those of euphony, could not have found a more fitting image in which to describe the glimpse of authentic nature between the trappings of convention. We refuse entirely to believe that the sylph who makes a convincing appearance in the earlier part of the poem had anything to do with the chiselling of its closing simile.

In *L'Ébauche d'un Serpent*, one of his more ambitious pieces, M. Valéry departs from his habitual theme and re-writes the temptation of Eve in an allegorical poem, part drama part burlesque. The Serpent, who is the principal character in the poem, opens with a monologue in which he apostrophizes his ally the Sun, whose office it is to mask the flaws of creation. He then proceeds to enlarge upon the mistake of God in creating Time, Causality, and Number, and afterwards to recount his seduction of Eve. At the close he bursts out into a paean to the Tree of Knowledge.

The main sentiment which we experience in reading this brilliant *tour de force* of versification is one of admiration for M. Valéry's instrumental powers. If an old story had to be told afresh it could not have been presented in a garb more unfamiliar or woven of rarer tissues. But has the author in effect anything new to say to us about the old problem of good and evil? There is nothing fresh to be said on that ancient theme and M. Valéry's answer that pride, the sin of the mind, is the sin *par excellence* which opens the gate to all others is only what the Catholic Church has taught throughout the ages. It must not, however, be expected of *L'Ébauche d'un Serpent* that it will contain either a philosophy or a moral message. What it contains and is intended to contain is some very good French writing. Here are some specimens accompanied by Captain Wardle's excellent English version:

The Serpent apostrophizes his ally the Sun:

> Soleil, soleil! Faute éclatante!
> Toi qui masques la mort, Soleil,
> Sous l'azur et l'or d'une tente
> Où les fleurs tiennent leur conseil;
> Par d'impénétrables délices,
> Toi, le plus fier de mes complices,
> Et de mes pièges le plus haut,
> Tu gardes les cœurs de connaître
> Que l'univers n'est qu'un défaut
> Dans la pureté de Non-Être!

> Sun, sun! O thou resplendent fault!
> Sun who on death a mask doth set,
> Beneath a gold and azure vault
> That roofs the flowers in council met;
> By rapture veiled in mysteries,
> Proudest of my accomplices,
> And highest snare that's known to me,
> Thou guardest lest the heart should guess
> The Universe only to be
> A blemish in pure Nothingness.

The Serpent describes his methods:

> Je vais, je viens, je glisse, plonge,
> Je disparais dans un cœur pur!
> Fut-il jamais de sein si dur
> Qu'on n'y puisse loger un songe?

Qui que tu sois, ne suis-je point
Cette complaisance qui poind
Dans ton âme, lorsqu'elle s'aime?
Je suis au fond de sa faveur
Cette inimitable saveur
Que tu ne trouves qu'à toi-même.

I go, I come, I glide, I dive,
Vanish into a heart that's pure!
What heart could ever so endure
That no dream lodged therein would thrive?
Be who you may, is that not I
The dawn of your soul's complacency
Whenever to self-love inclined?
I am at bottom of its favour
That inimitable savour
That only in yourself you find.

It requires indeed a certain violence of adjustment to attune oneself even to the simplest of M. Valéry's poems. The reader has an uneasy suspicion that the meaning which seems to him to be probable may not in fact correspond to the intention of the author, or that there may be undertones of significance only to be appreciated by the schooled ear of the initiate. The poet also has the perplexing habit of introducing dialogue into his Odes without any visible indication either as to who it is who is speaking or as to when his allocution begins or ends, and our perplexity is increased by the fact that in the Valerian poetry the gift of speech is not confined to human nature. In this respect M. Valéry allows himself the widest allegorical latitudes.

The admirers of Edgar Allan Poe, a name to conjure with among the French symbolists, will recollect how in *The Murders of the Rue Morgue* that remarkable man, Monsieur C. Auguste Dupin, indulges in a brilliant feat of thought-reading as he walks one night with his friend down a long dirty road near the Palais Royal.

'He is a very little fellow, that's true, and would do better for the Théâtre des Variétés,' observes the amateur detective after fifteen minutes' silence.

'There can be no doubt of that,' I replied unwittingly and

not at first observing (so much had I been absorbed in reflection) the extraordinary manner in which the speaker had chimed in with my meditations. In an instant afterwards I recollected myself and my astonishment was profound.

'Dupin,' said I gravely, 'this is beyond my comprehension. How is it possible that you should know that I was thinking of . . . ?'

. . . 'I will explain,' he said, 'and that you may comprehend all clearly, we will first retrace the course of your meditations from the moment in which I spoke to you until that of the rencontre with the fruiterer in question. The larger links of the chain run thus—Chantilly, Orion, Dr. Nichols, Epicurus, Stereotomy, the street stones, the fruiterer.'

The links in M. Valéry's chain of thought are sometimes of the same order of heterogeneity. Most of them, no doubt, can be discovered by the exercise of attention and ingenuity; but failing any assistance from the author himself there will probably always remain a residuum of obscurity calculated to sustain the conjectures of conflicting schools of interpretation. In fact

> Aux meilleurs esprits
> Que d'erreurs promises!

Of the two graceful prose dialogues, written in the Platonic manner, *L'Âme et la Danse* is the more original in substance, containing as it does that thought of the perpetual transmutations of life, action passing into rest, rest into action, which is central in Valéry's philosophy, and finding in the movements of Athikte, the consummate dancer, neither, as one opinion would have it, the very image of love, nor, as another contended, the bodily displacements visible to the eye, but the bare expression of that metamorphosis which runs through all nature. In *Eupalinos*, Socrates and Phaedrus discuss architecture, Phaedrus recalls to the memory of Socrates the memory of Eupalinos of Megara, the architect of the Temple of Artemis the Huntress, one of whose precepts was that in execution there was no such thing as detail, but that everything was important. He then recalls how Eupa-

linos had said that his delicate temple of Hermes was the
mathematical image of a girl in Corinth whom he had happily
loved. Thereupon Phaedrus compares the temple to a nup-
tial chant, a thought pleasant to Eupalinos, who proceeds to
divide buildings into three classes, those which are dumb,
those which speak, and those which sing. The creative art
behind the singing building is compared to an ecstasy or to
the possession of the loved object in sleep. In those moments
a wealth of mysterious and superabundant favours comes to
the architect. Thence the dialogue wanders away to speculations as to the relations of music and architecture, and of
both these arts to the basic science of geometry and afterwards we are led on to consider the difference between mechanism, life, and personality (a theme with regard to which the
prudent reader will prefer to have recourse to Dr. J. S.
Haldane), and the comparative advantages of speculation
and action. Socrates says that the choice lies between being
a man or a mind, and the dialogue concludes with a paean in
favour of a life of action and commending the art of construction as the most complete form which human activity
can take.

The idea, which is touched on in this dialogue, that there
is no difference in quality between the creative impulse of
the artist and the man of science was elaborated in a youthful
essay on Leonardo da Vinci, and is the theme of an interesting conversation reported by M. Lefèvre. Here Valéry observes that works of art interest him less in themselves than
for the reflections which they suggest as to the manner in
which they are produced. 'I like', he continues, 'to try to
represent to myself their embryonic state. Now in this state
the distinction between the *savant* and the artist vanishes.
Nothing remains but the play of excitement, of attention, of
mental accidents, and conditions. True, the constructions of
science are impersonal, but every act of a scientific con-
structor is the act of a personality. The style of a mathematician is as recognizable as the style of an artist. Poincaré
does not write like Hermite. There are even national styles
in mathematics. In Algebra itself nationality reveals itself.'

The infinity of accidents too, which determine the shape of an ode or a sonnet, play an equally influential part in the development of a science. Practice suggests some problems. Chance observations have been made at such and such a time, singular minds have manifested themselves at certain points of history. From the state of scientific knowledge at any moment it would be quite impossible to deduce the order in which the successive discoveries have been made or the causes which have prompted them. It is the same with poetry, which also is the victim of a myriad chances. Least of all does the poet know whither the Muse may lead him.

The conclusions of sound mathematical reasoning are clear. Not so, for the most part, the results of the artistic impulse applied in the Valerian manner. Why is this? The poet admits his obscurity, does not seek to defend it, but searches for an explanation, as if the obscurity of his poem were some natural phenomenon with which he was personally unconcerned. There are, he announces, three causes. The first is the difficulty of the subject-matter. States of thought and feeling can only be defined in terms of their relations and combinations, and these are unprovided with an exact and clear-cut nomenclature. The second is the number of independent conditions which the poet is expected to satisfy if he wishes to comply with the rules of classic prosody. The third cause for obscurity is a compound of the other two, the length of time which the author is compelled to take in elaborating a poetic text. It will be seen that Sheridan's 'damned easy reading, damned hard writing', is the converse of the experiences of M. Valéry's readers. The harder he writes, the more difficult he makes his writing for them. If he spends four years on the text of an Ode, his readers will probably need five years to understand it. In a word, M. Valéry does not correct and refine to clarify the meaning for his reading public, but on the contrary to deepen it or else to improve the musical effect of his verse. Neither of these operations conduces to greater intelligibility.

What else does all this mean than that M. Valéry has set himself an impossible task? His music must be flawless, his prosody classical, his theme the transmutations of human consciousness under successive stimuli from without and within. Need we wonder if, laying so great a burden on his shoulders, M. Valéry more often than not fails to win his way to clarity. The attempt to express in a lyric as musical as Schubert, as formal as Hérédia, such minute psychological changes as fill Proust's operose and interminable novels, this, if a gallant, is surely a forlorn enterprise. It is a remarkable feat of literary tact that, despite all these self-imposed and harassing conditions, M. Valéry should have published so much verse which can be read with pleasure and even with admiration. However little we may be disposed to accept the doctrine of the symbolists or the theory of *La Poésie pure*, or however little interest we may take in the introspective and psycho-physical content of so much of M. Valéry's verse, we cannot deny that upon occasions he can write 'pure poetry' not only in the Valerian but in the ordinary sense of the term. Here is an image of Narcissus approaching the lake in the stillness of evening:

> La voix des sources change, et me parle du soir;
> Un grand calme m'écoute, où j'écoute l'espoir.
> J'entends l'herbe des nuits croître dans l'ombre sainte,
> Et la lune perfide élève son miroir
> Jusque dans les secrets de la fontaine éteinte . . .
> Jusque dans les secrets que je crains de savoir,
> Jusque dans le repli de l'amour de soi-même,
> Rien ne peut échapper au silence du soir.
> La nuit vient sur ma chair lui souffler que je l'aime.
> Sa voix fraîche à mes vœux tremble de consentir:
> A peine, dans la brise, elle semble mentir,
> Tant le frémissement de son temple tacite
> Conspire au spacieux silence d'un tel site.

The unearthly magical effect of the still moonlight summer night on the soul of the lover as he approaches the image of the beloved, his ear attuned to every faint rustle of the breeze, is drawn with a beautiful delicacy.

Two large questions of aesthetics are naturally raised by the technique of this fastidious and original artist. The first is the question whether the poet can hope to produce the kind of appeal which is made to the ear by the musician, and if so, whether this should be his single aim. The symbolists among whom M. Valéry served his literary apprenticeship answered both these questions in the affirmative. If romantic musicians like Berlioz and Wagner could instil into their operas some of the specific effects of literature, they saw no reason why the poets should not take their revenge. Writing of the young literary men of the eighties and nineties who threw themselves with passion into the symbolist movement, M. Valéry says: 'We were nourished on music and our literary heads dreamed of nothing save of extracting from language almost the same effects as were produced upon our nervous systems by sound alone. Some worshipped Wagner, others Schumann. Seldom has more fervour and courage, more theory, knowledge, pious attention or debate been concentrated on the problem of pure beauty than during those few years. It was attacked on every side . . . some conserving the traditional forms of French verse tried to eliminate descriptions, maxims, moral reflections and purged their poetry of almost all the intellectual elements which music cannot express. Others gave to every object an indefinite signification presupposing a hidden metaphysic. They made use of a delicious ambiguous material, peopling their enchanted parks and evanescent woods with an entirely ideal fauna. Everything was an allusion. Nothing was content with just being. In those kingdoms all hung with mirrors everything thought; or at least everything attempted to think. Then there were some magicians, of a more independent and rational temper who attacked the ancient prosody. There were some for whom the colour of sound and the combining art of alliteration seemed to have no further secrets. They deliberately introduced into their verses the *timbre* of the orchestra; they were not always mistaken. Others learnedly recovered the spontaneous naïveté of the ancient popular poetry. Philology and phonetics were cited at the eternal debates of these rigorous lovers of the Muse.' Looking back upon the movement of his youth which has left so strong and enduring an imprint upon him, M. Valéry is bound to admit the failure of symbolism to establish itself. The effort to obtain pure poetry has been too arduous, the ideal has been too high, the results have been adjudged almost inhuman. The successors of the symbolists have neither endured their torment nor adopted their delicacies, and sometimes see licence in experiments which were regarded by the pioneers as a new kind of rigour.

The poets of to-day, he admits, open their eyes upon the accidents of Being where the symbolists in their effort to stand close to the essential heart of things had advisedly closed them.

In spite of this clear-sighted analysis, so much of the spirit of 'pure poetry' in the technical sense of that phrase continues to inform the verse of M. Valéry that his readers are still entitled to ask the question which was addressed to Mallarmé and his disciples. Can poetry produce the effects of music? If so, should it sacrifice clarity to sound? Now it is obvious that poetry being expressed in words cannot produce exactly the same effects as music, which is expressed in notes. Its effects may be analogous but they are not identical, just as the so-called song of the nightingale, being incapable of being taken down in musical notation is not in itself music though it has an effect analogous to music. But the fact that poetry cannot reproduce the exact effect of music on the nervous organism is no reason why it should not attempt to capture for itself as much of the specific musical influence as its medium admits of. Poetry, however, can never be 'pure' in the sense in which music is pure, because, do what the poet may, every word used in a poem is a complex of associations reaching out in every direction beyond the sphere of poetry. It is vain to attempt to exclude the accidents of Being from poetry. They come rushing back into the field of consciousness with every noun or adjective. Since then the specific emotional effect at the command of the musician is out of reach of the poet, is it wise for the poet to throw away the specific effect of poetry which is out of reach of the musician? By aiming at 'pure poetry' he does this, for he sacrifices articulate meaning in the hopes of reproducing an emotional state to which the instruments at his disposal are inherently unequal.

Let it not, however, be imagined that the symbolist movement was wholly barren. It was a great merit in this school of artists that they laid stress upon the value of the musical element in poetry and set themselves down to a passionate search for new and subtle harmonies in verse which had hitherto eluded the ear of the poet. They carried their movement to great and in some cases to fantastic extremes, but there can be little question that they have enriched the life of French poetry with new and unsuspected melodies, urging to a still further point the reaction against the rhetorical and romantic schools which was begun by Baudelaire and continued by Verlaine, and making a decisive break with the clear apodeictic spirit which for many centuries has ruled supreme in every province of French literature. Valéry would not now count himself among the symbolists, but he is a child of the movement, and has the better right to profess pure poetry since by the law of intellectual affinities he moves in the sphere of pure mathematics. Geometry and Poetry are old allies; and this poet, who is also a geometrician, has already given us a small body of poetical work at once so intellectual and so melodious that the jealous portals of the French Academy have been opened for his reception. His verse is confessedly difficult, but perhaps for that very reason, and because it evades the clear concrete outlines of everyday life, it has a curious power of transporting the reader into a magical world of its own in which there is nothing common and nothing definite, but only a phantasmagoria of haunting images passing before the eye to the sound of delicate unearthly music and with just so much of consistency and permanence as belong to the scent of flowers in the night breeze or to the ethereal tissues of a dream.

THE BURDEN OF HUMANISM

BY

ABRAHAM FLEXNER

The Taylorian Lecture 1928

PREFATORY NOTE

WITHOUT meaning to make any one else responsible in any measure for the substance of this lecture, it is only fair to say that I have enjoyed the opportunity of discussing its contents with Professor H. G. Fiedler Dr. E. A. Lowe, Professor Gilbert Murray, Professor Sir Charles Sherrington, and Professor Graham Wallas, to all of whom I am very grateful.

A. F.

16 *November* 1928.

THE BURDEN OF HUMANISM

I PROPOSE to consider to-day the peculiar burden laid upon humanism by developments that are non-humanistic in their essential character. It is the merest truism to say that the outstanding features of modern life are science, industry, and democracy. Obviously, within the limits of a lecture I cannot discuss all three. I shall discuss science and humanism somewhat fully, industry and humanism briefly; democracy and humanism I cannot touch at all.

May I ask you to note, as I begin, that I am speaking of science, industry, humanism—not, in the first place, of the scientist, the industrialist, the humanist; of them, as persons, I shall have something to say as I proceed; but my immediate concern is not with persons, but with great movements in the realm of thought and action.

Science, as science, deliberately limits its range of interest. It is concerned with phenomena, concerned to collect data, to ascertain relationships, to interpret, logically and imaginatively, what it has thus gathered. Here, then, is one essential limitation to its scope: its exclusive pre-occupation with data and their interpretation. There is still another, that is even more germane to my theme. Science is a two-edged sword. It is capable of doing harm as well as good, and science, as science, cannot, must not, ask which is likely to result. For example: science has had its repercussions throughout the entire range of human activities, affecting our thinking as well as our doing; it has largely—alas, not yet wholly— destroyed the puny notions within which religion, philosophy, and history respectively once led a relatively easy intellectual existence. With no more knowledge than was available two hundred years ago, one could and generally did regard the physical world as a tight little box or ball, four thousand

years old—and that notion suited well the mental indolence
to which men are prone. So, again, within the same little
ball, ethics and philosophy were relatively easy; a historian
could within prison walls write a history of the world—Sir
Walter Raleigh did it—and a physician could prescribe his
nostrums without scepticism, because he was so largely
ignorant of the make-up and workings of the human body
and the impotence of his drugs. These are, I say, puny
things; and science has done well to destroy them by enlarging the scope of human knowledge, human effort, human
thought, human imagination. The fortunate ones who heard
Professor Shapley's Halley Lecture last term will realize how
science has given wings to the human spirit: the endeavour to
reach the poles by sled or aeroplane or to climb Mt. Everest
is not to be despised; but it is child's play compared with
that adventuring into the infinite, in space and in thought,
upon which astronomy, physiology, and mathematics have
for several centuries been embarked.

But while, on the one hand, science is, without making this
its object, thus freeing the human spirit, it is also ministering
with absolute impartiality to the worst that is within us.
Physical chemistry reveals unbelievable force within the
atom: it is to physical chemistry immaterial whether the
outcome is a new philosophy of creation or hideous instruments of destruction for the next war. That is no business of
physical chemistry; its business is to go on unravelling secrets.
Every discovery that comes out of the laboratory is, as a
matter of fact, seized upon simultaneously by persons who
make good use of it and by persons who make the worst
possible use of it. Science has brought the world closely
together, for ill as for good. It has made human life safer and
longer, for good and for ill; it has enabled more people to live,
for good and for ill; it has introduced labour-saving devices
and speed, for good and for ill; it has got rid of pestilence and
infection, for good as for ill—for the bacteriology which has

destroyed typhoid in peaceful cities has made possible war
on a previously undreamt-of scale. It has all but destroyed
quiet and solitude—for the good, perhaps, of the lonely settler, but assuredly to the detriment of the thinker who needs
calm and repose, and of those who could once refresh mind
and body in the silent depths of the Canadian 'bush' or on
the edge of an Alpine glacier. On the whole, mankind has
doubtless gained—gained greatly. Science assumes that, in
the long run, its successes will be beneficent. But this is
a very general assumption, anterior to all scientific effort
whatsoever, and not pertinent to any particular activity or
undertaking. Moreover, that assumption once made, it must
be laid aside; it cannot be suffered to influence specific doings.
Science goes its way, dealing now with this problem, now
with that, regardless of proximate use or ultimate bearing.
It is no concern of science as such that the diplomatist, business man, warrior, statesman, or inventor may, thanks to
it, perpetrate or scheme atrocities from which, objectively
viewed, every sane and civilized person recoils. Nor does
science deserve any credit for the optimistic interpretation
which a humanitarian age has placed upon the doctrine of
evolution. That, as Santayana says, 'is a notion that has
nothing to do with natural science'.[1]

Scientific method, in the sense in which I have been discussing it, is as valid in the field of humanism as in the realm
of physics or biology; indeed the Germans have a single word
—*Wissenschaft*—covering both. For humanism must, like
natural science, procure data, generalize, interpret. Pains-
taking, sometimes monumental, works bear witness to the
efforts of humanism to obtain accurate data: historic sites
are excavated to procure the contemporaneous records and
relics of ancient events; manuscripts are deciphered and
compared; inscriptions are copied and photographed; dust-
covered archives are searched. Work of this kind corresponds

[1] *Reason in Science* (New York, 1906), p. 108.

in the field of humanism to the scientific endeavour to observe phenomena: it is, in the proper sense of the term, scientific— the search for facts in the realm of the human spirit upon which generalization, hypothesis, interpretation may safely rest. A library is a laboratory. Philology in the technical sense is science, not humanism. The intellectual processes operating in excavating below ground are precisely the same as those operating in the observation of the heavens. More- over, both humanistic and scientific studies have often suffered in the same way from inadequacy of data, from erroneous observation, from premature generalization, from unjustified interpretation. 'A series of judgments, revised without ceasing, goes to make up the incontestable progress of science. We must believe in progress, but we must never accord more than a limited amount of confidence to the forms in which it is successively vested.'[1] This statement is equally true of pathology and history. Both tend to run in grooves, out of which only giants have been able to lift them, for there are fashions and patterns, difficult to change, in the natural sciences, as in literature, history, politics, or art.

In revulsion from the easy interpretations of previous generations, the scientific side of humanistic studies has therefore in the last century been strongly emphasized. This has been thoroughly sound procedure. In humanism as in science men had gone too far on the basis of insufficient data. They had, and they still have, to address themselves to the task of learning the facts about man and his spiritual productions with all possible accuracy and fullness and with total disregard of consequences to established beliefs, customs, or practices. There is therefore a science of history, a science of Assyriology, as impartially devoted to just finding things out as the science of physics. In deciphering an inscription or subjecting the Bible to textual criticism, humanism has as

[1] Duclaux, *Pasteur—The History of a Mind* (translated by Smith and Hedges, Philadelphia and London, 1920), p. 111.

little concern for consequences as geology when it unearths
fossils that upset the Book of Genesis, or chemistry which
is ultimately responsible for the use of gas in warfare.

I have just said that science and humanism face the same
perils in the interpretation of data. The biographers of Pasteur, to whom I shall have occasion to recur, quite candidly
show that he was sometimes wrong about facts and correct
in his inferences, occasionally right about facts and wrong in
his inferences, even though usually, in the end, as far as he
went, right as to both. But the point is that, using not only
judgement but imagination, he had to interpret as well as
unravel—the mere accumulation of data is insufficient—and
that he could go wrong in either adventure or in both.
Humanistic studies face the same problem, even though the
humanistic problem be more complex, as human beings and
human society are more complex than atoms, bacteria, and
stellar systems. For humanism, like science, has not only to
describe, it has to interpret beyond the point at which details stop, though, as in science, that point is being steadily
pushed forward. To take examples from history: Cromwell
and Napoleon and Lincoln and Bismarck and Lenin were
results of specific antecedent causes and factors, many of
which can be definitely ascertained; but assuredly ante-
cedents, opportunities, conditions cannot yet be formulated
in terms that would satisfy a biologist or even a psychologist
—not to say a physicist or chemist; again, they produced
results—but results that depended in each case on individuality—on a peculiar type of intelligence, moral sense,
ambition, purpose, wit, will—that are thus far indescribable.
They had not only social and environmental histories that
may be quite adequately portrayed—see, for example, Sand-
burg's account of the prairie years of Abraham Lincoln—
but they have each histories, family and individual, social,
psychological, physiological, and anatomical. The results of
the impact when an individual of unknown idiosyncrasies—

a Socrates, Shakespeare, Napoleon, or Lincoln—crashes into history require interpretation, but with great risks. The current of events, which has been moving in a certain channel, is suddenly and incalculably wrenched from its course; thus the emergence and consequences of personality are with our present resources for investigation to a considerable extent accidental. And what is true in history is still more true of literature, art, music—of the Homers and Shakespeares and Goethes and Heines, of Michael Angelo and Bach and Wagner, whom up to a certain point one can account for—but who, beyond that point, are, as far as our present powers of analysis and expression go, still mysteries, inexplicable and unpredictable. Wit and technique are gradually narrowing this realm; but we have as yet far to go in eliminating the imponderable from the humanistic as from the scientific field.

I mentioned industry as characteristic of the modern age. Industry, mere industry, industry as such, is primarily concerned in satisfying needs or in creating needs that its products may satisfy. It is a fine thing when its activities give improved shelter, clothing, food, abolish famine and even the danger of famine. Like science, industry is entitled to the assumption that on the whole its activities are beneficent. None the less, industry, *quâ* industry, is engaged in making profits. Hence industry, which, like science, has plainly accomplished so much that is good, has always been more or less ruthless—at one time frankly so, nowadays sometimes more subtly. The same business activities, that have made food and clothing cheap or accessible, and that once exploited children in factories, now make peons of African natives and thoughtlessly destroy Oxford's superbly beautiful countryside. 'Since the war', exclaims your Slade Professor of Fine Arts, 'we have built a million houses; at how many of those can we look without shame and disgust?' Niagara is hopelessly disfigured by the base uses to which paint and electricity have been put. Sitting in a railway carriage on the Continent, I once overheard an American lady upbraid Germans, because the Germans, like other Europeans, permit women to do the hard work of the fields—to plough, to harvest, to tend the cattle, regardless of the weather. The German lady responded: 'Do you really think these women out here in the open, enjoying sun and sky and air, would be better off operating a cotton machine, in a hot factory, with thousands of others, similarly occupied in a deadening, mechanical routine?' Industry does not as industry ask these embarrassing questions. It produces, produces, produces; distributes, distributes, distributes; advertises, advertises, advertises; silk and shoddy; tinsel and gems. Ours is the age of the machine; and the machine, as machine, is efficient, not sensitive. Indeed, the well-being of a given society, even the vigour of humanistic studies, may to-day depend indirectly upon mass production, well distributed in the world's markets.

It is therefore plain that neither the unravelling of Nature's secrets nor the application of knowledge to practical ends carries us as far as we are impelled to go. The passion for knowledge as such—any sort of knowledge—is, of course, as pure a passion as human beings are capable of indulging. But when every riddle due to ignorance has been solved, and all the facts about all phenomena are known and applied, what then? The accumulation of information, the knowledge of relationships, the industrial application of knowledge to practical ends of one kind or another must be appraised. Within science itself, within industry itself, there is neither apparatus nor inclination to appraise what science and industry do. And there must not be. The thoroughness and impartiality of science would suffer, if its task were complicated by the necessity of thinking of the worth or use of what it is doing; it is its task to find things out, and there its task, *quâ* science, ends.

If science and industry are held down to their essential part, it becomes clear that somewhere a rational system of values must be developed, outside science as such, outside industry as such, and yet ultimately operative within both. It is this sense of value that will make distinctions and thus determine the direction of human development. The assessment of values, in so far as human beings are affected, constitutes the unique burden of humanism. Science, I have said, is concerned with the phenomena, with happenings—in the remotest fixed stars, on our own planet, within our own bodies, in our personal and social relations. But while the task of the scientist, as scientist, leaves him there, the completed task of the humanist carries him farther. Sooner or later the humanist, as humanist, must concern himself with worth-whileness; he must raise the question of value, not only in the particular field in which he operates scientifically, but elsewhere. There is no moment at which the scientist, as scientist, calls the law of gravitation reasonable or absurd ; he is indifferent as to the beneficence of atoms or germs. He asks, 'Is this true?', not, 'Is this beautiful or good?' He is satisfied when he understands and ceases to be puzzled. Not so the humanist. He must, to be sure, understand, as best he can; but, beyond this, he cannot ultimately help—it is inherent in the very word 'humanism'—distinguishing between the beautiful and the ugly, the noble and the base, the far-sighted and the immediate, the serene quiet of the depths, and the noisy and meaningless tumult of the surface. The humanist has nothing to tell the scientist about science; indeed, as I have pointed out, in one important aspect of his own work he takes a leaf out of the scientist's book. But whenever consequences ensue and action results, humanism rightly intervenes. Is this good or bad? Beautiful or ugly? Wholesome or unwholesome? Worth while or not worth while? Broad or narrow? These are questions that humanism cannot avoid. It is hopelessly lost, if prejudice influences or abbreviates the initial investigation of facts, creations, and situations; it falls short, if it is ultimately without concern about them, and from this point of view the applications of science are answerable to the humanistic spirit. The physicist lays bare facts and relations which the inventor ingeniously turns to use. The facts and relations are *per se* valuable; is the invention—telephone, subway, motor-boat, what not? It is the interpreter of ideals who must tentatively answer 'yes' and 'no'. Are these worth while? The humanist answers both 'yes' and 'no'. Yes, in so far as labour and sheer difficulty are reduced, in order that men may be freed to love, think, meet, co-operate, associate, enjoy; no, in so far as mere speed and noise have been converted into human obsessions. An amusing and significant story illustrating the point is told of the late Dr. Booker T. Washington, the great negro, who founded Tuskegee Institute. Dr. Washington tried to keep in touch with his former pupils by visiting them from time to time on their farms and in their homes. On one occasion, a former student, exhibiting to his revered leader a model pigpen, explained that he had discovered that, if corn were first softened in hot water, a pig could digest it in half the time. Dr. Washington's quick comment—'What's a pig's time worth any way?'—went to the heart of the whole speed craze. What's it worth any way? In this age of increasing complications—more movement, more comfort, more contact, more books, more business, more territory, more people, more students, more money, more of this, that, and everything, the question has got to be put insistently and courageously, 'What's it worth to mankind any way?' And the humanistic spirit must answer.

I have tried to point out, first, that as fact-gathering and interpreting activities, science and humanism are one; further, that, sooner or later, humanism must do what science as science does not do—it must raise questions of relative or actual value, beauty, wholesomeness. Now science and humanism take concrete form in persons; and persons are neither simple nor single-minded. Persons try to be whole, try—or should try—in different moods or for different purposes to detach themselves from one attitude and to embrace another. Scientists and humanists alike have, as persons, preferences, interests, and capacities that belong to various categories. The scientist, having emerged from his laboratory, may allow his humanistic instinct to have play; the humanist has not gone to the limit unless it *has* played. That, I think, marks a genuine distinction.

The necessary detachment and indifference of science can best be realized through the study of some supreme scientific intelligence. Pasteur lends himself admirably to this study. His life is an open book; its events have been admirably recounted by his biographer, his son-in-law, Vallery-Radot; the history of his mind has been clearly traced by Duclaux, his pupil and successor. Pasteur was a decidedly complex personality: an intensely patriotic Frenchman, concerned alike for the glory and the material prosperity of his country; so sensitive that he could scarcely endure the thought of experimentation upon animals; endowed with imagination, the value and the danger of which he well knew; in the depths of his nature, profoundly religious. Yet he was above all a scientist, bent upon ascertaining the truth; and in so far as truth was concerned, everything else was, for the time being, non-existent for him. It is interesting to observe that one whose doings transformed important industries and wrought unspeakable blessings to suffering mankind was not originally interested in either prosperity or health. He saw in course of time—in some instances he foresaw—the medical, humanitarian, and economic implications of his work. But these were not his primary concern. 'A disease, as a disease, did not interest him deeply. . . . That which interested him was the pathological conflict between the physiological properties of the micro-organism and of the cells of the tissues.'[1] Pasteur's insatiable scientific curiosity was both prior to and independent of his patriotic and humanitarian impulses.

Something similar happens in industry. Consciously or unconsciously the medieval craftsman was a humanist, not a merchant or a manufacturer; he cared nothing for mass production; he created works of art. But, quite obviously, he fitted only into an unscientific and an undemocratic age; most people simply 'went without'. Science and democracy introduce an era when everybody wants things and can get them. They are produced cheaply and in enormous quantity by the machine. That is the motivation alike of Manchester and Grand Rapids. I leave the humanitarian to deal with the ethical and sanitary problems created by the factory; the burden of the humanist is increased by the necessity of contributing an aesthetic value to its products. Industry, like science, is thus answerable to standards and ideals which lie outside and beyond it and which it is the concern of the humanist, now and then in the person of the industrialist himself, to create and to apply. It is interesting to observe the extent to which the humanistic spirit has invaded the factory. Many examples could be cited: let me give two or three. An artist in wrought iron—Brandt—has shown in Paris that the factory can turn out an abundant and a beautiful product; Mr. Henry Creange, French by birth, American by adoption, has shown that the demands of an almost insatiable market for silk can be satisfied as tastefully with the huge output of the factory as by the craftsmen of Lyons. Mass production had quite destroyed the art of printing. A few craftsmen have, however, arisen in the new world as in the old, who are endeavouring to conquer the refractory press. One of them, an Oxonian, has in an exquisite little volume written on the battlefields of Macedonia described

[1] Duclaux, *loc. cit.*, p. 280.

with perhaps excessive modesty the early steps of the humanistic conquest:

> 'It is a melancholy and humiliating truth that the history of
> printing is a long decadence. Even in the mechanics of printing we
> cannot to-day surpass the pioneers of the fifteenth century. We
> cannot achieve a finer paper or a cleaner impression. Our best
> types are modelled on theirs; and in the use of our tools, in all the
> rules of the art, we toil painfully in their wake. A great scholar and
> accomplished collector used to say that his study of early printing
> had cured him of the vulgar Radicalism of his youth. The early
> printers had the tradition of the scribes in their souls, and so the
> new art found its perfection at a spring. It has been in a slow
> decline for four centuries; and the best that we can do now is to
> follow the old models, and adapt the old methods, with what
> intelligence we may command.' [1]

The industrial museum, which began in Germany and is
gradually spreading over the Western World, represents an
effort to merge into the consumer, who, as such, merely
wants goods, and the manufacturer, who, as such, wants
merely to make and to profit by them, the humanist who
holds that things shall have meaning and beauty as well
as use.

The distinction which exists between science and humanism is thus capable of being softened, even turned to advantage
within the realm of industry. For the humanist may, as I
have pointed out, not only affect industry; the industrialist
may in the process of humanizing his operations promote the
primary ends of industry. Photography, building, engineer-
ing may accomplish their primary purposes all the better, all
the more profitably, by being sensitive to aesthetic considerations. On the other hand, they can never lose sight of
the limits within which industry must operate: for on the
whole and in the long run industry must pay. The spectre of
the market is always there; education may drive it back; it
cannot be exorcised. Industry cannot be humanized to the

---

[1] R. W. Chapman: 'Old Books and Modern Reprints', in *The
Portrait of a Scholar and other Essays* (Clarendon Press, 1920), p. 50

point at which its products are so lovely or its methods so humane as to result in bankruptcy.

The sources of the criteria which the humanist applies are not transcendental; they lie, according to my thinking, deep in the human soul. Humanistic authority springs from human tradition, human reflection, human reason. I do not close my eyes to the difficulties arising from differences of taste. But, somehow, in the progress of time, though a permanent dead level is never attained, the wheat is separated from the chaff, and ideals, while remaining personal, attain the quality of not being merely our own transient selves. *These ideals are in the special custody of the humanist,* however often he has himself fallen short in range of sympathy and understanding. He may not be dogmatic in applying them, for they are not immutable and he may err; but with all respect and deference, it is his task to see things in perspective, to measure tentatively the work and doings of the human spirit, scientific, practical, and humanistic as well. To be sure, the oftener a humanistic strain is present in the scientist or the business man, the better; I am not suggesting that the professional humanist can alone possess good taste. There have been humanists whose methods were highly scientific but whose taste was execrable. But my point is that the roundly developed humanist is necessarily concerned with meaning and beauty, whereas the scientist has, as scientist, to be careful not to become entangled in either. And the extent to which applied science and industry and human life in general are significant and attractive may depend on the authority which humanistic studies are able to obtain. 'The teacher of literature', Professor Lowes of Harvard once wrote to me, 'ought to have vision and imagination closely akin to the vision and imagination of a poet, for he has to transmute the raw materials of scholarship into instrumentalities for the interpretation of an art. The qualities which he must exercise in acquisition are the qualities which attach to rigorous scientific method; but the faculties brought into play in application are not so much the faculties of the scientist as of the artist.'

That the humanist must assess values would, I assume, be universally admitted in reference to antiquity. No one questions that it is the proper concern of the humanist not only to understand Confucius and Homer and Plato and Cicero and Erasmus, but to interpret, appreciate, and appraise them and the civilization out of which they sprang. With similar objectivity and lack of personal interest historians record and judge the doings of peoples, of Assyrians, Egyptians, Hebrews, Greeks, Latins, Huns, and the various medieval nations. Is the case different when modern or contemporary nations, personages, or events are in question? Of course, the past looks easier. Is the difference as marked as appears? Is it not perhaps simplified for us by ignorance and imagination? To be sure, time, the inexorable humanist, has done deadly work. The flimsy building has collapsed; the demagogue has been shown up; the poor colours have faded; the meretricious lyric has ceased to charm. But difficulties enough remain. Adequate data are almost never obtainable; pitfalls, due to mere ignorance, beset every inch of the road; current prejudices may even influence judgement.

The humanist, dealing with the contemporary world, faces other problems. He may not lack information, but he does lack perspective; and his feelings are less easily discounted. Nevertheless, the abundance of available data, the possibility of first-hand knowledge of men, books, opinions, social conditions, give him tremendous advantages. Of these opportunities, the scholar is sometimes slow—often too slow—to take advantage. Perhaps the conservatism of the university atmosphere is responsible for his timidity. In any event, a German writing of Shakespeare sees him against a narrower background than when he writes of Homer or Plato; when the Englishman writes of Goethe, he deals with a great man, a great author, with contracted grasp of the picture. The closer one comes to our own times and our own people, the narrower, the more particularistic, humanistic studies tend to become. One easily forgets one is English or German or American when one writes of Egypt or Troy; one does not readily forget it, and few try to forget it, when writing of recent events, current topics, or current literature.

The perfect humanist, *quâ* humanist, would not fear to appraise Gilbert and Sullivan as objectively as he appraises Aristophanes; he would be as little excited about Bolshevism and Socialism, Protestantism and Catholicism, as he is about Guelph and Ghibelline, Cavalier and Roundhead, slave-holder and abolitionist. The living author must be seen, larger or smaller, against the background of his nation's and humanity's achievement; the living statesman must get his stature by comparison with Pericles and Caesar; current events must be ranged beside the already historic comedies and the tragedies for which useless wars have been waged, useless horrors endured, useless sacrifices made. The final panorama of Childe Roland need not be postponed until the present has become part and parcel of antiquity:

> There they stood, ranged along the hill-sides, met
>> To view the last of me, a living frame
>> For one more picture! in a sheet of flame
> I saw them and I knew them all. And yet
> Dauntless the slug-horn to my lips I set,
>> And blew.

Endeavours of the kind I am now discussing belong under modern conditions to universities. As a matter of fact, the past cannot really be comprehended without them; but regardless of the past, they are appropriate to universities, just because universities have no responsibility for action or policy, but complete responsibility for ascertaining, telling, and interpreting the truth—the truth in respect not only to stardust and atoms, but to pictures and poems and politicians and economic theories, present as well as past. Do what we will, we shall not correctly anticipate the judgements of time and history; but frail and faulty as we are, we can do much better than we have done or are doing. Finality is possible in neither scientific doctrine nor in humanistic evaluation; but both are necessary to progress in clearer thinking. The saturation point of fact once reached, the finished scholar may not, I think, shrink from a philosophic attempt to set a value on the subject of his study—to see it in perspective, to estimate its value; and the fact that subsequent generations may revise his judgement does not render his effort superfluous.

A few years ago I was seated at dinner next to a distinguished Oxonian. The conversation turned on the subject of books about various nations written by foreigners. 'No one', said he, 'but a Scot or a German can write a good book about England, and a German has done it'. On inquiry I learned that my neighbour referred to a recent work, entitled *England*, by Wilhelm Dibelius. A few weeks later I met Dibelius himself in Berlin, talked with him about England and Germany, and procured a copy of his book. I have no opinion as to the qualifications one must possess in order to do justice to the English people. But the substance of the preface to this study of England made upon me a profound impression. It keeps on recurring to me: 'Germany has been at war with a people whom Germany did not understand and who did not understand Germany.' In the century or half-century preceding the war, what did the humanists of the great English, German, French, and American universities do to appraise these nations and to interpret them to one another? Perhaps in any case their efforts would have been vain; perhaps business and dynasties and newspapers and politicians and soldiers and seamen, working in the grooves in which men work, would nevertheless have steered the whole civilized world upon the rocks, uncertain when or whether it will be seaworthy again. But in any event humanists might have had clear consciences. They are not now entitled to them. Goethe was studied in England, Shakespeare in Germany and France; but the larger issues were ignored, left to practical men. I am not supposing that the humanist must be denationalized; I am only asking that he take as broad and as critical a view of modern life and culture as he takes of ancient life and culture; that he should not wait a century or two until the present has faded into antiquity before trying to be judicial, before trying to interest himself in the whole of a given civilization. As it turned out, professors everywhere were little broader than Nelson's captain, who is reported to have said, 'My lord, I have no prejudices, but God knows I hate a Frenchman.'

Plato suggests that the world had better be governed by scholars; but, as I have already pointed out, scholars may be influential, precisely because they have no responsibility for policies. They occupy for this reason a peculiarly strong position; their interest is in interpretation and evaluation and not merely in particularistic facts or laws; the world might therefore conceivably be governed by wiser and better men, if in the universities, through which most of the governors and many of the governed pass, a group of men, caring about values, expounded truth rather than glory; if professors of German and French and Spanish and English were human beings—humanists—before or besides being Germans, Frenchmen, Spaniards, Englishmen, or Americans. In that case, the world would not care less for science than it does or should care—for it is far from caring enough; but its actual fate would not be so largely committed to practical men who care altogether too little for science, still less for humanism, and altogether too much for the uses, individual or nationalistic, to which exploited science and industry can be put.

An American, addressing Englishmen, I cannot refrain in passing from giving a concrete example of a task from which the larger humanism is at this moment shrinking. The war lifted large masses of mankind out of what I have called its groove. To what extent has it lifted the governors? The kind of performance that we have been witnessing in the last few years, as between Washington and London, to mention only ourselves, raises a question as to how far the politicians and the services, civil and other, of the two countries have travelled in their thinking, comprehension, and technique. To be sure noble documents are signed and on festal occasions enlightened language is uttered; but then even Napoleon insisted that his empire stood for peace. So, in the era following, did battleships; so apparently they still do. In my opinion, the governors and warriors of the two countries have not yet been humanized to the point of seriously undertaking to comprehend one another, and, alas, they possess an extraordinary capacity for assimilating to their own viewpoint the more or less humanized output of the universities of the two nations. When will humanism be powerful and realistic enough to reverse the fatal process?

I am urging, as you will perceive, a broader, deeper, and more fearless conception of humanistic studies—urging that, without interfering with the specialized or scientific interests of the archaeologist, the palaeographer, or the historian, humanism should, further, charge itself with the appreciation of the present as well as of the past, of the value of science, of the value of industry, of the soundness, comprehensiveness, justice, fairness, worth-whileness of government, ours, yours, other nations'. Scholars are prone to take pride in withdrawing from the world of their own day; they let it alone; and the world is, in my opinion, much the worse for that.

The claim of a larger scope for humanistic enterprise goes hand in hand with vigorous encouragement of science and industry. It is idle to rail against either. The world went bankrupt on sheer ignorance of fact. Inevitably the pendu-

lum swung in the opposite direction. We have therefore
entered upon an era of science, mechanism, machine-pro-
duction, with all the social and aesthetic consequences and
problems therein involved. No merely pedantic, antiquarian,
intolerant, resistant, or unsympathetic type of humanism is
going successfully to impose a scheme of values on the
tremendous energy that is being released. With mounting
zeal men have sought to know more and to use what they
find out; with utter *naïveté* the responsibility for government
has been devolved upon the masses. As a matter of fact,
though knowledge and democracy have both achieved obvious
triumphs in both intellectual and social realms, neither from
knowledge as such, nor from democracy as such, does salvation spontaneously come: salvation is a thing of the spirit,
a thing of purpose, a thing of value. The ultimate control of
the physical and social forces which the last two centuries
have released depends therefore on an assertive humanistic
spirit; and among the assertive humanists one must, as I
have already intimated, count not only the professional
humanist—he may not even belong to the number—but any
person—scientist, statesman, or layman—who, divesting
himself of his prejudice or prepossessions, surveys his work
and that of others from the standpoint of its value to civilization.

Of the teaching of modern subjects, it can, I think, be
fairly said that thus far literature, language, and history have
been largely viewed as ends in themselves and but rarely as
means for that profound sympathy and comprehension
which Dibelius seeks.

The history of the Taylor Institution, like the history of
all modern subjects, shows the obstacles encountered by the
development of humanism. It is only within the last twenty-
odd years—too late to count yet for much in its effect on
present-day affairs—that this institution, devoted to the
teaching of modern languages and literatures, has notably

expanded; even for this limited function, its facilities are sadly inadequate. What is one to say of the capacity of other university departments here and elsewhere to extend their scope, so that nations, which are becoming increasingly interdependent, may not only know of one another's master-pieces in literature or art, may not only seek at one and at the same time to promote trade and intercourse, but really to understand one another? No modern university in any country is, as far as I know, equipped properly to undertake this larger function; nowhere could the effort be more hope-fully made than here at Oxford, which educates so large a proportion of the Englishmen who govern the Empire, its dominions, and dependencies, and, perhaps most important of all, are the means of communication between the Empire and foreign nations.

And it is not only with respect to foreign nations that the humanist will be fearless and candid; it may be more difficult, but it is assuredly not impossible to be objective with respect to one's own nation. It can no longer be left to superficial travellers to give their hasty and misleading judgements of other peoples—usually playing up to their own inborn nationalistic preferences; nor can it be left to the hundred per cent. German, Frenchman, Englishman, or American to value his own nation and thus confirm the unthinking in their native prejudices. What Bryce in his day did for the United States, what Dibelius has done for England, English, Ameri-can, French, and German scholars must endeavour to do for their own, as for other, countries. That is the burden that rests upon the shoulders of humanism in a world that will become a chaos if men do not strive to understand both themselves and one another.

To the preceding discussion it may, I think, be fairly objected that it has kept too closely to what Mr. Graham Wallas has called the 'anthropomorphic plane': it has tried to analyse and to conceive abstractly the working scientist, the working humanist. I have done this in order to bring into sharper relief the importance of appraisal detached from the mere search for knowledge or its application. Now let me, in concluding, add that there come supreme moments to the rare genius—philosopher, scientist, poet—to Plato, Newton, Descartes, Einstein—when, in the white heat of intellectual and spiritual passion, all distinctions melt away, when philosopher, scientist; and artist are one. It is not without significance that an English poet, searching for expression adequate to his ecstasy, found it in the rapture of the astronomer and the explorer:

> Then felt I like some watcher of the skies
>   When a new planet swims into his ken;
> Or like stout Cortez when with eagle eyes
>   He star'd at the Pacific—and all his men
> Look'd at each other with a wild surmise—
>   Silent, upon a peak in Darien.

At the level of intense feeling and deepest penetration, even human values dissolve, and things are what they are for their own sake and that alone.

CHEKHOV

BY

OLIVER ELTON

———————

The Taylorian Lecture 1929

———————

CHEKHOV

ANTON PAVLOVICH CHEKHOV died young, at the age of forty-four, in 1904, thirteen years before the Revolution. His life as a writer opens with the eighties; it covers the reign of Alexander III, the period of continuing repression and reaction, and also the first ten years, in appearance more hopeful, of Nicholas II. Much of his work reflects the disheartening aspects and temper of those times. As a story-teller he is the chief figure in the interval between two generations. He began just when Dostoyevsky died, in 1881. True, some two of Chekhov's elder contemporaries, Leskov and Garshin, were still in their prime; and another, his friend Korolenko, was long to outlive him. Tolstoy, who did not die till 1910, was still great, productive, and dominant in his later phase. For all this Chekhov, as a novelist, seems to be the truest representative of his time. His younger associates, Kuprin, and above all Gorky, begin a new chapter in the art. I will not venture to fill in this literary perspective. It has been done, and done with authority, by our best guide, Prince Mirsky, in his *Contemporary Russian Literature*. Prince Mirsky shows us how Chekhov strikes a Russian critic with a wide outlook. I will only try to show reason for the attraction which he exerts upon ourselves, an attraction which I believe will last; for this, in the case of a foreign author, is the only real question for all but professed students.

In his own country Chekhov is a classic, but the classic of a pre-diluvian past with which the present has broken; of an age far more remote in spirit than the age depicted in the *Forsyte Saga* is to an English youth to-day. In 1892 he remarked that he had been translated into all languages—'except foreign ones'; adding, however, that he had long ago been translated into German, and that the Serbs and Czechs were encouraging, also the French. In England he was little known during his lifetime. His own ideal of a translation, he says, is that it should be 'something light and ethereal, like lace-work'; he would surely have approved the versions of

Mrs. Constance Garnett. To her, above all, we owe our
acquaintance with his best plays and stories; and we can also
read in English, translated by various hands, many of his
best letters. These are delightful; they are usually cheery,
sometimes melancholy, explosive, ebullient, full of light jest,
and free-spoken; the reserve of the artist is not there and is
not wanted. Chekhov held it his duty as a writer never to
intrude upon the story; 'not to judge his own characters, or
what they say, but to be a dispassionate witness'. He claims
for one of his plays that he 'has accused nobody, and
justified nobody'. In his letters we read of his way of life,
of the sports and scenery that he loved, of his friends, of his
vehement practical activities, of his canons of art, of his
faith and his code of conduct. Chekhov is, above all, un-
pretending, and he would have laughed at the overdone,
semi-mystical laudations of some of his admirers, English
and Russian.

II. Anton, the third in a family of six, was born in 1860 in
Taganrog, the big commercial port on the Sea of Azov. The
grandfather had bought himself and his children out of serfdom twenty years before the Emancipation. The father kept
a grocer's store; but the business went downhill. He was
a cultivated man, devoted to music, especially to church
music; the home was cheerful, though strict and patriarchal,
and is well depicted by Anton's youngest brother and biographer, Mikhail. It was also religious; and Anton became
deeply familiar with the services, the ritual, and the church
hymns. He was overfed with piety, and said that in their
childhood they had all felt like 'little convicts'; he was to
abandon all formal belief; but he can portray the world of
a monk or pilgrim and the soul of a good ecclesiastic. 'Our
talent', he says, 'comes from the father's side; our heart and
spirit come from the mother's.' From the mother came also
his open, regular, harmonious, attractive features, so unlike
the tortured lines of Dostoyevsky. The face, said Korolenko,
had a touch in it of 'the simple-souled village lad'. His mother
also inspired in him a hatred of oppression, and a regard for

all defenceless things, birds and beasts. No novelist has shown a nicer and less sentimental insight into children.

When Anton was sixteen the household broke up; the parents went to Moscow and found it hard to live. The boy was left at school; and while there, as at college afterwards, he gave lessons, like many a Scot or American, in order to pay his way. Then he went to Moscow, studied medicine, and in 1884 was qualified. For many years he practised, and in his writings he uses his professional experience to the utmost. He often owns his debt to his calling, which trained the artist in scientific accuracy. Medicine, he says, was his lawful wife, literature his mistress. In this instance the two loves harmonized unusually well. It might be added that Chekhov's step-mother, not an unkind one, was journalism—comic journalism. Before he could earn medical fees he had to live by his pen. Deep down in him, though in moods of depression overlaid, is the humorist and mocker who keeps his own secret. For some five years he tossed off hundreds of little sketches for sheets that bore such titles as *The Dragon-Fly*, or *Chips*. At first they are mere chips, light vaudeville stuff; scores of them are of no account. We are startled by stray flashes, and that is all. Soon the flashes multiply, and within a few years we recognize a master of the edged and humorous anecdote. It had to be very brief, two or three pages. These conditions determined the scale of Chekhov's narrative art. The germ is the anecdote; out of this grows a short, then a less short, story. His longest tales are never longer than a short novel. Even these, he was to complain, were too long. *The Steppe*, he says, somewhat unjustly, is a string of separate pictures, not *one* picture 'in which all the details, like the stars in heaven, blend into a common whole'. He could make a beginning and an ending; but when he came to the middle, then, he says, 'I *champ*'. Most of his early works have no more middle than a wasp, and they never lack the sting. For some years comedy rules, or rather farce; but Chekhov's peculiar sombre presentment of life is soon to be discerned: the luminous grey texture, full of sparkles when it is held in the right light. This quality was evident by the year 1886, which was a critical one in Chekhov's artistic career.

III. In that spring he was stirred—'struck', he says, 'as by lightning', by a letter that came from a novelist of old standing, Dmitri Vasilievich Grigorovich. Chekhov had already attracted notice; he had quitted the cheap press, and entered into relations with Alexey Sergeevich Suvorin, the editor of the chief daily, the *Novoe Vremya*. To Suvorin, who was to be his intimate friend for many years, a multitude of his letters are written. But no one yet had told him that he was an artist, ahead of all his coevals. He replies to Grigorovich in a strain of gratitude and self-reproach. He has been, he says, careless; he has not respected his own gift; he has never taken more than twenty-four hours to write a story. Still, he adds,

'I have always tried not to squander upon a tale the images and pictures which were dear to me, and which, God knows why, I have saved up and carefully stored away.'

Thus encouraged, he went on producing, still upon the smaller scale; eighty or ninety tales, including some of his best, are the fruit of the next three years. He had always had a passion for the theatre; and, besides sundry farces and vaudevilles, he wrote, during this period, two plays; these are *The Wood Demon* (afterwards re-written as *Uncle Vanya*) and *Ivanov*. By this time he had a serious public; his life had many facets; he travelled to the Crimea; he had delightful country quarters in a village of the Ukraine; he was welcomed in Moscow by the men of letters; his correspondence becomes profuse, and cordial, and bitter and gay. But I pass over this chronicle, in order to linger upon Chekhov's greatest personal adventure.

IV. Towards the end of 1889 his mood was depressed and diffident; it is mirrored in *A Dreary Story*, in *The Seizure*, and in *The Princess*; and his health was irregular. He had, some years before, begun to spit blood; he was a consumptive; but he took little notice of his symptoms; and he had in fact, fourteen more years to live. He now went off at a tangent suddenly. From the first he had a warm place in his heart for the criminal in exile. One of his early anecdotes tells of a thief planted in Siberia who is dreaming at Eastertide of home and of the Russian spring. The local doctor is frigid to him, and refuses to ask him to a meal; but does ask another, a more important thief—more important, because he has stolen *more* and on a grander scale. The smaller thief had stolen in order to supply a heartless spendthrift wife, who was left behind. But behold, she now appears in Siberia, under the wing—of whom but the larger thief? The husband, who can do nothing, in a fit of fury kills his landlord's pet bird, is turned out of his lodging, and is last seen in the cold looking for a new one.

Now, in 1890, Chekhov picked up some books on Russian criminal law; and we see him fired with the disgust of the reformer who is justly ashamed of his country. To Suvorin he breaks out:

'We have let millions of people rot in prison; have let them rot at random, without reflection, and barbarously. We have hunted people in fetters through the cold for tens of thousands of versts; have infected them with syphilis, have perverted them, have multiplied criminals; and we have put the blame for all this on the red-nosed prison superintendents. Now all educated Europe knows that the blame is not on the superintendents but on all of *us*. Yet we take no interest; it is no affair of *ours*.'

Chekhov resolved to see for himself. He started alone, with no official blessing or credentials, on a trip of some 2,000 miles across Siberia, in vehicles and on river steamers, to visit the notorious convict settlement of Sakhalin (Saghalien). The journey out is told in his letters; his report is given in his book *Sakhalin Island*. This monograph is a sober and dreadful indictment. Its interest, no doubt, is largely historical and sociological; only stray extracts exist in English; it is, none the less, a real book and a revelation of the author. We are too apt to associate Chekhov's name with his helpless or baffled dramatis personae, and it is refreshing to see him at work in real life.

It took him six weeks to cross Siberia, and he passed

through alternate layers of hell and paradise. One paradise was on Lake Baykal; another, on the River Amur, where he passed through a lovely land, on the edge of China, far from officialdom. Before this he had made his way through mud, and flood, and cold, and dirt, and vermin. Once he had had to cross the great river Irtysh:

> 'The further shore is steep; the near one slopes; and it is gnawed away, slippery to look at, and repulsive; not a trace of vegetation. The turbid, white-crested water lashes it, and flings back angrily, as if disgusted at having to touch the ungainly slimy bank, on which, I should think, nothing could live but toads and the souls of murderers. The Irtysh does not clamour or roar; it seems as if, down at the bottom, it were hammering upon coffins.'

Chekhov was well received in Sakhalin, and stayed three months; he explored the whole inhabited part of the island, which was then entirely Russian soil. There were about 10,000 convicts of various grades. He had free access to all but the political prisoners. He visited, he tells us, every household, and made an elaborate census, on cards, of names, ages, occupations, creeds, marriages, and no-marriages. After doing a certain time in jail the male convict became a settler, planted out on the island; and then, after doing more time, he might be free to go back to the Siberian mainland. Chekhov describes the whole social economy; the handicrafts, the hunting and fishing, the diet; the punishments, the fates of the runaways, and, in his grimmest chapter, the position of women. The female convicts were not locked up, but distributed to the settlers for service and housekeeping; they were far outnumbered by the men. In one of the lighter passages Chekhov describes how the males, in their best clothes, assemble to inspect the newly landed criminals.

> 'They are turned into the barrack of the women and left alone with them. For the first quarter of an hour the indispensable dues are paid to confusion and embarrassment. The "bridegrooms" loaf round the plank beds, say nothing, and morosely eye the women, who sit hanging their heads. Each man makes his choice, without sour faces, and without smiling, quite gravely, in a "human" fashion; paying attention to their plainness, to their advanced age, to their jail-bird aspect; he scrutinizes, and he wants to guess by

their faces, which of them is a good housewife? Then one of them, young or elderly, "seems to him the thing"; he sits down by her and starts a heart-to-heart talk. She asks, Has he a samovar? How is his hut roofed, with planks or with thatch? To this he answers that he has a samovar, also a horse and a second-year calf; and his roof is planked. Only when the housekeeping examination is over, when both of them feel that the affair is settled, can she bring herself to put the question: "But you won't offend me?" The talk comes to an end. The woman is enrolled to settler so-and-so, in such and such a settlement; and the "civil marriage" is completed. The settler makes his way home with his consort; and, as a finale, hires a cart, often with his last coin, so that the mud may not splash their faces. At home, the woman's first act is to get the samovar going; and the neighbours, watching the smoke, say enviously, that so-and-so has got a wife already.'

Chekhov appears to have seen everything in the island except an execution. He saw men chained to wheelbarrows; he heard a long story from a murderer; he was present at an appalling flogging; he reports a conversation with a boy of ten who did not know his father's name, but only that the father had been killed by the mother, who was now doing time in Sakhalin, and living with a man. Later, Chekhov finds himself in a little graveyard, and his musings, we may think, would have appealed to Thomas Hardy:

'There is no need for any one to remember all these people, lying under little crosses: murderers, runaways, whose fetters used to clatter. Maybe, somewhere on the Russian steppe, some old wagoner, by the woodpile or in the forest, will relate, for sheer weariness, how in their village there was once a robber, so-and-so. The hearer, looking into the darkness, will shiver, a night-bird will cry at the moment; and that is all their funeral service.'

He returned, again through paradise, by Ceylon and India; and on reaching home he tried, through friends, to interest the empress in the lot of the children in Sakhalin; of these, he said, he 'cherished no little hope'. It is not clear what came of his efforts, or of his book, which is stated to have perhaps influenced certain changes that were made in the convict régime. The years that followed were full of public well-doing. Chekhov was active in the work of famine relief. In 1892 he bought a small farm at Melikhovo, in the province of Moscow: he converted it into a beautiful place; and it became, also, a head-quarters for action. The cholera threatened that region, but Chekhov worked successfully to avert it. He gave much medical advice. He had never been canny or economical, and once said that his money 'flowed away as quick as a perch that has bitten at the tail of a pike'. He founded a library in his native Taganrog. He could also set others to work. He built schools, built belfries; and received from the peasants the grateful token of the bread and salt. He held offices in the local administration. He threw himself into the work of the census, which brought him, as Mikhail Chekhov marks, closer to the life of the people, and made him 'a deeper and more serious writer'. His later fuller narratives, such as *Peasants* and *In the Ravine*, testify in their stern faithful way to these experiences.

V. After Sakhalin the stories became fewer; often they are longer than of old, and darker in tint. Chekhov is more preoccupied with the lot of humble persons, and with social problems, about which his characters discourse at length. Sometimes they talk too long; the problems have now lost their interest. Still the author, true to his principles, takes no sides. He must not insinuate an opinion; his task is simply to show how two Russians *would* debate about God, or pessimism, or the future life, or money matters, or the land. But there is no doubt as to the direction of his sympathies. He became, more definitely and openly, Liberal. During the Dreyfus business, he was wholly with Zola, whose *J'accuse* he found like a 'breath of fresh wind'; and he quarrelled sorely, for the time, with his friend Suvorin, the temporizing editor of the *Novoe Vremya*.

In the nineties Chekhov wandered a good deal in the search for health. At last he had to leave his beloved Melikhovo; in 1898, he was driven south; and he finally settled, with his sister and his now widowed mother, at Yalta in the Crimea. In that region he bought a property; and his life under the hot skies, and by the sea (which he once compares to 'blue vitriol') is mirrored in several stories, such as the well-known small masterpiece, *The Lady with the Dog*. He was much engrossed with the drama; after various failures, Chekhov's reputation was crowned by the success of *The Gull*, of *Three Sisters*, and of the *Cherry Orchard*. In 1901 he married the actress Olga Leonardovna Knipper. His wife continued in her profession, and the couple had often to live apart; but the marriage brought happiness to Chekhov, to judge from the multitude of his letters that have been published by his widow. They do him all honour, and show his gusty, gallant, and humorous spirit; but should love-letters be printed? During these years he often saw the aged, the still all-overshadowing Tolstoy, who was ill, but who was to survive Chekhov by six years, and who, if with certain reserves, admired his work. For a long time, says Chekhov, Tolstoy had influenced him deeply; but at last he broke away from the Tolstoyan code, and became disgusted with the ethics of *The Kreutzer Sonata*. Still, he loved no man more; without Tolstoy, he exclaims, they would all be as sheep without a shepherd; and, while he is alive,

'every kind of literary bad taste and commonness, everything that is insolent or lachrymose, will be remote and deep in shadow.'

During his latter years Chekhov was surrounded by younger writers: among them were Bunin, the poet; Kuprin, the gifted writer of short stories; and Gorky, whose talent Chekhov saluted and who has left the best literary etching of his friend. To read him, says Gorky,

'is like a melancholy day of late autumn, when the air is clear, and sharply limned upon it are the bare trees, the close houses, the greyish men and women—all so strange, lonely, immovable, and powerless.'

This is half the truth; it expresses one of the moods that Chekhov's writings induce. In 1904, still hopeful and full of plans, he went to the Black Forest to recruit, and died at Badenweiler. He was buried in Moscow beside his father.

VI. From first to last, Chekhov is a humorist; humour strikes across his gloomiest plays and stories like a line of sparkles on a tarn. In his early anecdotes it is rampant satire. His favourite victims are the official and professional classes, incompetent, servile, and absurd. We are still in the world of the rigid hierarchies originally designed by Peter the Great. Drink, too, is everywhere in Chekhov's pages, reeking,—drink on its ludicrous, or on its fatal side. Two advocates, 'in a superior frame of mind', blunder homewards, but into the wrong garden, and are entangled with the poultry in the darkness. A sanitary commission on circuit is detained by good cheer, and never gets to work. A coroner and a doctor driving to an inquest are diverted by weather, by hospitality, and by an amorous adventure which comes to nothing; they never reach the body. A defending counsel, day-dreaming about his children and also about a gipsy girl, drowses in the court and forgets his brief; suddenly he wakes, and sees that very girl in the witness-box. Or certain judges, in their private room, refuse to do business and talk only about eatables. In other legal scenes the point is the comic blank unintelligence of the prisoner. In *The Malefactor*, a peasant is being tried for unscrewing a nut upon the railway line. His defence is that he wanted a nut, and nothing else, for fishing, as a weight; for a nut is hollow, and it is heavy; and a nail is not hollow, and would have cost money. The court points out that he might have derailed a train and killed people. He only grasps the word 'kill':

> 'The Lord forbid, Excellency! Why should I kill? Am I not bap-
> tized? Am I a bad lot? Thank the Lord, I have lived all my life
> and have not only never killed but never had such an idea in my
> head.'

He is led away, still babbling. This tale was based on fact.

One of the best-known of these anecdotes is *The Chameleon*. The chameleon is a police inspector on his round. In the square he comes upon a small tradesman, who is pointing a bleeding finger and holding on to the hind legs of a dog. The inspector, indignant, says that the beast must be killed, and that he will teach people to let their dogs run about loose. But—whose dog is it? Some one says that it is the General's. The chameleon changes at once; tells the bitten one that he is lying, and that he had really torn his finger on a nail. Then it seems that the General has no such dog; and the chameleon is again sympathetic with the victim. But is it, perhaps, *Mrs.* General's dog? Her cook says, 'No.' 'Kill it!' says the inspector. 'Ah,' says the cook, 'but it *is* the dog of Mrs. General's brother, who has just arrived.' The chameleon makes a last quick-change. 'Doggy', he says, 'is all right: so lively! the naughty thing is angry'; and he turns on the wretched tradesman: 'Thou shalt hear from me presently!' and the crowd laugh.

We seldom ask a lettered Englishman whether he has heard that really good story about a Mr. Bumble or a Mr. Squeers. Chekhov's humorous yarns are no doubt equally familiar to a lettered Russian. But I take my chance of their being strange to some of my hearers, and will retail one more. This is called *The Anna on the Neck*. It is of later date (1895); it is an interlude, amidst a series of longer weightier narratives (*Three Years, My Life, The House with the Mezzanine*), and the old gaiety is renewed, but with a difference. The 'Anna' is the name of a decoration; it is also the name of the young wife in the story. She has been married, for the benefit of her indigent family; married to a rich elderly official. He is mean and pedantic. His wife's father is a tippler; and to this old man he doles out, along with a small loan, a heavy lecture on his habits. Anna gets no money from her husband; only rings and brooches, which, he remarks, are good things to keep against a rainy day. Anna's instinct is to live, to enjoy, to spend, and to spread her wings. She is sorely 'hadden doun'; but as they travel, on the dismal wedding-day, she has one moment of pleasure. At a wayside station she comes by chance on a crowd of cheerful young friends who wish her joy. This incident we remember afterwards to have been a good omen. At last her husband is forced to take her to an official ball, and also to give her a proper dress. To his amazement, as he stands about and nips brandy, Anna is at once the queen of the evening. She dances and flirts with the officers, and with a young gallant, who had been one of the party at the railway station. Above all, she is noticed by His Excellency, at the request of his wife, and triumphs at the charity bazaar. 'For the first time in her life she felt she was rich and free.' But Anna is no mere butterfly; and there is the true thrill of comedy in the three words that she flings, on the next day, at her husband: 'Blockhead, get out!' The tables are turned; she now spends what she likes and goes where she likes. The official world, his only world, is now against the husband. Yet he has his long-coveted reward, the ribbon and medal of the Anna of the second class; and His Excellency vents his time-honoured joke: 'Now you have three Annas, two on your neck, and one in your buttonhole.' Anna is last seen driving with her gallant. Her old father, jubilant, tries to call out to her something cheerful, in the street, while his young children take his arm, and entreat him: 'Daddy, you mustn't! Daddy, that will do!' Chekhov likes, at the finish, to throw in a bitter word that carries the imagination forward.

VII. He could write a tale for children; there is a delightful one, done in pen and ink with comic drawings, and reproduced in his correspondence. But, in his books, the children's tales are not tales for children. Now and then he is tragic, I will not say theatric; a desperate young boy shoots himself; a nurse-child, also desperate, kills an infant. In contrast, there is the merry picture of the loto party. Four small creatures, all under ten, are playing late at night for farthings while the parents are out; we listen to their chatter, and each of them is distinct. One cares only for the coin, another only for the game, another for neither; and the youngest, 'a regular little animal', only cares to watch for the quarrels of the rest. The cook's son joins in. They are last seen asleep, tumbled together upon a bed. It is a picture by an Old Master; Chekhov was then twenty-six.

Of the same date is *A Trifle from Life*, which illustrates well enough Chekhov's chosen method of winding into his subject. He likes to begin, in his own words, with 'life level, smooth, and ordinary, just as it actually is'. We are mildly interested; and some hints are dropped, which we do not notice until later. Then, at some point, there is a slight sudden swerve,[1] a *clinamen*, from the straight course, and the suspense is awakened. Then, at or near the close, a sudden phrase is heard, which drives in the point like a syringe. A youngish man, one Belyaev, ruddy, well-fed, and callous, is paying a chance call upon a mistress, a married lady, of whom he has long been weary; the husband has disappeared. Belyaev finds the eight-year-old Alyosha, the lawful son, sky-larking about alone. They chat; Alyosha plays with the visitor's watch-chain, and is at last led to tell him, after exacting a promise of secrecy, something that mother must never know: namely how he, Alyosha, and his small sister, are regularly taken by nurse to a pastrycook's; and how there they meet—whom but the vanished father? We hear how father feeds them with pies, tells them to respect and obey mother, and laments that she has been ruined by Mr. Belyaev; and how Alyosha had told father that Mr. Belyaev was quite kind, and never shouted at mother. At this Belyaev is furious; his heavy vanity is inflamed; and, when the lady enters, he rates her viciously and charges her, wrongfully, and in spite of Alyosha's desperate signs and noises, with being privy to the business. She goes out in indignation. Alyosha, shaking and crying, exclaims, 'But you gave your word of honour!' 'Get away,' says the fellow: 'this matters more than any words of honour!' Here, and not in the injury to the lady, is the tragic moment. Alyosha, says the author (speaking for once in person),

> 'for the first time in his life was brutally up against a lie, face to face. He had not known before that in this world, besides sweet pears, pies, and costly watches, there are many other things for which there is no name in the language of children.'

The tale of innocence, in fact, becomes a tale of experience; and Alyosha finds, in the words of the poet Blake, that 'Cruelty has a human heart, and Jealousy a human face'.

VIII. It may not be out of place to quote at this point some

[1] This method is described at length by Mirsky, *Contemp. Russian Lit.*, 1926, p. 90, to whom I owe the hint.

sentences from Chekhov's letters that set forth his own code of
behaviour. They are found at wide intervals of date. In his
youth, writing to a brother, he describes what he calls
'educated people'. They respect, he says, human personality,
and their own talent; they are sympathetic, and that not
merely with cats and beggars; they fear lying like fire; they
abhor smells and dirt; they control their sexual impulses;
and they work incessantly. Elsewhere he states that his own
morality is very ordinary; he has failings in the matter of
eating, drinking, and dissipation; and yet he is quits; for
these sins have been paid for by their consequences. But he
has not broken the Christian rule; he has not lied, coveted,
flattered, or pretended. The result is neither plus nor minus;
he is just an ordinary person. In another letter Chekhov sets
up a much less negative ideal; it is, indeed, a confession of
the faith which lies behind all his art:

> 'My holy of holies is this: the human body; health; intellect,
> talent, inspiration; love; and the most absolute freedom—freedom
> from lies and violence. . . . Such is the programme I would keep to,
> if I were a great artist.'

This, we may agree, is a good working creed, on what are
called naturalistic lines. More than once Chekhov disclaims
any dogmatic belief. His mind was not, like Tolstoy's,
doctrinal. No one has a sharper sense that all things are
mysterious, than the born agnostic; and Chekhov liked to
say, 'You will never *understand* anything in this world.'
Intellectually, he came to cherish a faith in some very far-off
time when reason and science and goodwill and decency
would surely prevail. I will try to indicate, when I refer to
his plays, how this faith becomes charged with feeling and
expressed with many a beautiful, as it were musical, *nuance*.
Meantime, in his stories, he discloses a rare dramatic and
human sympathy with certain kinds of religious sentiment.
Two examples may be mentioned: *The Bishop*, written in his
last years; and the *Student*, written when he was thirty-four.
The old, wakeful, dying bishop, who has risen from the people,
remembers his whole innocent life and its vexations. One of his

troubles had been that every one insisted on treating him as a man of God, as a man of rank; no one would talk to him simply as a human being. On Palm Sunday he goes wearily through the long service for the last time. In the congregation he sees an old woman who reminds him of his mother; and his mother she proves to be. A simple creature, she is embarrassed when they meet; she is divided between the thought of her boy and awe in presence of the bishop. He dies and is forgotten; she goes home, and when she ventures to say that she had once had a son in the hierarchy, she is scarcely believed.

In the other tale a young divinity student is returning home on Good Friday to his native village. He is in a weary mood. He reflects that in the time of John the Terrible there had been just the same freezing wind, just the same poverty, ignorance, and sense of oppression; and so it always would be. He then visits an old village acquaintance, who had once been a nurse, and her stolid peasant daughter; and suddenly he tells them, hardly at all in Church Slavonic, but in simple Russian, the story of the Apostle Peter's denials, and how Peter went out and wept bitterly. The women look at him, are moved, and burst into tears. The student goes away and reflects. Why did they cry? Not because he had told the story in a touching manner. The reason must be that the incident has some relation to them, and to himself. Then he seemed to see an unbroken chain of events stretching from that day to this. He had touched one end, and the other end had vibrated. Truth and beauty had guided mankind in the court of the high priest, and so they did to-day. Then a sense of youth and happiness came back to him, and life seemed full of high significance. Chekhov ends there, and draws no conclusions.

IX. But I have left out the setting of this story, the landscape; and without his landscapes Chekhov is not to be understood:

'The thrushes were loud; and close by, in the marshes, some living creature was droning a lamentable note, as though blowing into an empty bottle. One woodcock lingered still, and the sound of a shot rattled gaily after him in the spring air. But when darkness had fallen on the wood, an unseasonable blast of cold piercing wind came from the east, and all was silent. Needles of ice lingered in the pools, and the wood became comfortless, deserted, and un-inhabited. There was still a smack of winter.'

This chastity in natural description, such as we find in our own Thomas Hardy, seems to be the birthright not only of the greater Russian novelists, of Turgenev with his unequalled music, and also of Tolstoy, but of writers less ambitious. The pictures of river and forest, of ice and snow, by Korolenko, are exquisite, and deserve translation. Chekhov keeps, perhaps more strictly than the rest, to his canon that all such descriptions should be brief, should eschew routine (do not talk, he says of 'silvered poplars'!), and should exist simply to quicken in the reader a mood in accord with the story; let him be able to see the scene, when he shuts his eyes! Chekhov was himself an open-air man. One summer he is in a country house, near a 'broad, deep, islanded stream', one bank steep and high and overgrown with oak and willow; boats on the water; the sound of frogs: and

'In the reeds some mysterious bird is crying like a cow shut in a stable, or like a trumpet to waken the dead, day and night.'

In the stories, nature seldom rejoices; or, if she does, it is often as a foil to the cruel formidable village life, such as is depicted in *Peasants*; or, at best, as a momentary solace to the eyes of the pauper woman who has been driven from the village. In *The Witch*, a whirling tempest of snow imprisons in their hut the sinister sexton and his wife, and intensifies their discord. The best of Chekhov's landscapes, like those of the exquisite poet Fet, are in twilight; one of them I will quote, in order to introduce another, and a profoundly characteristic, type of subject. The teller, in the story (an early one) entitled *Verochka*, is recalling an episode of his long past youth; and this is how it had finished:

'He paced back quickly to the garden. In the garden, and on the path, the mist had gone; and the clear moon looked down from heaven, as if it had been washed; the east was just overcast with fog. Ognev remembers his cautious steps, the dark windows, the heavy scent of heliotrope and mignonette. The familiar Karo wagged his tail amicably and sniffed at Ognev's hand. . . . This was the only living creature that saw how he twice circled the house, stopped at Vera's dark window, waved his hand, sighed, and left the garden.'

The youth, who was of a bookish, rather timid temper, had taken leave, perhaps for the last time, of a cordial friendly family, after a long stay. It will soon be, so he muses, only a memory, like that of a flight of cranes over the sky. He had had no thought of love-making. But we are told, slowly, and with every shade of delicacy, for the theme is difficult, how the young daughter of the house had walked with him to the wood to see him off; how at last, desperately brave, she let him know that she loved him; how the youth, astounded, could only answer haltingly, and she ran back in shame; and how he followed her later, to look once more at the blind house; and how, for this is the root of the matter, he became aware of what he had lost 'through impotence of soul and incapacity for the deep acceptance of beauty'.

'All the time, something had whispered to him that what he was now seeing and hearing was, from the point of view of nature and personal happiness, more serious than any kind of books and statistics.'

But he had sighed, retraced his steps as described, and then gone away for good.

X. I have been dipping, all the time, in a lucky bag in which almost everything is a prize. There are many stories by Chekhov in which the ruling conception is some kind of fatal error, or *impasse*, or spiritual deadlock: a conception that has been made familiar by his plays. Anywhere, there may be a spirit in prison: in a villa, a hut, a hospital, a factory, a monastery, the edge of a forest; or, most impassable jail of all, upon the open steppe. The walls may be poverty, or distance, or solitude; or the iron social scheme and the hardness of surrounding persons. Above all, they are raised by the want of wit, or of sufficient will, to push away and escape. There is only the *wish* to escape, and the ineffectual vision of some window, or outlet, which is too high to reach. The result, in point of art, is that the story has no definite issue or solution; and with such a story the healthy Briton is apt to be impatient. He fingers his moral muscles, and he says, 'Why don't they *do* something? How Russian! This is not a story at all.' Well, you have only to live a short time and look around you, to see that an *impasse* in life is not a specifically Russian thing. And certain also of our own writers have shown that it is not: Thomas Hardy and George Gissing and George Eliot. Lydgate, in *Middlemarch*, the country doctor with his spoiled ambitions and his cramp-fish of a wife, is a thoroughly Chekhovian figure. What is really Russian about the business is the peculiar artistic method, which our novelists have hardly carried so far, and its power of suggestion. It comes out clearly enough in the elaborate study called *My Life*; and this I choose out of many such studies, partly to prevent any bewilderment, but also because, like Chekhov's later dramas, it does not end quite blankly. In some cases it is hard to acquit him of being over-clinical; of feeling, and of giving, the pleasure less of a work of art than of a perfect surgical operation. The alienist in *Ward No. 6*, who in the end joins his own patients, and the old professor, in *A Dreary Story*, who finds that his powers are failing and that his only friend has become strange— these, for all their power, I would call clinical studies. It is otherwise in *My Life*.

Here the speaker is a young enthusiast of noble rank, who is moved to 'simplify' himself, to quit the bonds of his class, to become one of the people, and to work with his hands: he is a real historic type, which has a special name, *narodnik*. He is duly denounced by his father and bewailed by his sister. He becomes a house-painter; he is cut by his friends, and at first is treated with hardship and derision by his fellow-workmen. Then comes a gleam of hope. A brilliant girl, an actress, who has no social prejudices, falls in love with him, or with his ideas, and marries him—for a time. Some money is saved; they set up in the country, try to help the peasants, to build a model school, and they fail. The wife wearies and goes back to the stage. The man carries on work with his sister, who has now escaped from home; she too has been through the fire; she dies, leaving an illegitimate child. The man remains a foreman, by this time quite well regarded. Now and then he meets another woman, who has loved him; but they never come together. They are last seen walking to the sister's grave with the child. The bright spot is the child—the eternal question-mark; and we remember Chekhov's hopes for Sakhalin. So the tale ends, with the characteristic no-solution, and yet less hopelessly than usual. Who will say that this is not like life, not good and penetrative art?

XI. But how present a situation of this kind in a drama? The theatre seems to demand that something should really happen. I have left too little time for Chekhov's plays and will only touch on one feature of them, which partially answers this question. Acted in Russian, they have triumphed in London and abroad; the principal ones are also played in English. Even if never acted again, I think they must live as dramatic literature. I say nothing of Chekhov's excellent merry farces, *The Bear*, *The Proposal*, and the rest; he refused to take superior views and never lost his relish for simple fun. To his four serious pieces, *The Gull*, *Uncle Vanya*, *The Three Sisters*, and *The Cherry Orchard*, should be joined one more, the early *Ivanov*. There was a pre-ordained harmony between Chekhov's talent and that of the Russian Artistic Theatre, which made and saved his fame as a playwright; and a corresponding harmony, it appears, among the players themselves, none of them usurping the scene, and all of them, like an orchestra, subserving the effect. This, indeed, is in several cases a violent one; in *The Gull*, for instance, the climax is a suicide. But such an ending is no less foreign to Chekhov's proper craft than is the 'happy ending' which for centuries was part of the very definition of a comedy. His true achievement, and that of the players, was to carry across to the audience his peculiar strain of poetic musing and his picture of an action in which, externally, nothing is accomplished. To do this, to supply the want with some idea to which the imagination can return and fix itself, Chekhov came to employ an instrument which it is terribly easy to jar and even to make ridiculous. This is the symbol; or, to use a less abstract word, the burden or refrain. Sometimes, as in *The Gull*—and as in Ibsen's *Wild Duck*— the symbol is definite; it is in the centre of the stage. The shot bird is there; it is seen, and is at once appropriated to herself, by the chief sufferer. This is the stage-struck girl, Nina, who has been blandished by the second-rate celebrated author Trigorin, and misled into the wrong profession. She becomes an actress and finds she is a poor one. But the symbol here is somewhat intricate. Morally, it is Trigorin who has slain the bird. Literally, it is slain by Nina's young adorer, who has shot it, like the Ancient Mariner, in a fit of wantonness. She deserts this young man. At last she returns, and sees him again; but she will not have him, and vanishes once more into her blank existence. The sound of his pistol is heard outside the scene.

In *The Three Sisters* the refrain is different; it is the word *Moscow*. Moscow signifies the supposed brilliant life, the far-off Elysium, which haunts the fancy of the sisters, and which they never reach. Entangled by circumstance, they are left alone together in the provinces. But here the refrain, as in many a ballad, is only incidental; it does not touch the vital point. The play is not merely a study in disappointment; on the contrary, a saving faith, or hope, remains, distilled from the disappointment itself. Each of the sisters expresses this in her own way, while the military music is heard without. One, who is stupidly married, exclaims that now they must live after all, must begin to live over again. The youngest exclaims that they must work for others, and that some day the human race will understand why it has suffered. To the eldest, the schoolmistress, the music seems to offer a kind of explanation; we, so she muses, shall be forgotten, but somehow our troubles will make for the happiness of those who come after us. The play ends with her cry, 'If only we could know, if only we could know!' Stated thus, the conclusion may seem unhopeful enough, or unoriginal; the force of it is only felt as the climax of a drama that has been fully acted out, in what George Eliot somewhere calls 'a troublous embroiled medium', by a crowd of characters.

In *The Cherry Orchard* the refrain is given by the title; and here the symbol is again at the true centre of the action. The imagination of each character plays about it in a different way. The orchard, a very old one, unique of its kind, and now in full flower, is seen by the spectator through most of the play. It has to be felled, and the timber will be sold, in order to pay off the debts of the owner, the lady, no longer young, who has just come home after a long absence and a stormy career. The sight of it recalls her youth; the orchard is itself a happy thing; and she says to it, 'the angels of heaven have not left *you*'. She cannot believe that it must go; she refuses to take steps that will make the sale more profitable. To her friend the merchant, Lopakhin, it is simply an asset. To the elderly student, Trofimov, it is a symbol of old Russia, which is still full of beautiful things. But it is also dreadful; for the ancient cherry-trees, in the evening, seem yet to be dreaming of the heavy days of serfdom. He reflects that Russia can only be redeemed by suffering and labour. They all go away, except the aged servant whom they have forgotten; he has the last word; he hears the sound of the axes falling.

The Cherry Orchard was played for the first time in Moscow, in Chekhov's presence, six months before his death; he had hastened up from Yalta to watch and advise in the rehearsals. He was applauded, honoured, and fêted to the point of exhaustion. Several of the actors have left their recollections; and we are assured that Chekhov firmly refused to consider the play a pessimistic or gloomy study of Russian life. 'It has turned out', he wrote, 'not a drama, but a comedy, almost a farce'; and this is true. The whole atmosphere is gayer and brighter, the suggestion of a decent future is less remote, than in *The Three Sisters*. The young, irrepressible Chekhov, the playwright of *The Bear* and *The Proposal*, has half revived. It would therefore be false criticism to take leave of him too solemnly. In this play there is a governess who does silly conjuring tricks; a wonderful old uncle, who

eats candy, chatters about billiards, and makes a sentimental speech to a century-old bookcase; a drunken tramp
who frightens a lady and requests 'thirty kopeks for a hungry
Russian'; and a station-master who walks in and begins to
recite a passage from Tolstoy. There is comic love-making
between a maid-servant and a clerk. All this reflects a gentle
tint of mockery upon the sentiment itself; and yet, in Chekhov's manner, the sentiment, the deep musical theme, survives the test. In a letter written some weeks after the
performance, Chekhov advises thus, in his lighter, his native
strain,

> 'Above all, be cheerful; do not look at life so ingeniously; probably,
> it is in fact much simpler. Whether it, namely, life, which we can
> never know, merits all the torturing reflections with which our
> Russian spirits wear themselves down—why, that is still the
> question.'

And let me add a word from one of his private note-
books, which have been printed :

> 'In the next world, I should like to be able to think this about our
> present life: *There were lovely visions in it.*'

I do not like to speak here without offering a salute to the
memory of that distinguished scholar, critic, and teacher,
Professor Nevill Forbes. Of his service to Slavonic studies in
Britain, and especially in Oxford, much has been said by
those who are entitled to judge; and also, by those who knew
him, of his personal qualities. I am but one of many strangers
whose steps in the reading of Russian have been guided by
his books, and who can only regret that his voice is silent.

NOTE

Accent as follows: Alexéy Sergéevich Suvórin; Alyósha; Amúr;
Antón Pávlovich Chékhov; Azóv; Baykál; Belyáev; Búnin; Dmítri
Vasílievich Grigoróvich; Dostoyévsky; Irtýsh; Ivánov; Górky;
Korolénko; Kúprin; Lopákhin; Mélikhovo; Mikhaíl; *naródnik*; *Nóvoe
Vrémya*; Ógnev *or* Ognyóv; Ólga Leonárdovna Knípper; Sakhalín;
Taganróg; Tolstóy; Trigórin; Trofímov; Ványa; Yálta.

I have to thank Mr. N. M. Tereshchenko, B.Litt., for kindly helping
in these accentings and transliterations, and in several points of
translation.

GERMAN VISITORS TO ENGLAND 1770-1795
AND THEIR IMPRESSIONS

BY

P. E. MATHESON

The Taylorian Lecture 1930

GERMAN VISITORS TO ENGLAND 1770-1795
AND THEIR IMPRESSIONS

WHEN I received the invitation of the Curators of the Taylor Institution to give the Taylorian Lecture, though I felt unworthy of the honour they had done me I could not refuse an invitation coming from such a source. My enjoyment of modern languages, while it has been that of a dilettante rather than of a serious scholar, has been so much associated with this Institution and its staff that I welcome the opportunity of expressing my gratitude to them—not only to the eminent scholars who have been associated with its teaching, but to the Library from which I have had much help, especially in German and Italian.

It is more than fifty years since I attended as a freshman scholar of Balliol the German classes of that distinguished teacher Dr. Hamann and learnt from his notes on Lessing's *Laokoon* and Goethe's *Faust* to understand something of the contribution made to German and European culture by the greatest critic and the greatest poet of Germany. And, as I happen to have given some close attention to one aspect of that immensely interesting period to which these great masters belong I thought that I could best fulfil my debt by speaking to you to-day about a subject, not indeed of primary importance in the history of German or European thought, but still of significance as illustrating some of the characteristics of that age of transition—I mean the literature of German travel in the last quarter of the eighteenth century. The field is a large one and I can only attempt to deal with a few selected books and writers. I shall confine my remarks to German travellers in England. The visitors to England of whom I have to speak are four, and their visits all belong to the last thirty years of the eighteenth century: Carl Philipp Moritz (1757–93), whose *Travels in England in 1782* I edited for the University Press in 1924; his friend Dr. G. F. A. Wendeborn (1742–1811), for some twenty years pastor of a German congregation on Ludgate Hill; Johann Wilhelm von Archenholz (1741–1812); and finally G. Christoph Lichtenberg, Professor at Göttingen, who paid two visits to England, the first in 1770 and the second in 1774–5. His letters, together with letters to him from his friends, throw vivid side-lights on the English life of his time as seen by a man of science moving in scientific and fashionable circles.

But before I speak of the writings of these men I must say a few preliminary words, however inadequate, on the period of German life and thought to which they belong. In the famous letter of Frederick the Great to Hertzberg, published in 1780 but written much earlier, he expressed the low opinion of German letters natural to one whose education was wholly French, but that opinion was already out of date when it appeared, for the essays of Lessing and his plays had effected a change that heralded the great period of German creative literature and formed a new canon of German prose. Wieland (1733–1813), whose varied works, which had a wide circulation, expressed the rational humanism of his generation, was having his writings published by the enterprising publisher Georg Joachim Göschen. The life of that publisher by his grandson and namesake, sometime our Chancellor, throws light on the age of 'Aufklärung' and 'Sturm und Drang', and Wieland's relation to it: a versatile and prolific man of letters, but destined before long to pass into oblivion, for in 1773 Goethe's *Götz v. Berlichingen* followed a year later by his *Leiden des jungen Werthers* marked the advent of a genius who was to be the commanding spirit of the next generation and with his friend Schiller, but with a profounder influence, was to enrich the new age of German literature. Their activities were only just beginning, yet in spite of the division of the German world into a multitude of States the German-speaking peoples were finding courage to claim their place in European letters and to free themselves from the hypnotism exercised over them by France in the preceding two generations. The claim was made to a world in which literature was already beginning once more to be an international bond. Leibniz (1646–1716) from Hanover and Berlin had already profoundly influenced European thought. It is true that his works that stirred the world were written in French and Latin, but he had already prophesied a great future for the German language, and now in 1781, the year of Schiller's *Die Räuber*, Kant's *Kritik der reinen Vernunft*, called out by the writings of our own Locke and Hume, opened a new period in the philosophy of Europe. The effective influence of this new factor in European thought was yet to come, but three other writers in that century had already moved England and Germany as well as France—Montesquieu, Rousseau, and Voltaire—and all three had visited England, a fact which shows that the interests of thinking men were beginning to overpass national boundaries. Their works and Adam Smith's *Wealth of Nations* all had a European vogue. The fact that a *European Magazine* was started in London at this time illustrates the new and wider outlook that was becoming general.

But we are concerned now rather with general literature than with philosophy and economics, and in that field the interaction of England and Germany was already remarkable. The publication of Bishop Percy's *Reliques of Ancient Poetry* and of Macpherson's 'translations' from Ossian gave an awakening impulse to the study of early German literature, and our poets and novelists had already won many readers in Germany through translations. Shakespeare's plays had gained a permanent hold on the German public, and Milton was widely read. Moritz, you will remember, carried Milton's poems in his pocket on his travels. The novels of Richardson and Fielding and Sterne had a wide and enthusiastic circle of German readers; the *Vicar of Wakefield* was a German classic, and Young's *Night Thoughts* were in the hands of all lovers of poetry in Germany and had profoundly influenced Moritz, as we know from his *Anton Reiser*.[1] Moreover, the alliance with Prussia under Frederick the Great had brought Englishmen and Prussians into close contact in the field, and though the British contingent consisted largely of foreigners

[1] Translation in *The World's Classics*, 1926.

under British officers, English regiments had fought by their side. Germany was no longer the unknown country that it had been and the advent of the Hanoverian line in England had made the contact of the two countries more intimate. These were among the reasons that made Englishmen and Germans inclined to visit one another's countries. There was another reason. This was an age of travel. We are familiar with the signs of it in England. The adventurous spirit that led our ancestors in the sixteenth century to the Pacific and the Spanish Main was finding a new outlet for its energy in other directions, in Anson's and Cook's voyages round the world and, rather later, Mungo Park's travels in Africa. Two Germans, Reinhold Forster and his son George, had taken part in Cook's second expedition, and the son had recorded their experiences. On the shelves of an Essex country house a few months ago I came across some handsome quarto volumes, dated 1753, *An Historical Account of the British Trade over the Caspian Sea with a Journal of Travels through Russia into Persia and back again through Russia, Germany and Holland* by Jonas Hanway, Merchant, whose life of mixed adventure and philanthropy, ending in a monument in Westminster Abbey, is one of the most varied in the *Dictionary of National Biography*. He deserves to be remembered for one sentence of perhaps unconscious humour: 'I was told in Brandenburg that Hanoverian women were remarkable for their beauty; but I confess I could not discover any such women; it is true that my eyes were then extremely weak.' These and the travels of J. Carver 'through the interior parts of North America' were among the more distant and perilous adventures, but curiosity and the passion for movement were in the air. Not only did English noblemen make 'the grand tour' in Europe as part of their education, but individual Englishmen were freely exploring their own and neighbouring countries and recording their impressions. We have Boswell travelling in Corsica, Johnson and Boswell in the Western Isles, William Gilpin, Prebendary of Salisbury, 'in several parts of England, particularly the

Mountains and Lakes of Cumberland and Westmorland'. There is Dr. John Moore whose *A View of Society and Manners in France, Switzerland and Germany* had reached a fourth edition in 1781, and finally the travels of Arthur Young a few years later, which have given us a vivid picture of France before the Revolution.

It was in this atmosphere of curiosity that here and there a German, conscious both of kinship and difference from the Englishman whose writings he had read, alive to the stirring movement of English life, and particularly to the contrast between Germany with its multitude of petty States and rigid monarchies, and England with its free Government, thought it worth while to travel in England and record his impressions. The traveller might be, like Moritz, a schoolmaster on holiday, escaping from the drudgery of the Graue Kloster in Berlin, to face the highway with a change of linen in his capacious pocket. He is called 'a poor, obscure German pastor', by the writer of the introduction to the first English edition of 1795, unaware that his veiled autobiography, *Anton Reiser*, had by this time won him the friendship of Goethe, and through Goethe a Professorship in Berlin, ended by his premature death in 1793. Or the traveller might be, like Wendeborn, a resident of long standing, in spiritual charge of the German colony in London; or like von Archenholz a professional soldier who had seen service in the Seven Years War. And to complete the picture given us by these writers of professed books of travel we have the occasional visitor, like von Lichtenberg. Moritz's *Travels in England in 1782* is probably known to most of my audience and I have little to add to what I said in my introduction to the edition of 1924. Its chief merit is its simplicity, its power of calling up a scene, and its genuine human sympathy. Archenholz from the superior height of noble Hanoverian birth writes somewhat contemptuously of this foot traveller, who did not know that in England you must ride or go by coach and that walking 'is not done': but Moritz's mode of travel brought him experiences that riding would not have procured him and his style, though in places it has been sophisticated[1] by his anonymous translator or editor or both, is effective for his purpose. It is a great testimony to his adaptability and his knowledge of English that in the few months he was in England he saw and learnt so much. His sympathy with the English character and his mastery of English made him a good observer. He knew what to look for and asked the right questions. I will give as a specimen of his style his description of a scene at a Westminster by-election, when he listened to the candidate's (Sir Cecil Wray) speech from the hustings and heard his election declared:

> When Fox, who was amongst the voters, arrived at the beginning of the election, he too was received with an universal shout of joy. At length when it was nearly over the people took it into their heads to hear him speak, and every one called out 'Fox! Fox!' I know not why; but I seemed to catch some of the spirit of the place and time; and so I also bawled 'Fox! Fox!' and he was obliged to come forward and speak. When the whole was over, the rampant spirit of liberty and the wild impatience of a genuine English mob were exhibited to perfection. In a very few minutes the whole scaffolding, benches and chairs and everything else was completely destroyed, and the mat with which it had been covered torn into ten thousand long strips or strings, with which they *encircled* or enclosed multitudes of people of all ranks. These they hurried along with them and everything else that came in their way, as trophies of joy: and thus, in the midst of exultation and triumph, they paraded through many of the most populous streets of London.

This lively picture will appeal to any one who has seen, as I have done in Nottingham, a riotous election in the 1860's before the Ballot Act reduced elections to order. Moritz had humour and an eye for a scene. He was a good traveller and what our friends across the Atlantic call a good 'mixer'. One could have wished that on his coach-ride to London from Northampton by way of Newport Pagnell he could have turned aside a few miles to the village of Olney and compared

---

[1] The editor from time to time added epithets which were not always happy. The 'snow' on the hills above Chatsworth becomes 'eternal snow' at Midsummer.

notes with Cowper, on English society and English manners.
They would have parted good friends, unless Cowper's stern
counsellor John Newton had intervened to save him from
latitudinarian heresy, for there is much in *The Task* and the
Tirocinium that would have appealed to Moritz.

Wendeborn was much more than a mere traveller in England, for he had spent twenty years here as pastor of a
German church on Ludgate Hill and had a very thorough
knowledge of London and some parts at least of England,
and had a good acquaintance with the English language and
literature. He wrote a Grammar for English learners, and
a book, written first in German (1780–4) and then in a shorter
form in English (1794) on the state of England, its religion,
learning and art, from which, besides valuable statistics on
trade and manufacture much entertaining information may
be got. As I have already given some account of this book in
the *Cornhill Magazine*[1] I shall speak chiefly to-day of his
shorter book on England, containing the story of his travels
in some of the Southern and Western counties (published in
1793). A word first on his *Grammar*. I have had the seventh
edition of it in my hands, dated 1819. In his preface to that
edition Wendeborn says: 'When the Author first published
the Grammar it was with a hope that in the course of a few
years in England, a country so famous for the improvement
and patronage of arts and sciences, the language and literature of the Germans would become an object of importance.
What he then only wished for, has since been realized to his
utmost expectation.' His grammar no doubt contributed
to this result.

In his book of travels his general attitude is that of his
ampler work on our country—admiration for England and
its people, with an observant eye for the weak points in
English learning and society, but, from the nature of its
subject it is mainly concerned with the incidents and humours
of the road, and with the inhabitants and manners of our
watering-places. From his chambers in New Inn, where he

[1] December 1928.

seems to have been very much at home, he set off by coach
from the White Horse, the starting-point of many travellers,
to go to Bath and Bristol, Southampton, Portsmouth, the
Isle of Wight, and Brighton. He gives a very genial account
of his adventures. He is careful to disclaim any idea of Anglo-
mania. 'I had no notion', he says, 'of writing a romance to
please the idle, or to confirm the foolish ideas of those who
know, or desire to know, no better, who regard England as
the Eldorado of Europe, and its inhabitants as demigods;
truth, so far as I could discover it, was the object of my
observation.' The reference to Eldorado finds a significant
supplement in a remark towards the end of his book, where
Wendeborn warns his correspondent (for the book is written
in the form of letters to a friend in Germany) not to send too
many letters to him, on which he had to pay postage, introducing visitors from Germany, in the fond belief that England
is full of rich Germans, ready to patronize literature and art
in the person of the needy immigrant. It is not so. 'Our
Germans here,' he says, 'except a few people of repute, whom
Heaven has rarely blest with abundant means, are ignorant
folk. Those who have a fortune by trade do not trouble
about the sciences or arts, of which they know nothing, for
they think money very unprofitably spent unless it gratifies
their foolish pride or their greedy appetite.'

Our traveller is mainly concerned in this book with
manners, modes of travel, and hotels, but at certain points
his journey brings him in contact with public events. Thus
at Portsmouth he records the recent concourse of people to
see the fleet that had been got ready to send to Russia and
had lain at Spithead in battle order and deplores the misery
of the sailors who had been unexpectedly discharged when
the expedition was abandoned. But his most exciting meet-
ing was with a brisk young man whom he met on the coach
between Bath and Bristol

who had just returned from a journey to France and had been
in Paris when the King was detained at Varennes and brought
back. He said that he had lately danced at a ball at Bright-

helmstone given by the Prince of Wales, with a French Duchess, who, when she found he was intimate with the leading members of the patriotic party in Paris told him she must take care what she said to him. He had relieved her anxiety by saying that, like a good Englishman, he was an aristocrat among aristocrats and a democrat among democrats. If this conversation really took place I believe his account of it, for very few Englishmen who have anything to do with trade and manufacture, any more than the Episcopal clergy and the nobility, with perhaps a few exceptions, favour the French Revolution.

The traveller handed round a French assignat for five *livres*, and after a discussion on the chances of its ever rising to par like the American paper,

> a substantial man of business who looked like a Dissenter gave his opinion that the present form of Government in France would be less harmful to England than her wars. 'If the British and French nations made a law for themselves, to under-take no conquests and to wage no wars but defensive ones . . . and to reduce to order any disturber of the peace, do not you think that the wars that have done so much harm would be stopped and an end would be put to the perpetual disorders that now infest Europe, so that in future large standing armies, so oppressive and exhausting to nations, would become un-necessary?' For this reason he would support the French Revolution.

Wendeborn's comment is worth noting.

> The Dissenter in the main was right and I think that if Mr. Fox and his party had been in office when the Revolution began, the Revolution would have benefited and order and quiet would soon have been restored with English support when the new constitution was established. I have many reasons for thinking that Mr. Pitt, if he were not Minister, would think and express himself like Mr. Fox in regard to the French Revolution.

I leave this speculation to the historians. At Old Sarum he comments on the evil of our rotten boroughs, and speaks with some sarcasm of those 'both here and abroad, who in spite of such obvious defects and abuses, proclaim the English constitution a marvel of wisdom and justice. No part of it needs such drastic reform as the representation of the people.' He is a sharp critic of the conduct of foreign affairs.

> The people, who have not the least idea of the power and interests of the European States, echo the Parliamentary debates and talk with a serious air of the danger threatening the 'Balance of Power', and allows money to be voted from its pockets to maintain it, with the help of the member for Old Sarum and the like.

His conversation in the Isle of Wight with an Englishman who had spent nine years in Madras and Bengal confirms his opinion of the shortcomings of the government, but he adds that 'his judgement on the character and conduct of Hastings as the first Governor, was very different from that expressed by Burke and others who are at present conducting the case against him. He assured me that those whom he had ruled there were for the most part well content with him and still hold his name in high esteem.'

On the whole his sympathy is with the Whigs and humanitarians. He has little respect for the weaknesses of Royalty and a low opinion of the pluralist parson. Hunting and sport he cannot away with, and racing he thinks bad for man and beast. But what he most misses in the west country, and it is to his credit, is the company of learned men and learned books. Unfortunately Dr. Douglas, Bishop of Salisbury, of whom he speaks with great respect, was away from home when he was there. But the main part of the book, apart from description of towns, is taken up with the road and its incidents. He pities the horses, which he considers badly over-driven, and has a horror of 'crooked and winding ways'. He describes the different ways of travel—private carriage, post-chaise, mail-coach, and wagon, and elects for the coach as cheaper and more sociable. But the privacy of the post-chaise is more suited to the English genius.

> Just as in travel abroad the English avoid *table d'hôte* and prefer to pay extra and dine alone in their room half as well as they would dine in company; just as in a coffee-house they choose an empty table and sit, read and eat at it; so they prefer to

drive alone and you will see many a man on the high road, alone or with one companion driving quickly past, yawning or sleeping or scowling as he goes, while the travellers by coach or mail shew a cheerful face and good humour.

It is not surprising after this to find that he considers our men have little faculty, compared with the French, of making themselves agreeable; he also thinks that the gossip and scandal at women's tea-tables is worse than in other countries. An English woman, perhaps, would have had something to say on the other side, after listening to the talk at a German Kaffee-Klatsch. He is very tired of the English dinner of roast meat and potatoes followed by cheese and strong beer, for which the guest has to pay more than he would pay in France for 'six courses and a bottle of wine', and he points out that the cost is increased by 'the silly English prejudice' that a gentleman should not question his host's reckoning. At the 'White Hart' in Bath he finds to his delight a room called a 'Common Room' in use, whereas 'in general, Englishmen as soon as they come to an inn ask 'Can I have a room to myself?' But at this inn there was sociable company which 'made up for the morose, reserved and foolish-proud air of the rest'. His journey had taken him through Salthill, where he saw Eton 'Montem', though he does not call it by that name; Reading with its ruined Abbey and its river traffic; Newbury, with its memories of the cloth-trade, to Marlborough, where he admired the mahogany of the old Castle Inn. From here he went on by Devizes to Bath and Bristol, and then by way of Salisbury, Southampton, and Portsmouth to Brighton, and so back to London.

Everywhere he keeps his eyes open and his comments show observation and shrewdness. He describes Bath very fully, the Bath of Jane Austen seen from a different angle, but the same in essentials, with its Pump-room and its boarding-houses, its Abbey and its 'bookshops where you can read books and magazines, and its lending libraries to fill the vacant hours of the idle with novels and entertaining literature; but there is no public library for students'. Here, as in London, he deplores the lack of meeting-places 'for scholars and men of learning'.

His account of Bristol is not the least interesting part of his story, for he gives a pleasant picture of a quiet evening with a Bristol family, contrasting it with the more fashionable and less rational entertainments of London.

> We sat down to tea at 6 and to my surprise and pleasure, when this was removed, the servant received no order to bring in the card-tables, but the women, younger and older, including four guests, sat round a small table and busied themselves with sewing, while the men formed a semi-circle beside them, and the time till supper passed in pleasant talk, in which the ladies bore a large part. In houses of less importance than this in London two or three card-tables would have been produced at once, as an antidote to boredom and to conceal the fact that the company was incapable of rational conversation and the clash of wits. . . . The supper was very good but not extravagant and the company parted at about 11, an hour when a London host would be putting supper before his guests.

We get a glimpse of one of the burning questions of that day in his condemnation of 'the abominable traffic with Africa', and his mention on Brandon Hill of a bonfire made by some young bloods of Bristol on the defeat of a vote for the abolition of the slave-trade. He is equally interested in the manufactures of Bristol, its sugar-refineries and glass-works, and in the country round it, for he drove out to King's Weston, one of Vanbrugh's houses (which readers of Miss Austen will remember), and from Pen Pole Point admired the beautiful view across the Bristol Channel to the Welsh mountains, with ships in the distance at anchor or under sail.

On his journey to Salisbury, for which he started at 6 a.m., not getting his breakfast till after the sixteen miles drive to Warminster ('for English maids and waiters are too fond of their morning sleep to leave their beds early to serve travellers') he was struck by the solitude of Salisbury Plain and the seriousness of the people at work. 'In Germany what a gaiety and cheerfulness prevail among the country-folk as they gather in the kindly fruits of nature! . . . but here I found nothing of the kind. No singing, no gaiety, no joking was to be seen.' Perhaps if he had seen them later in the evening or at harvest-home he might have changed his mind. It is not the Wessex of Thomas Hardy. Another thing that strikes him is the absence of women's labour in the country, except the immigrants from Wales and Ireland who come for the season. 'When you meet a family of Welsh girls dressed in their homespun and talking Welsh, which the English do not understand, they seem like foreigners.' Southampton, at that time mainly living on its fashionable visitors, (you may remember that Johnson's friend Bennet Langton went there in the season), has little to interest him, except the trade in wine and wool, but the view of the town with the sea and the New Forest in the background he finds charming. The Forest itself reminds him of a forgotten episode in German history. 'The poor folk from the Palatinate, who were sent to Georgia, were to have been planted as a colony in the New Forest. The scheme was a good one, but so much roguery was mixed up in it that it came to nothing.' A report of a recent Commission told him that the Forest was very badly managed and he could not forget that it was made to gratify a king. At Portsmouth he saw the *Brunswick*, seventy-four guns, then commanded by Sir Roger Curtis, the hero of the floating batteries at Gibraltar in 1782, and the *Barfleur*, ninety-two guns, taken from the French. He was pleased with the *table d'hôte* at the Crown, 'where you dine well and in good company, not only strangers but a number of ships' officers, some of them very agreeable. The presence of the hostess at the head of the table, with other ladies near her produced a certain decorum in the conversation.'

As he drives on to Brighton he speaks of the much-praised 'down mutton', much of which, so the story goes, comes by coach from London. Brighton does not come up to his expectations: 'without gardens and with hardly a tree within five or six miles; beaten by the south and south-east wind, in summer scorched by the heat; with nothing to occupy it but fashionable pleasures and distractions; a town where everything is extraordinarily dear, and landlords flay strangers in an unexampled manner'. After exposing his landlord's overcharges he turned homeward and as he approached London describes how 'the closer I came to London, the deeper I plunged into the swirl of its humanity and the clamour of its streets, the more delighted I was in a sense to exchange the quiet country for a noisy and restless capital. If you have for many years become used to the throng of London, the tumult in its streets and its thick atmosphere, it takes but a few hours to feel at home again even after an absence of several weeks or months.' Dr. Wendeborn, though he sometimes criticized our ways, had in his five and twenty years become a very complete Londoner. There is one very pleasant touch in his narrative that marks the carefulness of his observation. As he drives through the woodland on his way back from Brighton to London and thinks of the bakers whose fuel comes from that country-side, he describes one aspect of London at midnight which shows a nice observation and a feeling for the quieter enjoyments of life.

> One gets a pleasant change of smell at midnight when the bakers in the streets of this great capital begin to heat their ovens, in order to have their bread ready for sale in the early morning. At this hour the thousands of kitchens and stoves, which are fed with coal in the daytime, are no longer burning. The foul smoke of the coal fires, with which the city is covered eighteen hours of the twenty-four, has disappeared, the air begins to clear and the smoke of the bakeries, which are heated with wood instead of coal, spreads a very country-like smell in the neighbouring air. Those who walk at this hour through the streets, or open a window towards the wind, can well imagine on a summer night when the day's clamour is hushed, that they are in a village instead of amid a throng of more than half a million, who are wrapt in sleep about them in rank upon rank of close packed houses.

On the whole Wendeborn's view of England is that of a man familiar with English life, who appreciated its strong points: the healthiness of its open-air education and the frank manners of its citizens. He took pains to get at the facts of English trade and commerce and to convey them to his readers, and he was alive to the significance of the burning questions of the time—the American War, the trial of Warren Hastings and the whole subject of Indian government, the freedom of English institutions coupled with the corruption of Parliament and the small political weight given to the great towns. He had a low opinion of the English Church and its clergy, and saw that the Methodist movement was a natural product of the circumstances of the time. He criticized the want of learning in the English schools and Universities, while he admired the opportunity offered by the tranquillity of College life. With racing and sport in general he had no sympathy. While he admired the independence of the Englishman he found him reserved and unsociable, and he condemned the extravagance of his living and the monotony of his diet. He does not seem to have seen much of the best society of the time—we must look to Lichtenberg for that—but he was clearly very much at home among the merchant and professional class and recognized their good qualities, and his knowledge of English enabled him, like Moritz, to make himself at home in any company he frequented, whether it was the lonely young lady on the coach, the naval officers at Portsmouth, the mixed company in the inns, or the returned official from India and the young man who had just come from Paris in revolution.

I have next to speak of a man who shared many of the opinions of Wendeborn, and was not only socially his superior but also a much more important figure in the world of German letters. Johann Wilhelm von Archenholz was a man of many adventures. Flung into Frederick's campaign as a boy of seventeen after a short training in a Cadet School, he took part in the siege of Danzig and in several campaigns, retired from the army at the age of twenty-two with the rank of Captain and spent most of the remainder of his life first in travel and then in a variety of literary enterprises. He travelled in all parts of Germany, and in Holland, France, England, and Italy. He spent six years in England and his book *England und Italien*, published in 1787 and dedicated to Wieland, was the outcome of his experience. The book made a great success and was translated widely. But his English activities were much wider than this. He published a *Brittische Merkur* in German and English and for ten years after his book on England appeared continued his account of British affairs in a sort of Annual Register called *Annalen der Brittischen Geschichte*. In the *Annalen* he was helped on the literary side by J. G. Forster (1754–94) whom he had known in London, where Forster, after producing the account of Captain Cook's second voyage, already mentioned, was making a precarious living by translations and hackwork of various kinds, before he returned to Germany to more definite employment, but alas only to be swallowed up in the stormy waters of the French Revolution and to die in Paris at the age of forty, not indeed by the guillotine, but by an illness which no doubt was caused by his revolutionary adventures in Mainz and Paris.

Archenholz also published the *English Lyceum, or Choice of Pieces in Prose and Verse, selected from the best Periodical Papers, Magazines and Pamphlets and other British Publications* (Hamburg, 1787). The collection is rather a dull one, but is enlivened by some then unpublished letters of Sterne, Steele, and Johnson, a poem of Burns, a summary of Sheridan's speech on Warren Hastings, and an article on playwrights of the day—Colman, Cumberland, Murphy, Burgoyne, Mrs. Inchbald—and it no doubt served as a useful 'Reader' for students of English in Hamburg, which was at that time, from its comparatively liberal government, a lively centre of the intellectual life of Germany and through its commercial and social connexions mediated between the educated world of Germany and England. He edited a periodical, *Litteratur und Volkeskunde*, and was active in other magazines. Perhaps the most important of these and one which deserves mention, though much of it falls outside our period, was his *Minerva*, a magazine that attempted to give a contemporary view of European history and politics, though soon compelled to restrict itself to French events. He published it from Hamburg 1792 to 1809, and it was continued in Jena from 1810 to 1857, a long history for any periodical. It should be mentioned here both because it is an important source for our knowledge of the Revolution, and because it shows a change in Archenholz's attitude to England. He abandoned the favourable opinion of our country expressed in *England und Italien*. His sympathy with the Revolution until the violence of the Jacobins disgusted him and his sympathy, however qualified, with the Revolutionary government that followed turned him not indeed against the English people as a whole but against Pitt as War Minister, who he thought had refused to procure peace for Europe. This change of view was the more bitter to him as the hero of his book of 1787 was Chatham, for whose spirit and policy he had the deepest admiration. 'Never was such perfect unity of King, Parliament and People as during his glorious administration, which unhappily for England did not last long enough. Had it lasted only two years longer we should have seen no American War and Great Britain would now have reached a height of power, fame and prosperity, of which its position in 1762 was but a shadow.' I must not stop to give an account of his chief work, *Die Geschichte des Siebenjährigen Krieges*, which had a great circulation and in 1911 had reached a thirteenth edition. It was one of the sources for Carlyle's *Frederick the Great*.

During his stay in England he took Montesquieu for his political guide, and made a close study of the English constitution and its working. In politics his sympathy, like Wendeborn's, was with the Whigs. Into the three small volumes that contain the English part of *England und Italien* he manages to pack a vast amount of solid information. Like our other visitors he was attracted by the personal freedom of life in England. He approves the frank speech and independence of our people who, he says, are only on the surface rude and uncultivated, and he praises the even administration of justice.

'It is a truth that will not admit of doubt that no polished

nation was ever so free as the English at this day.' He refers
to the Habeas Corpus Act, the conduct of the Law Courts,
Trial by Jury, Representation in Parliament (with all its
corruption) and Liberty of the Press, but on the last he adds
an interesting note, ' I must say, to the honour of our country,
that, except England, there is no other kingdom in the world
where a man may write so many bold truths and discover so
many abuses as in Germany'.

He mentions with admiration the conduct of Lord George
Gordon's trial by Lord Mansfield. Presiding over his trial
'this magnanimous man forgot his burnt house, with its
precious library and rare manuscripts and works of art, the
loss of which was occasioned by the worthless Gordon, and
was simply a Judge, to give judgement according to law.
He treated the insane Gordon very gently, impartially
summed up all the evidence in his favour and acquitted
him.' The English, he says, are interested in politics, men
and women alike. They have a strong feeling of national
pride, and are generous for public objects. Voluntary contributions for the support of the Government in war-time and
for hospitals and other benevolent objects are common. He
illustrates the nice sense of national honour by the story of
the inn-keeper at Canterbury, who having charged the
French Ambassador, the Duc de Nivernois, fifty guineas for
a night's lodging, was ruined by being boycotted by the city
and county, who were shocked at his scandalous overcharge.
We are not inclined nowadays to think much of the eighteenth-
century system of police, but Archenholz is loud in its praise.

> For this excellent system of police, which combines the good
> elements of the Parisian system, stripped of its cruelty, with
> English laws, we have to thank Fielding the famous novelist,
> who was for many years chief Police Magistrate in West
> London. Here he studied the human heart and it was in this
> post that he acquired the extraordinary knowledge of men,
> extending over every rank and class, which we admire so much
> in his works.

The seamy side of English life has a special attraction for
him. He gives a list of the various types of London rogues:

Intelligencers, who cheat people with hopes of places; Setters who arrange fraudulent matches; Dippers, Trappers, Swindlers, Money-Droppers, and Kidnappers. He distinguishes the highwaymen from footpads and common thieves. A story of the politeness of the inferior class may illustrate his narrative style.

Though footpads are only underlings compared with the knights of the highway they have certain notions of honour, which lead them to act in a way that one may call a parody of virtue. An incident of 1786 will illustrate this. Near the North of London lies the pretty village of Islington. A lady, who had country house here was walking alone across the fields one summer evening when she noticed two suspicious persons approaching. They were joined by a third, who presently left the others and came towards her. She had presence of mind enough to act with decision; hurrying to meet the third man she addressed him with an air of confidence and begged him to protect her. 'You, Sir,' said she, 'look like an honest man, but I am afraid of those other two, whose designs I suspect. Pray, Sir, protect me.' 'Madam,' replied the robber, 'have no anxiety; take my arm and on my honour I will take you out of danger. As soon as I wave my handkerchief, the two men you are afraid of will vanish; they are my comrades, and we came intending to rob you, but your appeal to my protection has made all the difference for I am not such a rogue as to abuse your confidence.' He accompanied her home and when out of gratitude she offered him some guineas at parting, he rejected them with the remark that he had never in his life accepted payment for a service of honour.

Archenholz describes *con amore* the lighter side of London female society and speaks of the house of Mrs. Bellamy the actress, the Juliet to Garrick's Romeo, as 'the meeting-place of great and honoured men in all departments. She was a trusted friend of Young, Thomson, Littleton (*sic*) Garrick and Chesterfield. Ministers of State, Generals and Ambassadors visited her daily.'

The stage had a great attraction for him. He gives an account of Drury Lane, Covent Garden, and the Haymarket and their performances, among which he describes the new type of 'Entertainment', which is more a pageant than a

play and gives as an example the Shakespeare Jubilee of
1769, at Stratford, repeated next summer seventy-nine times
at Drury Lane. His comment on *The Beggars' Opera* has a
certain interest to-day.

> The robber's profession appears in a not ignoble light in Gay's
> famous Beggar's Opera, which is played some dozens of times
> a year in London alone and is a favourite of the British public.
> It is not to be denied that there is much to be said against its
> morality, but the extraordinary wit of the piece and the excel-
> lent music keep it permanently on the stage.

In the first volume of his *Brittische Annalen* von Archenholz
enlarges further on the variety of London amusements and
describes evenings of mixed entertainment, music and recita-
tion, in which actors took part, particularly the young and
popular John Henderson, 'the Roscius of Bath', an actor of
great promise, with a fine voice, who unfortunately died
young. He was so popular that he was given a monument in
the Abbey. There is an attractive portrait of him in the
National Portrait Gallery by his friend Gainsborough, in
which I take some personal interest as he was a cousin of
one of my great-grandfathers. It would be too long a task
to attempt to reproduce the picture of English manners as
Archenholz paints it: but I will call attention to some of its
characteristic touches. He praises the general good sense of
the commonalty: they are intelligent and judicious and be-
have well in a crowd and observe the courtesies of the street.
They love the open air, are the greatest walkers in Europe,
and delight in gardens. To threaten a public garden was to
risk a revolution. George II's Queen Caroline had proposed
to turn St. James's Park into a French garden and exclude the
public. Lord Chesterfield when shown the plans approved,
but when asked what it would be likely to cost replied (with
a happy play of words) 'Not more than three crowns.' This
answer saved the park.

Archenholz had a low opinion of the learning of the Universities, but admits that it is corrected by foreign travel.
Scotland, he says, has outstripped the south of England,

which is dulled by luxury. 'More true learning is to be found in Edinburgh than in Oxford and Cambridge taken together.' What does appeal to him is the fact that in England learning and science are not confined to a class. Scholars are not a race apart and the learned societies include men of all ranks in life. He applauds the fact that scholarship may be an avenue to preferment and instances the promotion of Prior, Addison, Locke, and Newton to public appointments. He would like to see the German Schröder, the interpreter of Shakespeare on the stage, honoured as Garrick and Mrs. Siddons are honoured in England. One of our great defects is our ignorance of foreign languages. Englishmen learn French, but not to speak it, and German is almost unknown. Yet, 'No one can properly judge the culture of a nation without learning its language: even the best translations are inadequate. Compliments paid to German literature by Englishmen and Frenchmen who do not know German, are, as a famous scholar observes, of no more significance than the signature "your obedient servant".'

London with its variety of life appeals to him strongly; particularly its social side: the multitude of coffee-houses, the variety of Clubs and Societies, for debate and politics and social purposes, the quantity of public dinners. 'Here the Englishman can air his political ideas, and indulge his inclinations and pay libations to his patriotism. He is in his true element. Anyone who observes these Islanders on such occasions will recognize that it is an unfounded prejudice that brands them as unsociable.' Nowhere perhaps does his appreciation of the independence of the Englishman and his social gifts appear more vividly than in his description of the King's Bench Prison with its society and self-government and its intolerance of encroachment, which he illustrates by the anecdote of an intrusive bailiff who was punished by being forced to swallow his parchment writ piece by piece!

He has a keen eye for the beauty and piquant dress of our countrywomen of all classes. 'The most elegant part of an Englishwoman's dress is her hat, which is usually adorned

with ribbands and feathers. . . . The art with which they
put them on is but imperfectly copied by foreigners, who
do not know how to derive from them all their magical
advantages.'

But a very substantial part of the book is devoted to a
description of British trade, the success of which is due to
'good laws, good government and an enterprising spirit',
and the working of British banks, and above all of the Bank
of England, to the importance of which he is very much alive.
He describes the crisis when the Duc de Choiseul tried to
ruin the Bank and was frustrated by the action of 'a
hundred and twenty of the richest business men in London,
who signed a document agreeing to accept Bank of England
notes as cash for three months. From that moment all
anxiety ceased.' He lays stress on the close connexion of
economics and politics, and gives the history of the Naviga-
tion Acts and traces their effect. One of the most striking
parts of his narrative in the first volume of *Brittische Annalen*
is his account of the outburst of British enterprise after
the American War. It is not without a moral for this
generation.

> The proud British manufacturers, always disinclined to take
> any steps to promote their foreign sales, lowered their tone,
> and sent their travellers round Europe, offering long credits
> and low prices even to retail dealers in small towns.

As a soldier he is interested in the British Army. He notes
the low repute in which the common soldier is held, deplores
the disgraceful sale of officers' commissions, which he regards
as a mean economy to save pensions, and explains the importance of the Militia. He describes a great review at Coxheath,
in 1787, a commonplace sight enough to a Prussian officer,
which evoked from the king the exclamation, 'O Amherst,
what a heavenly sight!' But his chief admiration is for our
Navy, whose strength he enumerates in detail. He describes
the great victory of Admiral Hawke over the Marquis de
Conflans on November 20, 1759, which cost France the loss
of Canada and the West Indies. The warm eulogy that he

pronounces on the British sailor will go to the heart of all
Englishmen.

> English sailors are a unique class. Bred from childhood more
> on sea than land, they are rough like the element. The stern
> discipline in English men-of-war, which has no parallel else-
> where, perhaps accounts in great measure for the wild deeds of
> sailors ashore: but with all their misbehaviour they very seldom
> do real harm and no class is more popular. Smollett has given
> masterly pictures of them in 'Roderick Random' and 'Pere-
> grine Pickle'. With all their roughness they combine courage,
> generosity, honesty and devotion.

It will be clear from this brief account of his book that
Archenholz was a good observer and that he understood our
temperament. He was no Anglomaniac, but he loved England. It was with no servile affection. He belonged, as I
have said, to a Germany that was becoming conscious of its
unity of race and language, and was already aware of the
great achievements of which it was capable.

> Thirty years ago, he says, if some obscure French journalist
> paid the least compliment to a German writer, the German
> thought himself lucky. We were childishly eager for praise
> from abroad. German literature was in its infancy, English
> everywhere unknown, while French literature had dazzled us
> for a hundred years. The French no doubt were our instructors,
> but the British even more so, as soon as Wieland took the great
> step of making Shakespeare known to us.

He appreciates Germany's debt to other nations, but he
prophesies that as Voltaire, Montesquieu, Rousseau, and
Helvetius have revealed England to Europe so will it be
with Germany in the next generation.

I find it hard to leave this congenial writer, but I must say
a few words on another visitor, whose letters give a somewhat
different view of English society—that of the man of science
entertained both by men of science and by the fashionable
world of London, and as a good Hanoverian from Göttingen
enjoying the patronage and society of the king. As Baron
von Pöllnitz remarked in the Preface to his *Observations on
his Travels* fifty years earlier, 'The Traveller judges of the

Nation where he is, by the Company he keeps', and 'A foreigner who takes up his Residence in the City of London will entertain a different Idea of the English from what another shall do who lodges at the St. James's end of the Town'. So far we have been in contact with' men whose acquaintance in England was mainly with the merchant class. Lichtenberg, who was an earlier contemporary of the three travellers already described, represents a somewhat different social type, and his associations in England were different.

Georg Christoph Lichtenberg (1742–99) has a place in the history of Physics as inventor of the 'Lichtenberg figures' but he was also a well-known man of letters. His writings, partly perhaps by reason of a fall in early days that made him a cripple, tended to satire. He is closely associated with Göttingen and its University and formed a link between Göttingen and the Royal family and scientific circles in England. His letters have been well edited by Albert Leitzmann and Karl Schüddekopf (Leipzig, 1901) and there is also a collection of letters addressed to him, edited by Hans Hecht (*Briefe aus G. Chr. Lichtenberg's englischem Freundeskreis*). He paid two visits to England, a short one in 1770, and a longer one of some months in 1774–5. He was well launched in London society of the better sort by his friendship with men of science; William Herschel, who had come from Germany as a young musician and was making a great name as an astronomer, though his discovery of Uranus was not till 1781: Sir Joseph Banks, F.R.S. and D.C.L. of Oxford, who had accompanied Cook in his voyage in the 'Endeavour' (1768–71): Solander, the Swedish botanist closely associated with Banks in his travels and afterwards Keeper of the Natural History Department of the British Museum; and the two Forsters, Reinhold and George, to whom I have already referred.

His letters continue till his death at the age of fifty-seven in 1799. The letters from London are chiefly addressed to his most intimate friend Johann Christian Dieterich, bookseller

in Göttingen, to which he had migrated from Gotha. Like
our other German visitors he was overwhelmed on his arrival
by the life and variety of London. In a letter to Christian
Gottlob Heyne, the distinguished Göttingen scholar, whom
many of us know from Carlyle's essay on him, and whose
daughter Lichtenberg had married, he thus sums up his first
crowded experience in 1770. 'I have seen the sea, some men
of war of 74 guns, the King of England in all his splendour
with his crown on his head in Parliament, Westminster
Abbey with its famous monuments, Paul's church, the Lord
Mayor in a great procession in a crowd with many thousands
round him, all crying "Huzza, God bless him, Wilkes and
liberty!" and all this in a week.' His adventures in sight-
seeing culminated in climbing to the top of St. Paul's, where
he drank his friend's health in cherry brandy. He had been
shown the sights by Lord Boston, and had friendly attention
from Lord Marchmont (the third Earl), whom we know from
his interview with Johnson in 1779 when he supplied him
with anecdotes of Pope. He gave Lichtenberg a low opinion
of the Royal Society, which he complained occupied itself
with trivialities. Lichtenberg finds Göttingen in good repute
in English society, but it would be more visited if a good
English or French 'Guide' were published. At present its
only visitors are young officers who come to learn German.
He himself had had such visitors to live with him. His
London life he found fatiguing and sighed for simpler living.
'I am obliged', he says to Kastner, another correspondent,
'to live too fashionably to learn much, and would give
a good deal to live here as quietly as I do in Göttingen.
I have to dress twice a day in different ways, and always
live and dine in large companies, and learn a new way of
life, which I shall never practice overseas.' Two things impressed him as they did Archenholz, the beauty of the women
of all classes, and the multitude of shops of manufactured
articles ready for sale. On his second visit (1774-5) he saw
England more at leisure. He spent some time at Kew near
the Royal Observatory and saw a good deal of the king

and queen, who treated him with great friendliness. On March 17, 1775, he writes:

> One day this week, when the planets were all in the sky at once, I was two hours with the King on the roof of the Observatory. I never saw him so cheerful and good-humoured: among other things, when I was looking very intently through a telescope he held his hat for a joke in front of the object-glass and when I did not at once discover the cause of its being darkened, he laughed not a little at my confusion.

To enlarge his experience he took a more adventurous journey than any of our other travellers and describes it in a letter to Schernhagen of Hanover. He dressed himself as a journeyman weaver, and with a couple of shirts and a collar, wrapt in a handkerchief, went by coach to Oxford, Birmingham, and Bath. Bath, he said, was the finest town he had seen. In Birmingham he visited Mrs. Baskerville (the famous printer himself had died that year) and saw many manufactures and machines that interested him, and was struck by the division of labour in the workshops. In Oxford his chief concern was a visit to Thomas Hornsby, Savilian Professor of Astronomy and first Radcliffe Observer. His observatory is 'as superior to that at Richmond as that at Richmond to that at Göttingen'. He was astonished to be told that the transit-instrument enabled the observer to see stars of the fifth or even sixth magnitude in daylight on a summer afternoon. In view of a recent controversy I quote the remark that follows. 'While I was in Oxford, the weather was not favourable enough for this. If this goes on astronomers like other artisans may go to bed at night.' Hornsby, it may be noted, promised to learn German.

But Lichtenberg's interests were not confined to science. He visits Yorick's grave in the churchyard of St. George, Westminster, and sends to Dieterich for the best edition of Voltaire's works for his friends the Irbys (Lord Boston's family). Above all he indulged his keen taste for the theatre; saw Garrick many times, and admired Thomas Weston in his clown parts; 'he is unique; Nature seems to have destined him to make others laugh without the faculty of laughing himself'. He evidently had an uncommon sympathy with English humour: among his miscellaneous writings none perhaps is more characteristic than his commentary on Hogarth's prints, which shows his insight into English life and manners. Like our other visitors he made a point of hearing the Parliamentary orators, and describes (March 6, 1775) a great debate in the House of Lords on an address from the Commons asking for strong measures against the Americans, when he heard speeches by the Duke of Richmond, Lord Camden, and Lord Mansfield. 'It was very dignified and moving, and everyone who hears I was there on that day thinks me very lucky.' His circle of acquaintance was wide, and he kept up his friendships long after his return to Göttingen. In June 1787 he writes to his friend Herschel: 'As soon as your forty foot telescope is ready I shall gird up my loins and go to England for a couple of weeks.' But this hope was never fulfilled. Lichtenberg's house in Göttingen acted as a sort of informal consulate or clearing-house mediating between England and Germany: he provides lodging for young Englishmen wanting to learn German, or receives inquiries of all sorts from England. Now it is John Garnett of Bristol who wants 'a light boy, who understands cleaning a horse', to enable him to keep up his German (22.10.80) and now Joseph Planta of the British Museum commending to Lichtenberg the *New Review* of Paul Henry Maty, his colleague. At all points we see him as the incisive, somewhat cynical critic, impatient of the sentimental proclivities of the *Hainbund*, the League of Poets, having its centre in Göttingen, with Voss as director and the Klopstock tradition behind it.

What do you think? he writes, in 1775, of the *Musen Almanach*? To my mind most of it is quite execrable, especially the Klopstock element and its imitations. Have you found a single new image in it? It is everlasting murmurs of the forest, silver clouds and oak trees, which we have had a hundred thousand times already, and they think to make it new by uttering it in a husky voice like the mysterious chant of a Sibyl. I prefer

Jacob Böhme to this sort of thing. By Jove, he could write whole quartos that no living soul understood except the initiated fools, and twenty Musen Almanach's won't weigh one quarto!

It was in keeping with this that when he founded the *Göttin-gensche Magazin* in 1780 with George Forster, his chief objects of attack were the sentimental school of poets and Lavater, whose extravagances he ridiculed. His sympathies are with the new movement represented by Goethe and Schiller. Goethe in 1796 sent him three volumes of *Wilhelm Meister* and they exchanged letters on light and colour. The double interest in science and literature was a bond between them. In Lichtenberg's letters from England his loyalty to friends and his literary interests come out in his letter to Heyne about his edition of Pindar, which had been well received in England, and his promotion of Dieterich's interest with the king, who was ready to favour him as 'ein ganzer Mann'. Later on we find him thanking Forster for his translation of *Sakuntala*, which with other Indian literature was then attracting attention, mainly through the influence of Sir William Jones of University College. Archenholz published one of his translations from the Sanskrit in 1789. Like Archenholz, Lichtenberg was a friend of the veteran Gleim, the author of the 'Grenadier Songs', who gratified him (1794) by a gift of porcelain on his wedding-day, at a time when the melancholy that darkened his later years was perhaps already coming upon him. 'I am moved to tears by the thought, "you cannot be such a nobody as you imagine when Gleim thinks of you and honours you". When everythi.:g has become indifferent to me except friendship and "laudari a laudatis" the effect of this thought is more than I can express.'

Of all the writers on England that I have discussed, Lichtenberg was the most cynical, but in acuteness of intellect he was the most distinguished, and his range of knowledge and interest make him a significant figure in the social and scientific intercourse between Germany and England in his time. If he seems wanting in feeling we must remember his physical infirmity. If he was at times violent in his criticisms he had the good sense to see the weaknesses of his friend Forster and to try to keep him in the right path. He had the great merit of vitality: nothing that showed ingenuity in mechanical contrivance or originality in literature or drama escaped him, the devices of John Harrison the clock-maker, or the art of Garrick, whom he praised in the *Deutsches Museum* (1776), or the skill of Mrs. Barry in using her arms on the stage, which he commends to the actresses of Germany, or Herschel's telescope—all appeal equally to that active mind.

It would be tempting to go on, but I must not wear out your patience. What I have already said will suffice to show that the personal links between England and Germany at this time were more numerous and vital than some of us realize. The interests of these visitors were not identical. Moritz was more attracted by our poetry; Archenholz and Wendeborn by our politics and institutions, Lichtenberg by our drama, and our equipment for manufacture and research, but all enjoyed the freedom of our everyday life and all helped to promote friendship between England and Germany by contributions of a genuine and practical kind, founded on personal friendship and interchange of courtesies and issuing in the publication of works that actively promoted knowledge and good will between the countries.

To-day, as in the age of Rousseau and the French Revolution, internationalism is in the air. There is much vague aspiration after a European mind and a cosmopolitan spirit. The problem before us is to combine nationalism in its best sense, the development of the best characteristics and capacities in each people, with the larger view of a common interest beyond the clamour of competition and conflict. Such a larger view can only be acquired by mutual knowledge among nations, and to this there is no short cut. It can only be acquired by serious study and by personal intercourse. It is because the writings of the men I have been describing illustrate the value of such intercourse that I have called your attention to them to-day.